Edmund Burke's

Reflections on the Revolution in France

July 2000

MANCHESTER
UNIVERSITY PRESS

(TEXTS · IN · CULTURE

SERIES EDITORS
Jeff Wallace and John Whale

FOUNDING EDITORS
Stephen Copley and Jeff Wallace

ADVISORY EDITORS
Lynda Nead, Birbeck College, London
Gillian Beer, Girton College, Cambridge
Roy Porter, Wellcome Institute for the History of Medicine
Anne Janowitz, University of Warwick

This series offers specially commissioned, cross-disciplinary essays on texts of seminal importance to Western culture. Each text has had an impact on the way we think, write and live beyond the confines of its original discipline, and it is only through an understanding of its multiple meanings that we can fully appreciate its importance.

ALREADY PUBLISHED

Charles Darwin's *The Origin of Species*
David Amigoni, Jeff Wallace (eds)

Adam Smith's *The Wealth of Nations*
Stephen Copley, Kathryn Sutherland (eds)

Niccolò Machiavelli's *The Prince*
Martin Coyle (ed.)

Simon de Beauvoir's *The Second Sex*
Ruth Evans (ed.)

Sigmund Freud's *Interpretation of Dreams*
Laura Marcus (ed.)

(TEXTS·IN·CULTURE

Edmund Burke's REFLECTIONS ON THE REVOLUTION IN FRANCE

New interdisciplinary essays

JOHN WHALE

editor

Manchester University Press
Manchester and New York

distributed exclusively in the USA by St. Martin's Press

Published by Manchester University Press
Oxford Road, Manchester M13 9NR, UK
and Room 400, 175 Fifth Avenue, New York, NY 10010, USA
http://www.man.ac.uk/mup

Distributed exclusively in the USA by
St. Martin's Press, Inc.,
175 Fifth Avenue, New York, NY 10010, USA

Distributed exclusively in Canada by
UBC Press, University of British Columbia, 6344 Memorial Road,
Vancouver, BC, Canada V6T 1Z2

British Library Cataloguing-in-Publication Data
A catalogue record is available from the British Library

Library of Congress Cataloging-in-Publication Data applied for

ISBN 0 7190 5786 8 *hardback*
      0 7190 5787 6 *paperback*

First published 2000

06   05   04   03   02   01   00   10 9 8 7 6 5 4 3 2 1

Typeset in Apollo by Koinonia, Manchester
Printed in Great Britain
by Bell & Bain Ltd, Glasgow

Contents

For Stephen Copley

Series introduction

Texts are produced in particular cultures and in particular historical circumstances. In turn, they shape and are shaped by those cultures as they are read and re-read in changing circumstances by different groups with different commitments, engagements and interests. Such readings are themselves then re-absorbed into the ideological frameworks within which the cultures develop. The seminal works drawn on by cultures thus have multiple existences within them, exerting their influence in distinct and perhaps contradictory ways. As these texts have been 'claimed' by particular academic disciplines, however, their larger cultural significance has often been obscured.

Recent work in cultural history and textual theory has stimulated critical awareness of the complex relations between texts and cultures, highlighting the limits of current academic formations and opening the possibility of new approaches to interdisciplinarity. At the same time, however, the difficulties of interdisciplinary work have become increasingly apparent at all levels of research and teaching. On the one hand the abandonment of disciplinary specialisms may lead to amorphousness rather than challenging interdisciplinarity; on the other, interdisciplinary approaches may in the end simply create new specialisms or sub-specialisms, with their own well guarded boundaries. In these circumstances, yesterday's ground-breaking interdisciplinary study may become today's autonomous (and so potentially circumscribed) discipline, as has happened, it might be argued, in the case of some forms of History of Ideas.

The volumes in this series highlight the advantages of interdisciplinary work while at the same time encouraging a critical reflexiveness about its limits and possibilities; they seek to stimulate consideration both of the distinctiveness and integrity of individual disciplines, and of the transgressive potential of interdisciplinarity. Each volume offers a collection of new essays on a text of seminal intellectual and cultural importance, displaying the insights to be gained from the juxtaposition of disciplinary perspectives and from the negotiation of disciplinary boundaries. The volumes represent a challenge to the conception of authorship which locates the significance of the text in the individual act of creation; but we assume that no issues (including those of interdisciplinarity and authorship) are foreclosed, and that individual volumes drawing contributions from a broad range of disciplinary standpoints, will raise questions about the texts they examine more by the perceived disparities of approach that they encompass than by any interpretative consensus that they demonstrate.

All essays are specially commissioned for the series and are designed to be approachable to non-specialist as well as specialist readers: substantial editorial introductions provide a framework for the debates conducted in each volume, and highlight the issues involved.

We would, finally, like to dedicate the series to the memory of our colleague Stephen Copley, whose insight and energy was its starting point.

Jeff Wallace, University of Glamorgan
John Whale, University of Leeds
General Editors

Acknowledgements

I would like to thank all the contributors for their patience and good humour during the long process of getting this volume into print. Vivien Jones and David Fairer were characteristically helpful and supportive. To Stephen Copley I owe (along with much more besides) the opportunity of editing this volume. I hope he would have enjoyed it. Given his untimely death, I can only dedicate it to him.

Abbreviations

All references to Edmund Burke's *Reflections on the Revolution in France* are to the edition (1989) by L. G. Mitchell which appears in vol. VIII of *The Writings and Speeches of Edmund Burke*, ed. Paul Langford and others (Oxford: Clarendon Press, 1981–) hereafter cited as *Reflections*. Other references to this as yet incomplete edition are given as *Writings and Speeches*. References to Burke's correspondence are to *The Correspondence of Edmund Burke*, ed. Thomas W. Copeland and others (Cambridge: Cambridge University Press; Chicago: Chicago University Press, 1958–78), 10 vols hereafter cited as *Correspondence*.

Chronology

with particular reference to this volume

1729 or **1730** Burke born.

1753 Jewish Naturalization Act.

1757 Burke's *Enquiry into the Sublime and Beautiful*.

1770 Burke's *Thoughts on the Present Discontents*.

1776 American Declaration of Independence.

1778 Richard Price's *Two Tracts on Civil Liberty, the War with America, and the Debts and Finances of the Kingdom*. Catholic Relief Act.

1788 Summoning of French States-General.

1789 Fall of the Bastille. Declaration of the Rights of Man. Price addresses The London Revolution Society.

1790 Burke's *Reflections*; Price's *A Discourse on the Love of Our Country*; Mary Wollstonecraft's *A Vindication of the Rights of Men*; Catharine Macaulay's *Observations on the Reflections of the Right Hon. Edmund Burke*.

1791 Tom Paine's *Rights of Man* Part 1; Burke's *Letter to a Member of the National Assembly*; *Appeal from the Old to the New Whigs*; *Thoughts on French Affairs*; Thomas Christie's *Letters on the Revolution in France*; James Mackintosh's *Vindiciae Gallicae*; Joseph Priestley's *Letters to the Right Hon. Edmund Burke, Occasioned by His Reflections*. Louis XVI's flight to Varennes.

1792 Paine's *Rights of Man* Part 2. Allied invasion of France. French royal family imprisoned. September massacres. Wollstonecraft's *A Vindication of the Rights of Woman*.

1793 Trial and execution of Louis XVI. The Terror. William Godwin's *Enquiry Concerning Political Justice*; Thomas Spence begins radical weekly *Pig's Meat; or Lessons for the Swinish Multitude*.

1794 Danton executed (April); Robespierre executed (July). End of Terror. Godwin's *Caleb Williams*; Wollstonecraft's *Historical and Moral View of the Origin and Progress of the French Revolution*. Ann Radcliffe's *The Mysteries of Udolpho*.

1796   Burke's *Letter to a Noble Lord*; *Letters on a Regicide Peace*; *Thoughts on Scarcity*. Revised edition of Godwin's *Political Justice*.

1797   Burke dies.

1798   Irish Rebellion.

1800   Act of Union with Ireland.

1807   William Hazlitt's *The Eloquence of the British Senate*.

1809–10 S. T. Coleridge's *The Friend*.

1817   Coleridge's *Biographia Literaria*; Maria Edgeworth's *Harrington*.

1819   Hazlitt's *Political Essays*.

1824   Thomas Moore's *Captain Rock*.

1829   Catholic Emancipation.

1830   Coleridge's *On the Constitution of the Church and State*.

1857–61 Henry Thomas Buckle's *History of Civilization in England*.

1858–60 Thomas Macknight's *History of the Life and Times of Edmund Burke*.

1867   John Morley's *Edmund Burke: A Historical Study*.

1878–90 William Lecky's *History of England in the Eighteenth Century*.

1879   Morley's *Burke*.

1914   Geoffrey Butler's *The Tory Tradition*.

1919   W. B. Yeats's 'The Second Coming'; 'A Prayer for My Daughter'.

1920   Harold Laski's *Political Thought in England: Locke to Bentham*.

1939   Philip Magnus's *Edmund Burke*.

1968   Conor Cruise O'Brien's edition of the *Reflections*.

1977   Ian Gilmour's *Inside Right*.

1

Introduction

JOHN WHALE

When Edmund Burke's *Reflections on the Revolution in France* appeared in November 1790 at a moment of impending political crisis it was greeted with an almost bewildering variety of responses – many of them negative. One of the most famous and most hostile – Tom Paine's *Rights of Man* – seized on its paradoxical and miscellaneous nature as if that were its weakest point. Addressing what he disparagingly calls Burke's 'paradoxical genius', Paine claims that: 'Mr Burke's Book is *all* Miscellany.'[1] The complex and competing variety of responses it has engendered – from the 1790s through the nineteenth century and to the present day – would suggest that the enduring significance of Burke's book might be said to have been made possible by its inherent variety. Its rich, contentious after-life – as a classic of conservative organicism; of English liberal society; of Natural Law; of counter-revolution; of political aesthetics; as the last testament of an aristocratic culture; as an expression of modernity and nostalgic national identity – might be traced back to Paine's disparaging description of its mixed and miscellaneous nature. Burke's deployment of a variety of styles and his choice of an apparently spontaneous, almost fatherly, letter to a young male friend in which to make his excoriating attack upon British sympathy for the emergent French Revolution have undoubtedly played their part in making this publication so amenable to a succession of different appropriations.[2]

On its publication, Burke's *Reflections* entered a highly charged political context. Relatively few positive public responses are documented, partly because, even before one considers the nature of the text, its author was already public property and immersed in a complex set of partisan, and sometimes simply prejudiced, relationships with people in power and with the print culture which surrounded him. If the *Reflections* can be said to have brought Burke a further instalment of notoriety rather than fame, it did so because he was already enmeshed in a set of public and political meanings which the text would itself inherit. The very target of Burke's polemic – those leaders of established and enfranchised political opinion who stood in the middle ground – would probably be the least likely to commit themselves to loud-voiced approval even if they assented to his anti-revolutionary argument. And given the way in which Burke had been vilified in the press (to the extent that his sanity was questioned), they would be less likely to do so. Even the ostensible subject of Burke's book – the French Revolution – was, in fact, determined by more local and more specific consider-ations. It takes its starting-point from the meeting held a year earlier (in November 1789) of the Revolution Society (composed of Dissenters and radical Whigs) and the speech, entitled 'A Discourse on the Love of Our Country', delivered to it by the leading radical Dissenter Dr Richard Price, in which he lent support to the newly emerged French Revolutionary leaders and made comparisons between their new constitution and the unwritten constitution of Britain. Burke's target, then, can be seen to be his own country's response to the French Revolution and its sense of its own constitution as much as the events unfolding in France. Even his most eloquent and angry rhetoric can be seen as specifically directed towards a particular, powerful section of British public opinion.

Such particularity and historical precision has, however, to take its place alongside the text's history of appropriations. Understanding Burke's *Reflections* must involve a double-act of the historical imagination, in order to do justice not simply to its immediate textual and contextual meanings, but also to its role in facilitating future modes of thought which might have migrated a long way from those Burke himself would have recognized or agreed with. To understand the variety and the paradoxical genius of Burke's *Reflections* (to invoke Tom Paine once more) one must also include the miscellaneous nature of its historical after-life.

The diversity of political appropriations which Burke has more generally undergone might also be said to derive from the *Reflections*. The 'liberal' Burke who spoke out for parliamentary independence and toleration against arbitrary forms of power, and against British policy in Ireland and India, had been admired by reforming Whigs. With the publication of this anti-revolutionary tract, many friends and admirers who had welcomed his support of the American Revolution – including Tom Paine and Thomas Jefferson – were left surprised and shocked. Burke's more obvious Whig characteristics – as a successor to Locke and as an exponent of the civilizing process of commerce and of religious toleration – are all more apparent in his pre-Revolutionary writings and speeches; and it is these which enabled him to be transformed, in the middle of the nineteenth century, into a liberal utilitarian precursor of John Stuart Mill. But it is Burke's sudden and aggressive stance in the *Reflections* against the new phenomenon taking place in France which has produced a greater diversity of admirers in subsequent political history. The *Reflections* has developed a complex and extensive legacy within conservative thought. Most notable here is the Tory appreciation of his apparent reverence for a hierarchical, organically complex society based on a fund of moral feeling supported by tradition, custom, and prejudice. His greatest legacy for conservative thinkers has been the argument for the political wisdom inherent in historically proven institutions and customs.

He has also been seen both as critic and as admirer of an emergent bourgeois order, someone with a distinctly ambivalent response to the capitalist market. And this tension between Burke the defender of a hierarchical establishment and Burke the market liberal is matched by the claim of a conflict within. Psycho-biographical readings of his life and career have emphasized this ambivalence, extending it beyond his overt political position as champion and scourge of a bourgeois order to encompass his attitude towards national identity as defender of the Whig oligarchy and as suppressed rebel against English rule in Ireland.[3] The prominence Burke gives to the role of feelings such as reverence and respect in the construction and maintenance of the social compact can make him seem like a pre-capitalist moralist or as a prescient precursor of the market who could, at one stroke, provide it with its psychological identity and its moral justification.[4] The 'manners' of Burke's civilization evident in his famous lament for the demise of the 'age of chivalry' in the *Reflections* could equally serve as the enabling subjectivity and the ethical, emotional back-up for the ruthless competition of the market.

In this way, Burke's *Reflections* provides the metaphysical dressing to many brands of conservative and liberal democratic thought. Its most impressive passages offer a compelling case for the need of a pleasing, even beautiful, covering for the stark and harsh realities of the compact the individual makes with the state. And this is the way the text is often used: as a means of providing an excuse for and an articulation of the moral, spiritual, and aesthetic 'cement' which binds the various levels of civil society together. Burke provided in the *Reflections* a vivid description of the compensatory realm of feelings which could keep the civic order intact and its populace self-consciously happy with their role in the order of things. The text simultaneously articulates and mystifies the feelings of a conservative mentality. Originally designed to protect the values and cultural symbolism of the ruling aristocratic elite of eighteenth-century British society, its historically specific hegemonic purpose can easily be transcended and transformed in order to serve other very different, but equally hegemonic ends.

Recent attempts to mobilize Burke's ideas (or, more frequently, to simply feed off the historical authority of his name), range from the suggestion that he provides the opportunity for a politics of the 'sublime of everyday life',[5] to Margaret Thatcher's enlistment of him as the first of 'the anti-Maastricht brigade'.[6] Although, over the last twenty years, Burke has been deployed most notably, amongst English Conservatives, by opponents of Thatcherism, who invoke him as a founding father of the middle way or even of a one-nation Conservatism,[7] it is not the *Reflections*, but *Thoughts and Details on Scarcity* which has lately loomed large in their attacks on the British welfare state and the Social Security budget.[8] When this has been the case, however, it has often been accompanied by a beguiling appeal to Burke's sense of a moral community of feeling, and his sense of attachment to the local and the particular. At least from the perspective of a divided Conservative Party in opposition, the *Reflections* seems to be serving a dual purpose: offering Burke's endearing image of the 'little platoon' in support of fear-inducing arguments about the new abstracting phenomenon currently taking place across the Channel, in which the Euro replaces the *assignat*; and, at the same time, justifying a continued attack on the 'cost of government'. Once again, the *Reflections* offers both the power and the compensation of a rhetoric of feeling in the service of a conservative form of social cohesion and national identity.

The prominence afforded to rhetoric by the *Reflections* in establishing such an aesthetic appreciation of civil society – the book's very literariness – has also engendered a complex set of responses over two hundred years. For all its success in terms of sales, and the admiration for the linguistic power of its author – in particular, for his style – the immediate response of Burke's would-be supporters and allies was profoundly mixed, often luke-warm, and frequently critical. In many instances there was a sense that the most passionate and melodramatic aspects of his book were a hostage to fortune. While many of Burke's prominent opponents and allies in the 1790s saw its rhetorical richness as a source of weakness, there were many who responded sympathetically (if often privately) to a text which not only asked for the outpouring of the outraged sensibility of its readers, but which also betrayed the active sensibility of its author in which he figured as the hero of a national romance. For an admirer like Frances Burney this meant that the *Reflections* was 'the noblest, deepest, most animated, and exalted work' she thought she had ever read;[9] for an opponent like Wollstonecraft it provided an opportunity to portray Burke as the victim of his own sensibility. She could turn the book's rhetorical extravagance back on its author and make him look like a libertine fantasist divorced from reality.[10] Satirical prints in the 1790s also exploited this aspect of the text by transforming Burke into a Don Quixote figure. He is presented in a number of prints in the guise of a ludicrous 'Don Dismallo' who pays homage to Marie Antoinette's Dulcinea. More famously, he is 'The Knight of the Woeful Countenance' riding out against the National Assembly armed with a bloody pen instead of a lance and carrying the shield of aristocracy and despotism.[11] This perceived gap between the book's stylistic energy and its political content is neatly captured in Pitt's response in a letter of 1795 in which he refers to the *Reflections* as a series of 'Rhapsodies ... in which there is much to admire, and nothing to agree with'.[12]

Through the nineteenth century acclaim for Burke as a literary stylist underpins the admiration of conservative Anglicans like Coleridge as much as parliamentary Liberals like Gladstone. Burke the political theorist and Burke the aesthetic rhetorician have often gone hand in hand. This meant that a middle-class radical like Hazlitt felt he had to draw a line between Burke's politics and his qualities as an imaginative literary writer.[13] The aestheticization of Burke in the Romantic period prepared the ground for a further level of de-politicization in the Victorian period when the pragmatic Whig statesman was often replaced by a disinterested, almost Arnoldian, free thinker, unsullied by the demands of party faction and scandal.[14] More famously, Marx saw in Burke's recognition of an emergent bourgeoisie, a political insight marred by a vision that was distinctly 'romantic'.[15]

This conflict of interests between Burke's political force and his literary identity has been replicated in the academic criticism of the *Reflections* which has been written over the last twenty years. Within the different disciplines of history, English studies, aesthetics, and political science, scholars have restaged and revisited this difficult and historically determined combination of politics and aesthetics. The ways in which the *Reflections* has been read have mirrored this tension.

Political scientists in both the nineteenth and the twentieth centuries have tended to read Burke's *Reflections* against the grain and turn it into a systematic or coherent work of political philosophy.[16] The book has also been granted another kind of power. With the hindsight of history, it has been afforded an almost metaphysical quality, an uncanny wisdom, which, given its own scathing attack on Enlightenment reason as a form of dangerous magic, is highly ironic. Burke's seeming capacity to predict the subsequent events of French history and their aftermath has led to an awed reverence for his historical prescience. In the Victorian period Burke was more generally accorded the status of a sage or prophet of culture. That Marxist critics have often, in their very different way, accorded his text a similar power, whether that be for his recognition 'that capitalism needed the sanction of tradition and habit'[17] or because the text reveals a suppressed rebel, suggests that the *Reflections* possesses a capacity to generate a response in its various historical readers which repeats the terms of its original debate.[18] Not only has the *Reflections* created the taste by which it is enjoyed (to use an idea deployed by two other notable conservatives, Wordsworth and T. S. Eliot) it also has the capacity to transcend the boundaries of the 'little platoon', the specific context, for which it was designed. To encounter the history of the *Reflections* through its subsequent life of two hundred years is to witness the repetition in many of its readers of that quasi-religious veneration which the book advocates on behalf of an English aristocratic culture that was under threat by the end of the eighteenth century.[19] It is as if the hegemonic power which is the historically specific and overt subject of many of its pages haunts the reading process for subsequent readers. Burke's text can easily become an object of veneration given its own gothic, organic, and labyrinthine structure.

Allied to this sense of the prescience of the *Reflections* is the status the text has been accorded as a significant marker in the birth of 'modernity'. Something of the same excessive, irrational veneration inheres in the powerful claims made for the *Reflections* as an articulation of a moment of modern historical consciousness: the point at which 'revolution' takes on a particularly modern, or Marxist, meaning and significance. 'All circumstances taken together,' Burke writes, 'the French revolution is the most astonishing that has hitherto happened in the world'.[20] To Burke's *Reflections*, some have argued, we owe the first announcement of the new concept of revolution as the radically and violently new – even if in Burke's express terms this is simultaneously registered as a fall, an apocalyptic end of culture and civilization, rather than the beginning of what we now understand as 'history'. Within the text, of course, Burke's famous advocacy of the local, specific, and actual as the starting-point of political identity stands in opposition to the deracinating cosmopolitanism of Enlightenment reason which he identifies with revolutionary France:

> To be attached to the subdivision, to love the little platoon we
> belong to in society, is the first principle (the germ as it were) of
> public affections. It is the first link in the series by which we
> proceed towards a love to our country and to mankind.[21]

So here too there is an irony, in that the *Reflections* announces a
new modernity, but it does so only to express its own alienation
from that modernity. This is compounded by the fact that
Burke's choice of chivalry as a means of defending the values of
civilization and the current mode of civil society is itself a sign of
historical alienation. For all Burke's insistence on continuity and
tradition, he invokes a version of the past which is incapable of
dealing with the present. At the same time as it announces a new
sense of history and modernity amid the nightmare of revolution,
it figures its own historical identity in terms of romance, a
manoeuvre which betrays its own belatedness and its own
nostalgia. Ironically, the *Reflections* presents its 'revolution' as an
apocalyptic end to European civilization and in the form of a
savage attack upon the limitations of Enlightenment reason.

And because Burke ups the stakes in this way – making a
case for the new French constitution being announced across the
Channel in Paris as the demise of 'chivalry' rather than the
beginning of 'history' – his *Reflections* moves into a different
dimension. In its delicious, elegiac imagining of aristocratic
culture it takes on an anthropological status, as if Burke is
marking down, at the moment of its destruction, the system of
beliefs which constitutes his culture. In so doing, he defines that
culture's identity through a process of aggressive differentiation
which invokes many of the 'others' of his time. In attacking the
intellectuals of the Enlightenment Burke invokes not only the
irrational demons of his own culture – the alchemists and magicians of Europe's irrational past – but also the demonic subjects
of its colonialist and emergently imperial present: the American
Indians and other native peoples who inhabit their historically
differentiated cultures. Declaiming against the effects of the
'barbarous philosophy' of the Enlightenment, Burke argues from
the position of 'this European world of ours' that 'we have
subtilized ourselves into savages'.[22] It is the Europeans, then, who
are in danger of exemplifying a state of barbarity masquerading

as improvement. In a string of comparisons Burke invokes 'a procession of American savages', 'Maroon slaves', examples of Turkish and Persian 'barbarous anarchic despotism' and, most memorably perhaps, the unnamed people who 'hack the aged parent to pieces, and put him into the kettle of magicians' with 'wild incantations'.[23] There is an interesting and, I think, challenging blurring of those subjectivities within his text. Because Burke's own culture is defined as belated – as chivalric – it stands in a provocative sympathy with the figures of 'savages' and 'primitives' used to debunk the innovators of Reason across the Channel.

In a similar way, the specific attack on French Enlightenment reason which features so prominently in the *Reflections* spills over into a more general engagement with the irrational. Burke's reverence for the sacred 'altars', 'hearths', and 'sepulchres' which form the focus of the domestic body politic, the 'bearings and ... signs armorial' of aristocratic culture, the watch-words and shibboleths of his own society, works in rhetorical tandem with his scathing attacks upon the superstitious and magical signs of his French revolutionary opponents: their spells, pills, 'mummy', and 'amulets'.[24] In his ascription of barbarous irrationality to French 'reason' Burke's text works its own form of magic: his words take on a talismanic and totemic power which supplements and undermines its dominant tone of assured reasonableness. This combination is present in Burke's famous rhetorical *tour de force* which introduces the assault on the royal apartments at Versailles. He presents his reader with a verbal picture of the massacre of the innocents which begins with 'History will record' – a phrase which is, at once, history and prophecy. In such a moment, Burke's rhetoric refuses and engages with the irrational.

Amongst literary critics, Burke's *Reflections* has proved to be a fruitful site of enquiry for an exploration of the relationship between aesthetics and ideology. For this reason, a common literary strategy has been to read the text through *A Philosophical Enquiry into the Origin of Our Ideas of the Sublime and Beautiful* (1757), written largely in the 1740s while Burke was still an undergraduate at Trinity College, Dublin. In such readings, the *Enquiry* provides a means of understanding the gendered nature of aesthetic experience and figures as the unconscious of an explicitly political *Reflections*. This has led to a rich critical literature on the gendered economy and sexual form of Burke's aesthetics, and, at least in part, accounts for the way in which the dramatic passages involving the Queen of France have become the most celebrated and analysed sections of the text. In particular, the scene Burke presents of an 'almost naked' Marie Antoinette fleeing her bedroom before 'a band of cruel ruffians and assassins' has been read as symptomatic of the text's equation of revolutionary energy with sexual energy, and of its symbolic representation of a patriarchal order under threat at its most vulnerable and disturbing point. This melodramatic and almost ritualistic stripping of the Queen restages the gendered terms of Burke's distinctions between the categories of the beautiful and the sublime made in the *Enquiry* and opens them up to further levels of anxiety, displacement, and contradiction.[25]

Such readings have not met with unanimous support, however. There is undoubtedly a historical daring (some might say violence) in coupling two of Burke's texts together in this way, especially when they are separated by nearly forty years. And a further danger lies in focusing on what are, for all their dazzling and emotive rhetoric, only a few brief passages in Burke's long book. But there is both historical precedent and good intellectual justification for such readings. Many of Burke's contemporaries in the 1790s used his treatise on the sublime and beautiful as a means of reading the *Reflections*, and the cartoonists of the period found some of their best visual opportunities in the passages involving Marie Antoinette. Some of Burke's most astute critics have been irritated by the amount of critical attention paid to these isolated and uncharacteristic episodes, but, ironically, they have produced some of their own best work when attempting to correct the balance. For example, one of J. G. A. Pocock's important essays on Burke reads these passages in the wider context of political economy.[26] Burke's insistence on manners, historically formulated as the code of chivalry, is not, Pocock argues, some vague reaching after an emotive trigger with which to unleash the enraged sensibility of his readers, but an integral part of his understanding of civil society. For Burke, in the *Reflections*, manners are the basis of that society and the means by which its life and development through commerce can take place. The long, perhaps less spectacular passages in the *Reflections* on the seizing of Church property and the raising of the new speculative currency of the *assignat* by the revolutionaries are, Pocock argues, intimately linked to the more melodramatic, theatrical moments of sensibility such as the much-quoted storming of the queen's bedchamber.

With the advent of poststructuralist forms of literary criticism in the 1970s, Burke's text began to be seen in a different light as both indicative and constructive of the meaning of 'revolution', which could now be conceived in a wider cultural context. The pamphlet war of the revolution controversy has been read, in poststructuralist terms, as a battle over key cultural signs and one whose main constituent or referent – 'the French Revolution' – is linguistically defined. The *Reflections*, in conjunction with the *Enquiry*, has also played a key role in many feminist rereadings of both male Romanticism and the Gothic. Similarly, Freudian readings have opened up our understanding of the *Reflections* to an appreciation of the dynamic and competing narratives of revolution, history and sexuality.[27]

Attention to its generic identity and form has liberated the *Reflections* so that it can be reimagined in other ways. If one of the reasons for the popularity of the book in the 1790s (at least amongst its admiring target audience) was its ease of access – the ability to read the familiarity of the letter form in a correspondingly desultory way – it has also to be admitted that this apparent casualness turns out to be one of the text's most complex aspects. Literary critics have stressed the generic instability of Burke's letter, the freedom it gives him to move from one territory, one topic, to another. If the letter form is a mark of Burke's ideological preference for the particular, local, and actual, it is also a sign of sensibility, a way of registering a heightened capacity for feeling which might stand against the systematic philosophers of reason. In this way, the form of Burke's text can signal his ideological position and give him the opportunity of making a virtue out of his strategic and apparently spontaneous reaction to the events in France.

A rather different focus on the genre of the *Reflections* is provided by Seamus Deane, who has recently used the book's epistolary character to rethink and extend its generic possibi-

lities.[28] Because of its urgent deployment of the 'actual' alongside
a process of differentiation between cultures, Deane feels able to
describe the *Reflections* as a work of travel literature akin to
Swift's *Gulliver's Travels*. This allows him to offer another
exciting way of conceiving of Burke's book as a seminal text
which constructs a national identity. He too engages with the
problem of Burke and modernity, but avoids having to subscribe
to the notion of the text's irrational, prophetic, and supra-
historical wisdom. His model allows him to conceive of the
Reflections in terms of a more dynamic concept of literary
influence and canon formation than would be available if he
simply saw it as an originary text. Deane refers, within the context of Irish literature and national identity, to the *Reflections* as a
'foundational' text. In this manoeuvre he emphasizes not only
the book's capacity to set in motion future orientations of Irish
literary and political history, but also its ability to rearticulate
the past. The text is now involved in making a narrative of Irish
literary genealogy which can alter the past as much as the
present in a dynamic version of literary influence and historical
consciousness.

Deane's imaginative reconfiguration and recuperation of
Burke's *Reflections* within Irish cultural studies is a good
example of the text's continuing capacity to generate meaning
and be the target of different political and literary appropriations. Anyone wishing to engage with the meaning of the
Reflections must now take this after-life on board. It should
remind us that the meaning of such a key cultural text is
something that can never be taken for granted or fixed at one
particular moment. Establishing the meaning and significance of
such a book now inevitably means having to engage with the
history of its appropriations.

The essays which follow in this volume reflect and extend recent
trends in critical and historiographical work on the *Reflections*
which have included a desire to return Burke to his original
historical context and to see him as a pragmatist whose writing is
strategic and provisional rather than theoretical and systematic. At
its best, this demand for precise historical scholarship works
alongside the need to address the ways in which Burke's text

both articulates and is mediated through theoretical modes of thought. Through their deployment of different methodologies the following essays offer further evidence of the variety of ways in which Burke's book can be interpreted and appropriated, both by examining its relationship with contemporary critical discourses and by analyzing the context in which it was read and understood when it made its immediate impact in the 1790s. Each of the contributors here is engaged in negotiating and traversing the interdisciplinary boundaries between history, politics, aesthetics, and philosophy. They engage in the various kinds of interpretive strategies that are most commonly associated with English studies and cultural studies; and they are all also interested in having to move between the different contexts in which both Burke's text and they themselves are situated. In their different ways, they acknowledge that reading the *Reflections* is no easy business; any reading of this text has to be argued for and struggled over, and the outcome will be understood against the history of previous readings.

The volume opens with an essay which offers a sharp rejoinder to those (mainly literary critics) who may have underplayed the rhetorical status of Burke's text: its persuasive relationship to the real events taking place in British and French politics. It closes with a plea for a reassessment of the way in which Marxist and Leftist criticism has approached this key conservative text. The first essay asks for a more informed understanding of the way in which contemporaries would have responded to Burke's language, the last asks for a revision of Burke's significance and usefulness within a particular branch of critique. Burke's *Reflections* is equally present in both. Two essays, which in their different ways deal very specifically with the book's reception in the 1790s, are those by F. P. Lock and Gregory Claeys. Lock concentrates on an eighteenth-century appreciation of rhetoric, its relationship to reading practices, the nature of politics and its engagement with the actual. Claeys engages with the variety of responses engendered by the *Reflections* in the 1790s and focuses in particular on the way in which Burke's text created a split amongst the Whigs which, paradoxically, prepared the ground for a later broadening of Whig philosophy and principles.

This complementarity of historical precision and the wider potential of the historical imagination is further exemplified in W. J. Mc Cormack's essay, which takes up the challenge of trying to understand the silence which surrounds Burke's *Reflections* in the Ireland of the 1790s in the years before the Act of Union. In this instance, the meaning of the *Reflections* resides in the structured and coercive set of relationships between state power and print culture, which can only be accessed, as the appendix to this essay makes graphically apparent, through painstaking research. From this example, it can be shown that a text's absence may be as significant and as informative as its more overt appropriation in print. Here the archival details of the Public Record Office are continuous with the later imaginings of Yeats.

Mc Cormack's essay on the 'absence' of Burke's *Reflections* in Dublin is nicely complemented by essays by Tom Furniss, Susan Manly, and Claire Connolly which ask us to reconsider Burke's response to national identity, toleration, and the Act of Union: and which add to our understanding of Burke's relationship to Ireland and Irishness. Burke's role in the debate about the burgeoning sense of national identity as it developed during the course of the eighteenth century, forms the basis of Furniss's enquiry as he reassesses the discursive history of ideas under-lying the exchange between the *Reflections* and Dr Richard Price's address to the Revolution Society. Manly's location of Burke's advocacy of toleration in relation to the key early eighteenth-century figure of John Toland provides a parallel historical per-spective which offers as much insight into Burke's adopted Englishness as it does into his problematic sense of Irish identity.

Burke's complex engagement with the issue of 'modernity' is a major concern of the essays by Kevin Gilmartin, Claire Connolly, and Angela Keane. All three address the force and the limits of Burke's historical imagination. For Gilmartin, in his account of print culture in relation to a Habermasian notion of the public sphere, Burke's *Reflections* fails to acknowledge the new role played by the emergent realm of letters and print. Burke's incorporation into future narratives of history is the concern of Connolly and Keane as they engage with, respectively, the Act of Union, and the imbrication of Romantic aesthetics with Marxist criticism. Connolly addresses Burke's deployment of the narrative of history, its 'proleptic wisdom', which can write the future as much as the past. The volume ends with a recommendation, within literary theory, to see the *Reflections* as a work of pragmatism which resists its subsequent Romanticization. Here once again we are presented with the complex double-life of the *Reflections*: its continuing capacity to engender readings which must negotiate between the local and the national, the provisional and theoretical, the material and the metaphysical.

Notes

1 Tom Paine, *Rights of Man,* ed. Henry Collins (Harmondsworth: Penguin, 1969), p. 138.

2 For an account of Burke's use of different styles in the *Reflections* see: Frans De Bruyn, *The Literary Genres of Edmund Burke: The Political Uses of Literary Form* (Oxford: Clarendon Press, 1996), pp. 165–208; Conor Cruise O'Brien, 'Introduction', *Reflections on the Revolution in France* (Harmondsworth: Penguin, 1969), pp. 42–56; F. P. Lock, *Burke's Reflections on the Revolution in France* (London: George Allen and Unwin, 1985), pp. 100–31. For an account of the critical history and contemporary responses to the *Reflections* see: Lock, *Burke's Reflections*, pp. 132–99; L. G. Mitchell, 'Introduction', *The Writings and Speeches of Edmund Burke*, vol. VIII, 'The French Revolution 1790–1794' (Oxford: Clarendon Press, 1989), pp. 1–51; Clara I. Gandy and Peter J. Stanlis, *Edmund Burke: A Bibliography of Secondary Studies to 1982* (New York: Garland, 1983); J. T. Boulton, *The Language of Politics in the Age of Wilkes and Burke* (London: Routledge and Kegan Paul, 1963).

3 See: Conor Cruise O'Brien, *The Great Melody: A Thematic Biography and Commented Anthology of Edmund Burke* (London: Sinclair-Stevenson, 1992); and Isaac Kramnick, *The Rage of Edmund Burke: Portrait of an Ambivalent Conservative* (New York: Basic Books, 1977).

4 See: David Bromwich, 'Remember! Remember!: Edmund Burke as the Last Defender of Pre-Capitalist Morality', *TLS*, 16 January, 1988.

5 See: Stephen K. White, *Edmund Burke: Modernity, Politics, and Aesthetics, Modernity and Political Thought*, vol. 5 (Thousand Oaks and London: Sage, 1994), pp. 83–90.

6 See: Robert Rhodes James, 'The Relevance of Edmund Burke', in *Edmund Burke: His Life and Legacy*, ed. Ian Crowe (Dublin: Four Courts Press, 1997), p. 145.

7 The main figure here is Ian Gilmour. See: Michael Gove, 'Edmund Burke and the Politicians', *Edmund Burke: His Life and Legacy*, pp. 154–5.

8 See: Michael Gove, 'Edmund Burke and the Politicians' , pp. 156–8; and, in the same volume, John Redwood, 'Edmund Burke and Modern Conservatism', pp. 193–5.

9   Frances Burney, *Diary and Letters*, ed. Austin Dobson, 6 vols (London: Macmillan, 1904–5), vol. 4, p. 435.

10 See: Mary Wollstonecraft, *A Vindication of the Rights of Men*, in *The Works of Mary Wollstonecraft*, ed. Janet Todd and Marilyn Butler, 7 vols (London: Pickering and Chatto, 1989), vol. 5, pp. 1–60.

11 See: Nicholas K. Robinson, *Edmund Burke: A Life in Caricature* (New Haven and London: Yale University Press, 1996).

12 See: J. Ehrman, *The Younger Pitt: The Reluctant Transition* (London: Constable, 1983), p. 80.

13 See: William Hazlitt, *Complete Works*, ed. P. P. Howe, 21 vols (London and Toronto: J. M. Dent and Sons, 1930–34), vol. 7, pp. 226–30, 301–13; vol. 12, pp. 10–14.

14 Something of this remains in Burke's standing in liberal constitutional thought. See: Stephen Macedo, *Liberal Virtues: Citizenship, Virtue, and Community in Liberal Consitutionalism* (Oxford: Clarendon Press, 1990), pp. 118–19.

15 Marx writes in *Das Kapital*: 'This sycophant who, in the pay of the English oligarchy, played the romantic *laudator temporis acti* against the French Revolution'. See: Karl Marx and Frederick Engels, *Collected Works* (London: Lawrence and Wishart, 1996), vol. 35, p. 748. See also: vol. 34, p. 269; and the *Manifesto of the Communist Party*, ch. 1 where they refer to his 'speculative cobwebs, embroidered with flowers of rhetoric, steeped in the dew of sickly sentiment'.

16 See: Peter J. Stanlis, *Edmund Burke and the Natural Law* (Ann Arbor: University of Michigan Press, 1958).

17 See: C. B. Macpherson, *Burke*, Past Masters series (Oxford: Oxford University Press, 1980), p. 71.

18 The most notable are Harold J. Laski, Conor Cruise O'Brien, Isaac Kramnick, and C. B. Macpherson. For Laski, see: *Political Thought in England: Locke to Bentham* (Oxford: Oxford University Press, 1920) and *Edmund Burke* (Dublin: Falconer, 1947).

19 Burke's figuring of the imminent decline of aristocratic culture could also be seen as strategic, given Linda Colley's claim: 'The last quarter of the eighteenth century and the first quarter of the nineteenth century witnessed, then, the emergence of a genuinely British ruling group. Nobles and notables closed ranks and became more homogeneous in terms of wealth, marriage patterns, lifestyles, and ambitions, thereby rendering themselves more secure in the face of extreme pressure from without.' *Britons: Forging the Nation 1707–1837* (London: Random House, 1994), p. 164.

20 *Reflections*, p. 60.

21 Ibid. pp. 97–8.

22 Ibid. pp. 128, 130, 137.

23 Ibid. pp. 117, 87, 176, 146.

24 Ibid. pp. 120, 121, 359, 368.

25 For the best examples of the way in which the sexual economy of this scene
    has been read see: Ronald Paulson, *Representations of Revolution (1789–
    1820)* (New Haven and London: Yale University Press, 1983), pp. 59–73;
    and Tom Furniss, *Edmund Burke's Aesthetic Ideology: Language, Gender and
    Political Economy in Revolution* (Cambridge: Cambridge University Press,
    1993), pp. 138–64.

26 See: J. G. A. Pocock, *Virtue, Commerce, and History: Essays on Political
    Thought and History, Chiefly in the Eighteenth Century* (Cambridge:
    Cambridge University Press, 1985), pp. 193–212.

27 See: Paulson, *Representations of Revolution*; Thomas Weiskel, *The Romantic
    Sublime: Studies in the Structure and Psychology of Transcendence* (Baltimore
    and London: Johns Hopkins University Press, 1985); Frances Ferguson,
    Solitude and the Sublime: Romanticism and the Aesthetics of Individuation
    (London and New York: Routledge, 1992); Neil Hertz, *The End of the Line:
    Essays on Psychoanalysis and the Sublime* (New York: Columbia University
    Press, 1985); Eve Kosofsky Sedgwick, *The Coherence of Gothic Conventions*
    (London and New York: Methuen, 1986).

28 Seamus Deane, *Strange Country: Modernity and Nationhood in Irish Writing
    since 1790* (Oxford: Clarendon Press, 1997). See also: W. J. Mc Cormack,
    *From Burke to Beckett: Ascendancy, Tradition and Betrayal in Literary
    History* (Cork: Cork University Press, 1994), pp. 28–48.

2

Rhetoric and representation in Burke's *Reflections*

F. P. LOCK

In *Rights of Man*, Thomas Paine repeatedly accuses Burke of using rhetoric to distort and mislead. He speaks of Burke's 'flagrant misrepresentations', his 'tragic paintings ... very well calculated for theatrical representation', his 'declamation and his arguments ... gay with flowers', his periods that finish 'with music in the ear, and nothing in the heart'. According to Paine, Burke uses neither 'the language of a rational man' nor 'the language of a heart feeling as it ought to feel for the rights and happiness of the human race'.[1] These protests against rhetoric, together with the use of a self-consciously 'plain style', constitute a recognizable, indeed venerable, rhetorical strategy. A familiar example is Thomas Sprat's *History of the Royal Society* (1667). Deprecating eloquence as inimical to truth and reason, Sprat announces that the members of the Royal Society are determined 'to return back to the primitive purity, and shortness, when men deliver'd so many things, almost in an equal number of *words*'.[2] Neither Sprat nor Paine questions the ability of language to represent reality. Rather, each claims that his own language is better able to do so than the language of his opponents. Where Sprat had condemned the word-spinning of the scholastic philosophers and the rhetoric of the Renaissance humanists as inimical to the project of science, Paine excoriates Burke for writing in a style more suited to romantic fictions than to serious political discourse.

Recent critics have given Paine's indictment a new gloss. Conceding the essentially fictional nature of the *Reflections*, they have treated the question of its veracity as unimportant. Thus Peter Hughes credits Burke with being 'deeply original in his creation of an order of experience that changes discourse into events, that abolishes any clear distinction between art and life, between words and acts'. Ronald Paulson describes Burke's 'poetic language and images' as 'self-generating in that they make little or no claim on the real world of what actually happened in the phenomenon called the French Revolution'. Tom Furniss concludes that Burke 'seems not to have been concerned with historical accuracy'; the *Reflections* 'emerges as a representation of the Revolution which abandons the "reflection" theory of representation, relinquishing any direct relation between representation and "object" or "event" represented'.[3] These are not unsympathetic critics. Their avowed aim is not to refute Burke but to unravel and even celebrate the complexities of the Burkean text. Though they do not constitute a school, they share certain aims. They seek to explore the psychological resonances and ideological contradictions of Burke's text, rather than what it purports to represent about the world. They bring to the *Reflections* expectations commonly associated with texts, and especially poetic texts, of the Romantic period. Hughes, for example, claims that 'Burke prefigures and Romanticism continues' a change from literature as mimesis to literature as expression: 'literary discourse becomes less and less a way of representing, a way of saying something else, and more and more an enactment of itself, a way of saying that becomes a mode of existence'.[4]

These readings confirm the status of the *Reflections* as a classic text, able to satisfy the demands of new modes of interpretation. Their emphasis, however, on the expressive elements of the *Reflections* obscures its rhetorical nature. Not that rhetoric and expression are necessarily incompatible: rhetorical texts may, intentionally or not, reveal character. Burke, however, was habitually so reticent about himself, and the *Reflections* is so overtly rhetorical a work, that expressive interpretations of it need careful scrutiny. The purpose of a rhetorical discourse is to persuade a particular audience. Most such discourses are highly referential, purporting, as the *Reflections* certainly does, to describe and interpret the real world. Admittedly, no one now reads the *Reflections* for information about the French

Revolution. Its interest has become comparable to that of a play or novel, independent of any relation between the fiction and external reality. For Burke's contemporaries, however, the accuracy of his representations was crucial. They were being asked to make judgements, which by 1793 amounted to war or peace, on the basis of the veracity of his description and the accuracy of his analysis. Historical understanding of the *Reflections* and the influence it exercized therefore requires careful attention to the means Burke employed to convince his readers of the truth of his arguments.

Especially problematic is the extent to which recent critics of the *Reflections* have drawn on Burke's *Philosophical Enquiry into the Origin of Our Ideas of the Sublime and Beautiful* (1757). This strategy, seeming to interpret Burke by reference to his own theoretical ideas, has proved so persuasive that its legitimacy and its methodology have passed unquestioned. As recently as 1960, Francis Canavan argued that, since Burke's aesthetics were irrational, while his politics derived from rational principles, his aesthetic theory could throw no light on his political ideas.[5] Neal Wood broke new ground when (in 1964) he proposed that, on the contrary, the categories of the sublime and the beautiful 'are a unifying element of Burke's social and political outlook', giving 'a degree of coherence and system to the welter of words which he bequeathed to mankind'.[6] The problem of coherence is an old one in Burke studies. Wood's attractive solution commanded widespread acceptance, and many edifices have been raised on his foundation. The 'long-established connection between Burke's *Enquiry* and his *Reflections*' can now be casually invoked as 'an obvious way of introducing a political base to the sublime effusions of power in later Romantic poetry'.[7]

This 'long-established connection' needs critical scrutiny. There is, for example, no justification for treating the *Enquiry* and the *Reflections* as the foundational documents of Burke's thought, as though he wrote nothing else of importance. More than thirty years separate the two works and, to judge by his rhetorical practice during the intervening decades, Burke's ideas about persuasion had changed significantly by the time he wrote the *Reflections*. In 1789, when Edmond Malone tried to interest him in revising the *Enquiry*, Burke responded that 'the train of his thoughts had gone another way, and the whole bent of his mind turned from such subjects'.[8] For Burke, then, there was no obvious link between the two works.

The main subject of Burke's *Enquiry* is human response to natural phenomena. Only a few pages are devoted to words, and most of what Burke says about them applies to poetry rather than rhetoric. To explain how words affect the imagination in contexts avowedly fictional (not with the power of words to make convincing representations of the actual), Burke advances a theory of words that is strikingly anti-representational. Speaking of what he calls 'compounded abstract' words (his examples are 'virtue, honour, persuasion, docility'), he asserts that 'whatever power they may have on the passions, they do not derive it from any representation raised in the mind of the things for which they stand'.[9] From this passage, critics have mistakenly inferred that Burke thought that all words operated in like manner.[10] Admittedly, there are instances in the *Reflections* of compound-abstract words used in the way Burke describes in the *Enquiry*. A notable example is the 'Society is indeed a contract' passage.[11] Such language, however, is found chiefly in a few epideictic passages, which serve to induce a mood or feeling rather than to advance a rational argument. For the most part, the style of the *Reflections* conforms to the canons of classical rhetoric, which placed a high value on vivid description, regarded as a powerful persuasive tool. Even Burke's opponents acknowledged this quality of his rhetoric. One of his 'characteristic excellencies', William Godwin thought, was 'vividness and justness of painting'.[12] In the *Reflections*, obscurity generally connotes a 'false' sublime. Thus 'in the fog and haze of confusion all is enlarged, and appears without any limit'. Nations wade into an 'ocean of boundless debt'. Burke uses the word 'sublime' itself in its traditional, Longinian sense of elevation. Sometimes its connotations are positive (as in 'sublime principles'), but more commonly it is applied in derision to the revolutionaries. Their 'sublime speculations' are equated with 'ranting speculations'. Geometry is a 'sublime science', and a revolutionary economist is found 'subliming himself into an airy metaphysician'.[13] Rarely does Burke use an image that would qualify as 'sublime' as the term is used in the *Enquiry*.

The discrepancy between the sublime of the *Enquiry* and the sublime of the *Reflections* has not passed unnoticed. Paulson, for example, distinguishes 'the sublime in which Burke himself is participating' from 'the sublime as a rhetorician's tool'. Slipping between Burke's experience of the Revolution and his depiction of it in the text of the *Reflections*, Paulson seeks to reconcile the two sublimes by arguing that Burke 'could come to terms with the Revolution by distancing it as a sublime experience, even while denying its sublimity and realizing that it might not keep its "distance"'.[14] Observing the contrast between the assumptions on which the *Enquiry* is based and the values promoted by the *Reflections*, Furniss attributes the discrepancy to 'both a logical and an ideological contradiction within the very structure and context of both the aesthetics and the politics'. He argues that Burke's rhetoric is 'energized because it recognizes and seeks to contain those contradictions without abandoning the ideology'.[15] Since Burke wrote the *Enquiry* as a work of philosophy, to detect 'contradictions' in its argument is indeed damaging. To discover 'contradictions' in the *Reflections*, however, or between it and the *Enquiry*, would matter only if the *Reflections*, too, were a work of systematic philosophy. Burke expressly disavows such a purpose. His rhetoric in the *Reflections* is intended not to 'contain contradictions' but to exploit simple but striking oppositions, between ideas and values that he expects his audience to recognize as good and bad, appealing and alienating respectively. Whether unsympathetic critics detect 'contradictions' in his system of oppositions is beside the point. The *Reflections* is avowedly a work of description and persuasion, which does not stand or fall by the canons of logic.

A work of persuasion is not, of course, exempt from close and careful analysis of its arguments and its evidence. Recent critics have conceded too much on this score, exaggerating the extent to which the *Reflections* exerts an emotive rather than a rational appeal. Gray and Hindson, for example, claim that, while the book contains 'factual error, unsubstantiated assertion, non-sequitur, incoherence, and platitude', these do not matter, because it was 'written to persuade the emotions, not to impress the intellect'.[16] This supposes an improbably low level of intelligence on the part of Burke's audience. Burke did not

expect to capture the emotions of his readers without also convincing them. He was writing in a rhetorical tradition which
accorded primacy to the rational appeal. At the head of the
tradition stands Aristotle, who defined the purpose of rhetoric as
securing a judgement (*krisis*).[17] Judgement here means a rational
process that weighs evidence, balances alternatives, and follows
objective procedures.

For Burke as for Aristotle, the emotional and ethical appeals
are subordinate means to enforce a rational judgement. Neither
envisaged audiences so weak-minded as to be convinced by a
primarily emotive appeal. Persuasion, in theory at least, was a
process of rational conviction. Burke probably imbibed this idea
at Trinity College, Dublin, during his undergraduate years.
Precisely what he was taught about rhetoric is not known. The
best evidence is the course of lectures by John Lawson, professor
of oratory, first delivered in 1750, and which were published
after his death. Burke left the college in 1748, too early to have
heard Lawson. Even so, since Lawson was himself a graduate of
the college, his lectures probably repeat much of what he (and
Burke) had learned as undergraduates.[18] Following Aristotle,
Lawson insists on the primacy of rhetoric's appeal to the reason.[19]
In his *Philosophical Enquiry*, Burke may seem to depart from the
classical tradition in emphasizing the power of the emotions
against that of the judgement. The *Enquiry*, however, is a
psychological study of the 'origins' of human responses. Indeed,
its concentration on 'natural' responses sets it apart from works
that analyse the responses of real audiences, conditioned by
education and social experience. Burke himself is explicit about
this. In the essay on taste prefixed to the second edition of the
Enquiry, he distinguishes between the operation of the senses,
the imagination, and the judgement. His theory assumes that
sense-impressions are virtually the same in everyone. The
imagination, too, he argues, is a more uniform faculty than the
judgement, the faculty that enables educated readers to give the
preference to Virgil over Bunyan. Imagination may be strongest
early in life; judgement matures with age and experience. This
contrast was a commonplace. Robustly sweeping away the
boyish Boswell's desire to retain the youthful pleasure of
'admiration', Johnson asserted: 'Sir, as a man advances in life, he

gets what is better than admiration – judgement, to estimate
things at their true value'.[20] The *Reflections* is addressed
primarily to the understanding or judgement, only secondarily
to the imagination. Readers are repeatedly invited to judge, to
discriminate between things that may look alike, and to estimate
them 'at their true value'.

Twentieth-century readers are unlikely to share Burke's
notion of 'true value'. His appeal to the 'spirit of a gentleman',
for example, is apt to appear quaint or anachronistic. Interpretation of the *Reflections* is therefore inescapably historical. The
work itself is so referential, so caught up in the representation of
contemporary events and with directing readers' responses to
those events, as to demand a historical understanding. Today's
world is so different from Burke's that even critics who believe
his ideas to be 'relevant' need to allow for historical differences.
Modern readers are especially liable to misconstrue Burke's
religious oppositions, for compared to his England, contemporary western societies are highly secularized and ecumenical in
their attitudes to religion. Burke exploits the widespread hostility to sectarians that had recently (1787–89) defeated proposals
to relax the penal laws against Dissent.[21] Few modern readers are
likely to share this hostility. A further source of difficulty is that
the most influential modern critical approaches to literature place
a high value on indeterminacy of meaning: on discovering
tensions, ambiguities, and contradictions in texts. This is a
disadvantage in interpreting didactic works such as the
Reflections.

Burke treats the idea 'that twenty-four millions ought to pre-
vail over two hundred thousand' as 'ridiculous', self-evidently
absurd.[22] Today, its truth seems axiomatic. To understand the
appeal of the *Reflections* therefore requires an imaginative
empathy with the audience for which Burke was writing, and to
whose feelings he appealed. These feelings he often identifies as
'natural'. Again, modern readers are likely to be sceptical of such
appeals to 'nature'.[23] Burke, however, could rely on his
audience's broad agreement with him about what was 'natural'.
The *Reflections* defines its intended audience by assuming certain
values and proposing to deduce certain conclusions from the
application of them to a novel situation. This technique is, in

Aristotelian terms, enthymemic. A truncated syllogism in which the major premise is omitted as too obvious to need stating, a logical enthymeme depends on unstated axioms. A rhetorical enthymeme similarly depends on audience and speaker sharing a belief in some general proposition from which particular conclusions may plausibly (though not necessarily logically) be drawn.[24] An example in the *Reflections* is the 'liberal descent' passage, in which Burke describes a highly aristocratic 'spirit of freedom', equipped with 'a pedigree and illustrating ancestors ... its gallery of portraits; its monumental inscriptions; its records, evidences, and titles'.[25] The appeal is to those who have, aspire to have, or defer to those who have, such possessions. Negatively, Burke uses traditional imagery to create a frightening picture of a world upside-down. In this nightmare world, fanatic preachers lead captive kings; men 'snatched from the humblest rank of subordination' usurp the place of legislators; and women are aggressive savages rather than objects of chivalric adoration.[26] On such passages, Frans de Bruyn comments that 'to speak of "inversion" ... is to adopt the point of view of the dominant political and cultural group in society ... the same events that he [Burke] by turns regards as farcical or tragic assume the shape of apocalyptic comedy when they are seen through the eyes of his political opponents'.[27] This is true, but hardly damaging. The 'dominant' group was precisely Burke's audience, and he set out to represent events from its point of view. His descriptions are so heavily moralized that the reader's only choice is to accept them or reject them. Burke thought and wrote in an intellectual and rhetorical tradition unafraid of such categorical value judgements, and confident of its own ability to discriminate between true and false, good and bad.

When Burke asks his audience to distinguish 'a spectacle ... resembling a procession of American savages' from 'the triumphal pomp of a civilized martial nation',[28] twentieth-century readers are likely to regard 'civilized martial' as an oxymoron. A modern anthropologist would probably regard both 'triumphs' as indeed functionally analogous. Burke's anthropology, and that of most of his readers, was unashamedly Eurocentric and hierarchical. He had no use for the incipient cult of the primitive, and in describing the French Revolution as a regression into barbarism, he was appealing to widely shared values. The moral economy of the *Reflections* depends on readers being able to distinguish a bad triumph from a good one. The procedure works like irony, requiring a knowing audience.[29] In the *Reflections*, Burke likewise assumes that readers will readily distinguish between appropriate and profane uses of biblical imagery and symbolism.

Not every rhetorical discourse supposes the possibility of dissent. Some rhetoricians employ an 'everyone will agree with me' strategy. Burke does not. Even his unintended audience, however, those who rejected his arguments and his images, shared more of his mental world than do modern readers. Burke's confident moralization is so alien to modern relativism that several recent critics have sought to recuperate Burke, and the *Reflections* in particular, by treating his oppositions (such as theatre and counter-theatre, piety and sacrilege, plague and panacea) not as hierarchical, moralized pairs but as equals that subsist in a 'mutually dependent system'.[30] This distinctively modern way of constructing the world, and of interpreting texts, is anachronistic as an account of what Burke was doing. Burke's oppositions did not appear problematic to his contemporaries. Whether they agreed with him or not, they construed the *Reflections* as Burke intended, as a rhetorical transaction, accepting or rejecting his interpretation of the Revolution and the propriety of his rhetoric as a mode of representing it.

The judgements that Burke invites the reader of the *Reflections* to make are of different kinds. To persuade his audience of the validity of his representation of the Revolution, Burke employs three main strategies. First, he incorporates much information about recent events in France and much detail about the new French constitution. The inclusion of such material strengthens his rational appeal. Second, the work is written in an overtly rhetorical manner, deploying emotional appeals calculated to work on the prejudices of his intended audience. Third, and serving to integrate the rational and emotional appeals, is Burke's ethical appeal, his foregrounding of himself and his own character and credibility. Only in analysis, of course, are these separable. In the experience of reading the text, presentation of fact and argument, appeal to emotions and values, and a sense of the speaker as sincere and trustworthy, are intertwined. The most memorable passages in the *Reflections* are the emotive high points. These, however, would not achieve their purpose without the background of rational argument and objective evidence. Long stretches of the *Reflections*, especially in the second half, are primarily rational in their rhetorical appeal. The account of the new French electoral system is an example.[31] This section, which analyses in a dispassionate manner several general questions about the nature of popular representation, is a model of rational argument. Readers may agree with some of Burke's objections, and disagree with others; debate is possible, even invited. The more emotional passages work differently. They demand total assent. If they fail to secure it, they are likely to encounter total rejection.[32]

The prime example of such a passage is Burke's account of the attempt to assassinate Marie Antoinette on 6 October 1789. He begins in a grand manner:

> History will record, that on the morning of the 6th of October 1789, the king and queen of France, after a day of confusion, alarm, dismay, and slaughter, lay down, under the pledged security of public faith, to indulge nature in a few hours of respite, and troubled melancholy repose. From this sleep the queen was first startled by the voice of the centinel at her door, who cried out to her, to save herself by flight – that this was the last proof of fidelity he could give – that they were upon him, and he was dead. Instantly he was cut down. A band of cruel ruffians and assassins, reeking with his blood, rushed into the chamber of the queen, and pierced with an hundred strokes of bayonets and poniards the bed, from whence this persecuted woman had but just time to fly almost naked, and through ways unknown to the murderers had escaped to seek refuge at the feet of a king and husband, not secure of his own life for a moment.[33]

Commentators on this passage have been reluctant to believe that anything like Burke describes could actually have happened. Even sympathetic critics have supposed that he invented or exaggerated. Paulson claims that there is 'no evidence of Marie Antoinette's fleeing "almost naked"'. Hughes believes that Burke's 'most brilliant and theatrical touches', including 'the phallic thrusts into the queen's bed', were invented. (Treating the *Reflections* as a novel, Hughes admires such imaginative details.) Charging that Burke 'exaggerates and dramatizes ... already histrionic counter-revolutionary reports', Furniss argues that, because Burke exaggerates so greatly, the 'distinction between his own historical veracity and the theatricality of revolutionary rhetoric – a distinction vital to his ideological project – thus threatens to collapse in its most critical moment'.[34] Furniss at least (unlike Hughes) recognizes how damaging, from Burke's point of view, is the charge that what he describes never happened.

The 'historical veracity' of Burke's account is indeed important. Readers must be persuaded that what he describes actually took place. As has often been pointed out, the centinel was not in fact killed (though his death was widely reported) but left for dead. This small error hardly subverts the general accuracy of Burke's picture. Several contemporary sources mention the queen's undress, and at least one describes the violation of her abandoned bed.[35] Yet the success of Burke's rhetoric in this passage does not depend on the details. Only a reader who refused to accept Burke's main point would fasten on trivial inaccuracies. Most English observers shared his sense of outrage. Mary Wollstonecraft, for example, was an ardent supporter of the Revolution and author of one of the first replies to the *Reflections*. Yet in a later work (written when opinion in Paris was more inclined to minimize the incident), she described the attack on the queen as 'one of the blackest of the machinations that have since the revolution disgraced the dignity of man, and sullied the annals of humanity'.[36] Even Paine could not openly condone the would-be assassins. In his highly sanitized account of the October Days, he omits the incident altogether (much as Burke ignores the taking of the Bastille).[37] The distinction that is 'crucial to his ideological project' is not between Burke's factual accuracy and revolutionary rhetoric, but between appropriate and inappropriate narrative styles and reader responses. Given an audience ready to condemn an early-morning armed attack on the queen's bedroom, Burke's hyperbolical style, far from calling his 'veracity' into question, serves to reinforce the reader's sense of the enormity of the outrage and of the strength of Burke's own feelings. Such an incident, the reader is meant to feel, calls for such language. The reader is invited either to agree with Burke's assessment of the October Days as a scene of almost unparalleled horror, or to regard them (with Price) as a proper subject for a 'triumph'.

Burke's rhetorical polarizing means that the *Reflections* can indeed be described as, in a sense, a 'dramatic' work. Burke himself uses theatrical metaphors to describe not only what was going on in France, but to characterize (for example) the role of Providence. There is some danger today of misunderstanding this rhetoric. For a variety of reasons, anti-theatrical prejudice has declined significantly. Acting is now a highly regarded profession. In 1790, the idea of an actor becoming the head of state of a powerful nation was unthinkable. Drama, which enacts and shows action in an apparently unmediated way, has largely replaced narrative as a way of representing and interpreting reality.[38] (Paine is a 'dramatic' writer in that he purports to show and affects not to have a persona.) Today, the trope of politics as a kind of theatre is a commonplace. Anti-rhetorical prejudice, by contrast, has massively increased. Oratory, now inescapably tainted with insincerity, unscrupulous manipulation, and even brainwashing, is viewed with suspicion. A rhetorician evokes distrust, whereas an actor is not thought to deceive, because dramatic representations are acknowledged to be fictions. The reverse was the case in the eighteenth century. Rousseau, for one, controverts the notion that the orator is like an actor. 'Quand l'Orateur se montre, c'est pour parler, et non pour se donner en Spectacle; il ne réprésente que lui-même, il ne fait que son propre rolle, ne parle qu'en son propre nom, ne dit ou ne doit dire que ce qu'il pense; l'homme et le personnage étant le même être, il est à sa place; il est dans le cas de tout autre citoyen qui remplit les fonctions de son état.'[39] Admittedly, Rousseau in this passage idealizes the orator in order to blacken the actor. Burke did not share this extreme anti-theatrical prejudice. He was a regular playgoer and admired good acting. Nevertheless, the distinction that Rousseau makes is one that he would have accepted. An orator is a citizen making truth-claims about the real world, whereas an actor counterfeits.[40] In the *Reflections*, Burke writes explicitly 'en son propre nom ... dans le cas de tout autre citoyen qui remplit les fonctions de son état'. Little as Paine thought it deserving of credit, he recognized that the *Reflections* was a 'publication intended to be believed'.[41]

The passage in the *Reflections* that has provoked the most incredulity from Burke's day to ours is also the most famous. It follows an account of the royal family's forced return to Paris, which Price had treated as a great 'triumph':

> I hear, and I rejoice to hear, that the great lady, the other object of the triumph, has borne that day (one is interested that beings made for suffering should suffer well) and that she bears all the succeeding days, that she bears the imprisonment of her husband, and her own captivity, and the exile of her friends, and the insulting adulation of addresses, and the whole weight of her accumulated wrongs, with a serene patience, in a manner suited to her rank and race, and becoming the offspring of a sovereign distinguished for her piety and her courage [Maria Theresa]; that like her she has lofty sentiments; that she feels with the dignity of a Roman matron; that in the last extremity she will save herself from the last disgrace, and that if she must fall, she will fall by no ignoble hand.
>
> It is now sixteen or seventeen years since I saw the queen of France, then the dauphiness, at Versailles; and surely never lighted on this orb, which she hardly seemed to touch, a more delightful vision. I saw her just above the horizon, decorating and cheering the elevated sphere she just began to move in, – glittering like the morning star, full of life, and splendour, and joy. Oh! what a revolution! and what an heart must I have, to contemplate without emotion that elevation and that fall! Little did I dream when she added titles of veneration to those of enthusiastic, distant, respectful love, that she should ever be obliged to carry the sharp antidote against disgrace concealed in that bosom; little did I dream that I should have lived to see such disasters fallen upon her in a nation of gallant men, in a nation of men of honour and of cavaliers. I thought ten thousand swords must have leaped from their scabbards to avenge even a look that threatened her with insult – But the age of chivalry is gone. – That of sophisters, oeconomists, and calculators, has succeeded; and the glory of Europe is extinguished for ever.[42]

Some of Burke's contemporaries found the rhetoric of this passage risible. In every case, however, they also disagreed with his interpretation of the French Revolution.[43] The first such critic was Philip Francis (the probable author of the famous *Letters of*

Junius of 1770–72), who read the *Reflections* before publication. Francis condemned the passage on Marie Antoinette as 'pure foppery'. Are you, he asked Burke, 'such a determined Champion of Beauty as to draw your Sword in defense of any jade upon Earth provided she be handsome?' Criticism always stung Burke to elaborate self-justification. In this instance, he retorted that Francis had misread the text, if he thought that the beauty, or even the virtue, of Marie Antoinette was at issue. Burke grounded his defence on the queen's 'high Rank, great Splendour of descent, great personal Elegance and outward accomplishments'. These, he argued, were 'ingredients of moment' in securing our interest and sympathy in 'the Misfortunes of Men'.[44] This is the elevated sublime of Longinus, not the fearful obscurity of Burke's own *Enquiry*. For modern readers, the notion that rank gives a special poignancy to suffering is alien and repugnant. Tragedy is now a thoroughly democratized genre. Even in 1790, an alternative 'bourgeois' tragedy was well established. Burke, however, remained loyal to the still-dominant classical tradition in which he had been educated, and expected his readers to respond to the classical notion of decorum which restricted tragedy to characters of high social rank.[45]

Burke's purpose in the evocative passage on Marie Antoinette was 'to excite an horrour against midnight assassins at back stairs, and their more wicked abettors in Pulpits'. Defending the propriety and the sincerity of his feelings, he drew a parallel with his reactions to literary tragedies:

> 'Whats Hecuba to him or he to Hecuba that he should weep for her?' Why because she was Hecuba, the Queen of Troy, the Wife of Priam, and sufferd in the close of Life a thousand Calamities. I felt too for Hecuba when I read the fine Tragedy of Euripides upon her Story: and I never enquired into the Anecdotes of the Court or City of Troy before I gave way to the Sentiments which the author wished to inspire; nor do I remember that he ever said one word of her Virtues. It is for those who applaud or palliate assassination, regicide, and base insults to Women of illustrious place, to prove the Crimes in the sufferers which they allege to justifye their own. But if they had proved fornication on any such Woman, taking the manners of the world and the manners of France, I shall never put it in a parallel with Assassination.[46]

Furniss uses this passage, together with the incident in *Hamlet* to which Burke alludes, to illustrate the 'theory of the theatrical nature of political figures and institutions' which he attributes to Burke. In his view, Burke, the 'sentimental victim of his own dramatic spectacle', asks readers to 'respond to the suffering of Marie Antoinette as if she were a dramatic character'.[47] On the contrary: Burke is responding to a 'real tragedy' in a way that he takes to be natural, not theatrical. To respond with sympathy to the distresses of a real queen is more 'natural' than to be moved by such misfortunes in drama. Tragedy in real life (as he had argued in the *Enquiry*) is more powerful than its representation in drama.[48] Burke uses the allusion to *Hamlet* to convince Francis of the genuineness of his feeling for Marie Antoinette, not to concede its theatricality. If I shed a tear for the fictional queen of Euripides, he argues, surely you can believe that I weep for the real sufferings of a real queen? In Shakespeare's play, Hamlet, comparing himself to the First Player, is disturbed by the incongruity between the ease with which the player can respond to a fictional situation with a real emotional response, and his own difficulty in doing anything about a real situation. The Player responds to the story of Hecuba because, so Burke believes, to be moved by the fall from greatness to misery is a 'natural' human reaction.

Burke makes the point explicitly in the *Reflections* itself:

> Some tears might be drawn from me, if such a spectacle were exhibited on the stage. I should be truly ashamed of finding in myself that superficial, theatric sense of painted distress, whilst I could exult over it in real life. With such a perverted mind, I could never venture to shew my face at a tragedy. People would think the tears that Garrick formerly, or that Siddons not long since, have extorted from me, were the tears of hypocrisy; I should know them to be the tears of folly.[49]

For Burke, politics was not a kind of theatre. The dispute between him and Price was not between different ideas of theatricality. Burke offers his readers a decorum for behaviour in the pulpit, which he accuses Price of desecrating; and a decorum for behaving towards kings and queens, whom he accuses the revolutionaries of basely insulting. These decorums are 'problematic' only to those who do not share Burke's assumptions and values. Burke's 'spectacle' is a rhetorical means to induce the same response in others. They will respond only if they are persuaded that Burke's feelings are themselves genuine. A commonplace of classical rhetoric is that, in order to move an audience, the orator must appear to be moved himself.[50] Quintilian provides an example apposite to the passage on Marie Antoinette. Explaining how a rhetorician can work himself up to an emotion real enough to affect his auditors, he recommends conjuring up such visions as will enable him to recreate the emotions which the real object of passion evoked.[51] Quintilian even confesses that he has often not only moved himself to tears by this method, but even turned pale and felt real grief.[52] Similarly, Burke told Francis that he wept at his own description of Marie Antoinette, both when he wrote it and 'almost as often' as he reread it.[53] In using hyperbole to achieve these effects, Burke was likewise following classical tradition. Aristotle did not approve of hyperbole, but recognized its rhetorical power to create an impression of anger. Thus he commends Homer for making Achilles reject Agamemnon's magnificent peace-offering in hyperbolical terms (*Rhetoric*, II. xi; 1413a). Later writers repeat Aristotle's point about the need to express emotion though appropriate figures, without any of his distrust of hyperbole. Thus Cicero, defending the free use of the emotional appeal, treats exaggeration as a stylistic resource ('Orator ... mala, ac molesta, et fugienda, multo maiora et acerbiora verbis facit').[54] Quintilian describes hyperbole as a lie without the intent to deceive ('mentiri hyperbolen nec ita, ut mendacio fallere velit').[55] Though his enemies liked to portray him as carried away by his passions or even mad, Burke was perfectly conscious of what he was doing: writing in a tradition that employed hyperbole to represent anger, indignation, and reactions to extreme situations.

Burke's rhetorical problem in the passage on Marie Antoinette was to create sympathy for a woman whose reputation was not, as Francis correctly noted, spotless. The first paragraph is constructed as a single paratactic sentence, to emphasize a sense of the weight of the queen's 'accumulated wrongs'. The topic of her distinguished ancestry allows Burke to introduce the (quite irrelevant) virtues of her mother, Maria Theresa, the late empress. Maria Theresa had enjoyed a reputation as a pious and courageous monarch. British opinion had strongly supported her against Prussian and Bavarian aggression during the War of the Austrian Succession. In a bold stroke at the end of the paragraph, Burke conflates three images: Maria Theresa (who had died in 1780); the stock figure of the Roman Matron; and the unfortunate Marie Antoinette herself. The fusion is tragic but not theatrical. For it to work, the reader must accept that the reality of Marie Antoinette's situation is such as might justify suicide as an alternative to a fate worse than death. In the second paragraph, Burke employs a different strategy to deflect attention from inappropriate images of the queen. He moves from 'I hear' to 'I saw'; from the present to 'sixteen or seventeen years ago'. Burke visited France in 1773. The deliberate vagueness about the date combines authenticity with immediacy; writing a letter, Burke does not feel the need to check his dates. In 1773 Marie Antoinette was a princess of eighteen, unsullied by the scandals that later besmirched her reputation. Although Burke's description has been much ridiculed, to evoke the appearance of a young princess surrounded at a respectful distance by a swarm of gallant admirers, his style is not inappropriate. Since the rhetorical purpose of the passage is to provide a contrast with the queen's present humiliation, Burke's description emphasizes elevation rather than beauty. Conventional Petrarchan images evoke an idealized *princesse lointaine*. The conceit figures the princess as Venus, the morning star, just risen; and as the goddess, just stepping out of her chariot. The reader is invited to sympathize with the once-adored young princess, formerly defended by the 'ten thousand swords' of the admiring cavaliers, now a matron threatened by the 'bayonets and poniards' of a gang of cruel assassins.

So emotionally intense and so obviously value-laden a passage divided readers on predictable lines. Those who were sympathetic to the Revolution ridiculed it; those with aristocratic prejudices warmed to it. Horace Walpole, despite being an inveterate enemy of Burke, even provided a testimonial to its accuracy as a representation. 'I know the tirade on the Queen of France is condemned,' he told Lady Ossory, 'and yet I must avow I admire it much. It paints her exactly as she appeared to me the

first time I saw her when Dauphiness. She ... shot through the
room like an aërial being, all brightness and grace and without
seeming to touch earth'.[56] The memoirist Nathaniel Wraxall, who
saw Marie Antoinette in 1776, provides another corroboration,
the more valuable for being unwitting. According to Wraxall,
Burke had 'overrated' her 'personal charms', which in his view
'consisted more in her elevated manner, lofty demeanour, and
graces of deportment, all which announced a queen, than in her
features or countenance'.[57] Wraxall wrote from imperfect
memory of the *Reflections*: these are precisely the qualities that
Burke celebrates.

In the *Reflections*, rhetoric and representation are inter-
dependent and mutually reinforcing. Those who agreed with
Burke's interpretation accepted the propriety of his rhetoric.
Indicative of the power of Burke's arguments and his evidence is
the number of replies that the *Reflections* provoked. Had it been
no more than the 'dramatic performance' that Paine pretended, it
would hardly have demanded refutation. Had Burke been no
more than (as Hughes claims) 'the chief actor in a drama that he
has also staged and written', he could safely have been ignored.[58]
In fact, so powerful a case did Burke make (though few of the
readers who agreed with it said so in print), that dozens of
supporters of the French Revolution took up their pens in
response. They all proceed from the assumption that Burke has
made a formidable case which needs to be countered with every
weapon, rhetorical as well as rational, at their disposal. They
subject Burke's use of evidence, his arguments, and his
conclusions to minute scrutiny. They do not treat the *Reflections*
as a cobweb of sophistry that can easily be brushed away. While
the power of Burke's rhetoric is what energizes the *Reflections*,
rhetoric can do little on its own. Burke's opponents recognized in
the *Reflections* a powerful and credible representation of the
Revolution. That representation deserves to be taken more
seriously. Paine's dramatic metaphor, overdeveloped by recent
critics, should not be allowed to delude readers into treating the
Reflections as a work of fiction.

Notes

1 *Rights of Man* (1791; Harmondsworth: Penguin Books, 1969), pp. 35, 49, 46, 45, 49. I am grateful to Mark Jones for his comments on an earlier version of this essay.

2 *History of the Royal Society*, II, xx, ed. Jackson I. Cope and Harold Whitmore Jones (St Louis: Washington University Studies, 1958), pp. 111–13.

3 Peter Hughes, 'Originality and Allusion in the Writings of Edmund Burke', *Centrum*, 4:1 (1976), pp. 32–43 (quotation from p. 39); Ronald Paulson, *Representations of Revolution (1789–1820)* (New Haven: Yale University Press, 1983), pp. 4–5; Tom Furniss, *Edmund Burke's Aesthetic Ideology: Language, Gender and Political Economy in Revolution* (Cambridge: Cambridge University Press, 1993), p. 150.

4 Hughes, 'Originality and Allusion', p. 32. Paulson speaks of reading Burke at 'a deeper level of consciousness', at which 'the illustrations and metaphorical decoration take us closest to Burke's true intention, often saying more than he may have meant to say'; *Representations of Revolution*, p. 66.

5 Francis P. Canavan, *The Political Reason of Edmund Burke* (Durham, NC: Duke University Press, 1960), especially pp. 40–1.

6 Neal Wood, 'The Aesthetic Dimension of Burke's Political Thought', *Journal of British Studies*, 4:1 (1964), pp. 41–64; quotation from p. 42.

7 Stephen Copley and John Whale, eds, *Beyond Romanticism: New Approaches to Texts and Contexts* (London: Routledge, 1992), Introduction, p. 8.

8 Printed in Sir James Prior, *Life of Edmond Malone* (London, 1860), p. 154. Burke made the same point in a draft letter, undated but assigned by the editor to 1795 in *Correspondence*, ed. Thomas W. Copeland and others (Cambridge: Cambridge University Press, 1958–78), VIII, pp. 364–5. These references lend credibility to Richard Payne Knight's assertion that 'in his latter days' Burke 'laughed very candidly and good-humouredly at many of the philosophical absurdities' of the *Enquiry*; *An Analytical Enquiry into the Principles of Taste* (4th edn, London, 1808), p. 28.

9 *Philosophical Enquiry*, pt V, sect. ii; ed. James T. Boulton (London: Routledge, 1958), p. 164.

10 W. J. T. Mitchell, *Iconology: Image, Text, Ideology* (Chicago: University of Chicago Press, 1986), p. 139, quotes this passage as though it applied to words in general. Furniss, too, makes Burke's theory more general than the text of the *Enquiry* warrants (*Edmund Burke's Aesthetic Ideology*, pp. 96–112).

11 *Reflections*, pp. 146–7.

12 *Enquiry Concerning Political Justice* (1793), ed. F. E. L. Priestley (Toronto: University of Toronto Press, 1946), II, 545, note. Paul Fussell, *The Rhetorical World of Augustan Humanism: Ethics and Imagery from Swift to Burke* (Oxford: Clarendon Press, 1965), shows how deeply traditional was

Burke's metaphorical language. Paulson, too, recognizes the 'extremely conventional literary elements' in the *Reflections* (*Representations of Revolution*, p. 65).

13 *Reflections*, pp. 98, 204, 143, 114, 222, 232.

14 *Representations of Revolution*, pp. 71, 67.

15 *Edmund Burke's Aesthetic Ideology*, pp. 69, 12.

16 Tim Gray and Paul Hindson, 'Edmund Burke and the French Revolution as Drama', *History of European Ideas*, 14:2 (1992), pp. 203–11; quotation from p. 204.

17 Aristotle, *Rhetoric*, II. i, 1377b.

18 *Lectures Concerning Oratory* (Dublin, 1758); modern edition by E. Neal Claussen and Karl R. Wallace (Carbondale: Southern Illinois University Press, 1972).

19 *Lectures on Oratory*, pp. 127, 165, 179, 215, 219.

20 Boswell, *Life of Johnson*, entry for 16 April 1775, ed. George Birkbeck Hill, revised L. F. Powell (Oxford: Clarendon Press, 1934–64), II, p. 360.

21 G. M. Ditchfield, 'The Parliamentary Struggle over the Repeal of the Test and Corporation Acts, 1787–90', *English Historical Review*, 89:3 (1974), pp. 551–77.

22 *Reflections*, p. 103.

23 Furniss, *Edmund Burke's Aesthetic Ideology*, especially pp. 11–12.

24 Lloyd F. Bitzer, 'Aristotle's Enthymeme Revisited', *Quarterly Journal of Speech*, 45:4 (1959), pp. 399–408.

25 *Reflections*, p. 85.

26 Ibid. pp. 116, 100–1, 93–4, 122.

27 Frans de Bruyn, 'Theater and countertheater in Burke's *Reflections on the Revolution in France*', in *Burke and the French Revolution: Bicentennial Essays*, ed. Steven Blakemore (Athens: University of Georgia Press, 1992), pp. 28–68; quotations from p. 43.

28 *Reflections*, p. 117.

29 The irony of Burke's first book, *A Vindication of Natural Society* (1756), assumes an audience able to identify an argument as inherently absurd. The assumption proved mistaken: to the second edition (1757), Burke added a preface explaining the ironic intent. By the 1790s, the book's ideas, far from seeming self-evidently absurd, struck a radical such as William Godwin as eminently sensible; *Enquiry Concerning Political Justice*, I, p. 13n.

30 Tom Furniss, 'Stripping the Queen: Edmund Burke's Magic Lantern Show', in *Burke and the French Revolution*, ed. Blakemore, pp. 69–96; quotation from p. 77.

31 *Reflections*, pp. 221–31.

32 Edwin Black observes, on an emotive, self-referential passage in a speech by Lyndon Johnson, that 'the auditor had to be moved by such depiction [of child poverty] or reject it altogether. No reserved response was possible short of disengagement'; *Rhetorical Questions: Studies of Public Discourse* (Chicago: University of Chicago Press, 1992), p. 27.

33 *Reflections*, pp. 121–2.

34 Paulson, *Representations of Revolution*, p. 60; Hughes, 'Originality and Allusion', p. 39; Furniss, *Edmund Burke's Aesthetic Ideology*, p. 154.

35 Martha Swinburne, an English visitor, uses the phrase 'in her shift'; 'Political Extracts from Mrs S[winburne]'s Letters from Paris in 1788 & 1789', Pelham Papers, British Library, Add. MS 33,121, fo. 16. According to the *Journal Politique-National*, the queen fled 'en chemise' (collected edition, vol. 2, no. 21, p. 243). Jean-Joseph Mounier describes the Queen as fleeing 'à demi-nue'; *Exposé de la Conduite de M. Mounier* (Paris, 1789), part 2, p. 26. A later account by Mounier describes the violation of the bed: 'les Brigands irrités de n'avoir pu la sacrifier à leur fureur, percèrent les matelats à coups de piques, & commirent d'autres indignités'; *Procédure criminelle instruite au Châtelet de Paris* (Paris, 1790), pt 3, p. 77.

36 *An Historical and Moral View of the Origin and Progress of the French Revolution* (1794); in *Works*, ed. Janet Todd and Marilyn Butler (London: William Pickering, 1989), VI, p. 206. Wollstonecraft's attack on the *Reflections* is *A Vindication of the Rights of Men* (1790); in *Works*, V, pp. 5–77.

37 *Rights of Man*, p. 63.

38 Black, *Rhetorical Questions*, pp. 147–70, speculates on the causes of this shift.

39 *Lettre à M. d'Alembert sur les spectacles* (1758); in *Œuvres complètes*, ed. Bernard Gagnebin and others (Paris: Gallimard, 1959–95), V, p. 74.

40 In 'Burke's Tragic Muse: Sarah Siddons and the "feminization" of the *Reflections*', in *Burke and the French Revolution*, ed. Blakemore, pp. 1–27, Christopher Reid quotes a passage from the *Enquiry*, in which a real-life orator is addressing a crowd, as though Burke made no difference between this use of language and acting (pp. 14–15).

41 *Rights of Man*, p. 50.

42 *Reflections*, p. 126.

43 Examples include *Strictures on the Letter of the Right Hon. Mr Burke, on the Revolution in France* (London, 1791), pp. 96–101; *Temperate Comments upon Intemperate Reflections, or, a Review of Mr Burke's Letter* (London, 1791), pp. 32–6.

44 Francis to Burke, 19 February 1790, and Burke's reply, 20 February; *Correspondence*, VI, pp. 85–92.

45 'Hints for an Essay on the Drama', in *Writings and Speeches*, I, p. 558.

46 *Correspondence*, VI, p. 90.

47 Furniss, *Edmund Burke's Aesthetic Ideology*, pp. 161, 159.

48 *Reflections,* p. 132; *Philosophical Enquiry,* I, sect. xv, p. 47.

49 *Reflections,* p. 132.

50 Aristotle, *Poetics,* 1455a; Lawson, *Lectures Concerning Oratory,* p. 252 (with an important qualification on p. 256); Hugh Blair, *Lectures on Rhetoric and Belles Lettres* (1783), ed. Harold F. Harding (Carbondale: Southern Illinois University Press, 1965), II, pp. 192–3.

51 Quintilian, *Institutio Oratoria,* VI.ii.26–36.

52 Ibid. 26.

53 *Correspondence,* VI, p. 91.

54 Cicero, *De Oratore,* I.li.221.

55 Quintilian, *Institutio,* VIII.vi.74.

56 Walpole to Lady Upper Ossory, 1 December 1790; in *Correspondence,* ed. W. S. Lewis (New Haven: Yale University Press, 1937–83), XXXIV, pp. 97–8.

57 Sir Nathaniel William Wraxall, *Historical and Posthumous Memoirs,* ed. Henry B. Wheatley (London, 1884), I, pp. 84–5.

58 Paine, *Rights of Man,* p. 59; Hughes, 'Originality and Allusion', p. 41.

3

The *Reflections* refracted: the critical reception of Burke's *Reflections on the Revolution in France* during the early 1790s

GREGORY CLAEYS

Completed in late August 1790, Edmund Burke's *Reflections on the Revolution in France* was published on 1 November at the comparatively expensive price of five shillings. Its appearance had been eagerly awaited for months by Burke's friends and political associates. They knew that the alarming rupture between Burke on the one hand and Fox and Sheridan on the other in the Army Estimate debates on 5 and 9 February 1790 – the moment Burke declared France should be 'considered as expunged out of the system of Europe ... as not politically existing',[1] the moment the *Reflections*, no work of scholarship, was almost spontaneously born[2] – would probably be rendered permanent by the work. This proved the case. Initially it was Burke who was isolated. But soon (though Pitt would still attempt a coalition with Fox)[3] the Whigs were rent asunder, and in both practice and theory British politics were swiftly transformed. Burke himself had been to a degree ambiguous at the outbreak of the Revolution.[4] Well aware of the implications and growing sense of public anticipation, he had laboured over the text, revising and redrafting until his exasperated printer, Dodsley, urged a conclusion. He was not, finally, completely pleased with the result; as he wrote to Windham (27 October 1790):

> I may have made some Mistakes, and I wrote sometimes in circum-
> stances not favourable to accuracy. I wrote from the memory of
> what I had read; and was not able always to get the documents
> from whence I had been supplied when I wished to verify my facts
> with precision. But I hope my errors will be found to be rather
> mistakes than misrepresentations. I am quite sure, that in most of
> my statements, I have shot short of the mark than beyond it.[5]

Much has been written on the immediate political results of
Burke's break from the Foxite Whigs; his antagonism towards
Sheridan,[6] whom he regarded as the real leader of a democratic
faction among the Whigs and against whom he had harboured a
grudge for several years;[7] his forgiveness by George III, whom he
had, 'almost mad'[8] himself, attacked so vehemently during the
Regency Crisis, and his reconciliation with Pitt, with whom he
was dining in friendly company within a year.[9] Less attention has
been devoted to how the *Reflections* was actually read. This essay
accordingly will examine some of the readings of, and reactions
to, Burke's *Reflections* during the period from 1790 to 1793. Its
purpose is to draw out the main themes which excited the
reaction of Burke's critics; to eke out, in other words, the
'meaning' of the text not as Burke construed it, but as critics,
hunting and picking at the ideas which most offended them,
conceived it, in order to define more exactly Burke's contribution to a contemporary debate, rather than to conservative
political philosophy.

The immediate success of the *Reflections* is undoubted. Seven
thousand copies were snatched up in the first week alone,[10] a total
of 19,000 in the year following in England and another 13,000 in
France, with about 30,000 copies being sold in Britain over the
next few years.[11] Many of the heads of state in Europe sent Burke
their thanks. The French princes, assembled at Koblentz,
extended their compliments through M. Cazales. George III had a
number of copies bound in brown moroccan leather which he
gave as tokens of honour, and reportedly said – it is a pity that
the dust-cover blurb had not yet been invented – 'that it was a
book which every gentleman ought to read'.[12]

Some of those Burke had aimed to please with the volume
responded effusively, like Sir Joshua Reynolds, to whom he had

sent a copy. Eulogies both public and private were common. Friends like Gilbert Elliot wrote of the book that he 'could not lay it down till I had finished the last page. I shall read it again immediately, with more deliberation and therefore, if that be possible, even with greater enjoyment; certainly with more profit ... Every Scholar, and every man who without deserving that name, has any relish for mental pleasures ... must make this book his companion and his constant resource ... Your book contains the fundamental Elements of all Political knowledge, and lays clearly open to us the just foundations of all Social wisdom.'[13] Horace Walpole was 'not more charmed with his wit and eloquence than with his enthusiasm, being particularly enamoured of Burke's description of Marie Antoinette, and 'the swords leaping out of their scabbards' – or which ought to have leapt out – in her defence.[14] Fanny Burney found the *Reflections* 'the noblest, deepest, most animated, and exalted work that I think I have ever read,' and thought that whatever might appear to be Burke's inconsistencies, 'When I read however, such a book as this, I am apt to imagine the whole of such a being must be right as well as the parts, and that the time may come when the mists that obscure the motives and incentives to those actions and proceedings which seem incongruous, may be chased away.'[15] Lord Auckland thought it 'a fine piece of eloquence and a splendid exercise of talents', if somewhat 'diffuse and flowery, like his speeches'.[16] Horace Walpole read it twice and found it 'Sublime, profound, and gay. The wit and satire are equally brilliant, and the whole is wise, tho' in some points he goes too far; yet in general there is far less want of judgment than could be expected from him.'[17] Burke's close friend William Windham thought that there had never been 'a work so valuable in its kind, or that displayed powers of so extraordinary a nature. It is a work that may seem capable of overturning the National Assembly, and turning the stream of opinion throughout Europe.'[18] Similarly Burke's friend Dr Thomas Barnard, Bishop of Killaloe, wrote that the *Reflections* was 'indeed a capital work. The facts are undeniable, the arguments impregnable, the stile inimitable, and the whole unanswerable.'[19] Edward Gibbon proclaimed himself 'as high an Aristocrate as Burke himself', and begged 'leave to subscribe my assent to Mr. Burke's creed on the revolution of France. I admire his eloquence, I approve his politics, I adore his chivalry, and I can almost excuse his reverence for church establishments.'[20]

Some who might be expected to be pleased, however, like Fox's friend the Prince of Wales, whose order had been so well served by Burke's efforts, reacted differently; 'How the Devil could your friend Burke publish such a Farrago of Nonsense?', he was reported to have said to Lord Thomond shortly after the book appeared.[21] Other readers from whom Burke had expected more reasoned approbation were also critical, notably Philip Francis, generally accepted to have been 'Junius', to whom, with Reynolds and Windham,[22] he had shown an early draft. Francis wrote that 'I find, (though with no sort of surprise, having often talked with you on the Subject) that we differ only in every thing.'[23] Francis particularly rejected Burke's famous description of Marie Antoinette at Versailles 'glittering like the morning star, full of life and splendour and joy', which evoked the famous phrase, 'the age of chivalry is gone; that of sophisters, economists, and calculators has succeeded; and the glory of Europe is extinguished for ever!':[24]

> In my opinion all that you say of the Queen is pure foppery. If she be a perfect female character, you ought to take your ground upon her virtues. If she be the reverse, it is ridiculous in any but a lover to place her personal charms in opposition to her crimes ... Look back, I beseech you, and deliberate a little before you determine that this is an office which perfectly becomes you. If I stop here it is not for want of a multitude of objections. The mischief you are going to do yourself is, to my apprehension, palpable. It is visible. It is audible. I snuff it in the wind. I taste it already. I feel it in every sense, and so will you hereafter; when I vow to God (an elegant phrase) it will be a sort of consolation for me to reflect that I did everything in my power to prevent it.[25]

What, then, of the critics Burke *might* have expected? Fox loudly proclaimed his views to be 'wide as the poles asunder' from Burke's. Privately he called the book 'Cursed Stuff'. In Parliament, debating the Quebec Bill, he said that, 'as soon as his book on the subject was published, he condemned that book both in public and private, and every one of the doctrines it contained'. He felt that 'his right honourable friend's conduct appeared as if it sprung from an intention to injure him, at least it produced the same effect, because the right honourable gentleman opposite to him had chosen to talk of republican principles as principles which he wished to be introduced into the new constitution of Canada, whereas his principles were very far from republican in any degree'.[26] His main line of argument against Burke thereafter was his political inconsistency.[27] Sheridan's thoughts were similar from February onwards.[28] At the famous meeting of the Revolution Society in which an argument broke out over the *Reflections*, the radical John Horne Tooke, taking a line favoured by many Dissenters, called it 'the tears of the Priesthood for the loss of their pudding'.[29] Yet the radical Whig leaders, like Fox and Sheridan, were not republicans, and while they would continue to espouse the cause of parliamentary reform, did not expect that an expanded franchise would introduce a novel political system. Temporarily divided from Burke over the nature and implications of the French Revolution, they nonetheless remained no great distance from him in many other respects, even with respect to the British constitution. This would facilitate the return of some Whig critics, after the mid–1790s, back to a Burkean camp which they still regarded as Whiggish, and indicates the degree to which Burke could be still read as innovating within Whiggism rather than rejecting it.

The early printed critiques of the *Reflections* were of the more ephemeral as well as the more extended, philosophical variety. While it is not possible here to summarize all of the arguments of these critiques of the *Reflections*, some sense of their main themes can be given. The first printed response of the *Reflections* was Mary Wollstonecraft's *Vindication of the Rights of Men* (1790),[30] the often-unread predecessor to the more famous second vindication, of the rights of woman. Wollstonecraft's line of attack is to accuse Burke of 'pretty flights' of prose which 'arise from your pampered sensibility', in other words, of romanticizing the old order and the monarchy in particular, which as 'hereditary property – hereditary honours' have in Wollstonecraft's view inhibited the progress of civilization. Like most of the opposition works of this period, Wollstonecraft's starting-point is an ideal of natural rights given to mankind by God, and not susceptible of substantial modification by prescriptive rights. Burke's 'servile reverence for antiquity, and prudent attention to self-interest' prevented him from seeing that an undue regard to prescription violated natural rights:

> Security of property! Behold, in a few words, the definition of English liberty. And to this selfish principle every nobler one is sacrificed. – The Briton takes place of the man, and the image of God is lost in the citizen![31]

Instead, the cultivation of natural rights is to foster a bold republicanism, the very antithesis of 'an unmanly servility, most inimical to true dignity of character', which is subverted by chivalry. (This would become a central theme in the second vindication.) Burke was merely inconsistent in having 'staunchly supported the despotic principles' of France compared with his defence of the American colonists.

Following Wollstonecraft several other brief responses to Burke merit mention. The historian Catharine Macaulay's *Observations on the Reflections of the Right Hon. Edmund Burke* (1790)[32] focuses on Richard Price's and the radical Whigs' interpretation of the 'Glorious' Revolution of 1688, which they believed France had emulated, Louis XVI having been 'cashiered' for misconduct by a National Assembly acting wholly within its rights, which included the formation of a new constitution, and a more popular form of government and ecclesiastical arrangements. George Rous's *Thoughts on Government Occasioned by Mr. Burke's Reflections* (1791)[33] charges the *Reflections* with retailing 'neither more nor less than the exploded doctrine of the old school revived in a new dress', i.e., the Toryism of 1688 which supported any form of despotism, rather than any form of Whiggism which opted for the cause of liberty. Rous took the view that despotic principles had so far penetrated the political and ecclesiastical system that their overthrow was inevitable, and that kingly power must rest upon popular approbation, the principle established in 1688 and reiterated in Price's 1789 sermon, the final cause of the composition of the *Reflections*. 'The whole fallacy of Mr. Burke's reasoning consists in confounding the right of the people with its abuse', Rous insisted, public happiness being the test of monarchical as well as any other form of government. Similarly Brooke Boothby's *A Letter to the Right Hon. Edmund Burke* (1791) defended Price's leading principles, justified the causes of inevitable revolution in France against 'an *unqualified* monarchy, a feudal nobility, a domineering hierarchy,' and praised 'the most magnificent spectacle that has ever presented itself to the human eye. A great and generous nation animated with one soul, rising up as one man to demand the restitution of their natural rights.' Burke seemed 'to have been so awe-struck with the magnificence of the court and so enamoured of the rising beauties of the Dauphiness' that he 'had no attention left to bestow on the people'. Nor was Burke consistent in his opposition to monarchical encroachments on popular power in the 1770s and 1780s, and in his prosecution of the arbitrary rule in India of Warren Hastings (a theme addressed in John Scott's *A Letter to the Right Hon. Edmund Burke* (1791),[34] and the views outlined in the *Reflections*. A defence of ideas of popular right and the choice of governors against 'indefeasible hereditary right' or 'divine right' was also at the centre of Benjamin Bousfield's *Observations on the Right Honourable Edmund Burke's Pamphlet* (1791), Charles Pigott's *Strictures on the New Political Tenets of the Right Hon. Edmund Burke* (1791), and other responses. Few of the shorter tracts on the *Reflections* fail to comment on Burke's view of Marie Antoinette, his apparent inconsistency in supporting the despotic rule of the *ancien régime*, his failure to appreciate the power of ecclesiastical 'superstition', in upholding the *ancien régime*, and his apparent opposition to the principles of 1688.

Amongst the more extensive responses to Burke four merit special attention: Thomas Paine's *Rights of Man* (1791–92), Thomas Christie's *Letters on the Revolution in France* (1791), James Mackintosh's *Vindiciae Gallicae* (1791), and Joseph Priestley's *Letters to the Right Hon. Edmund Burke, Occasioned by His Reflections on the Revolution in France* (1791). Paine's *Rights of Man* became of course much the most famous and most reviled of these, being mocked by many Whigs but sparking a popular movement of extraordinary importance.[35] I have analysed its themes and their reception extensively elsewhere.[36]

Christie's *Letters* focused on six themes: the general

principles of the *Reflections*, especially in contrast to those of 1688; the necessity of a revolution in France; the evils attending that revolution; the judicial and territorial changes made since; and the monarchical system. Taking his starting-point as Price's defence of natural rights, including a people's right to choose their own governors and frame their own government, Christie derided the view that the British constitution was unalterable, or based solely on prescriptive right.[37] The *ancien régime*, rotted throughout by corruption, was 'an arbitrary and wretched system of Government', and merited a 'radical reform' as Britain's had done a century earlier. Once this principle was acknowledged, the violent episodes of the Revolution, the occasional fury of the mob, paled into insignificance, and the right of the people to devize a constitution and assembly to their liking could be conceded.

Better known than Christie's *Letters* was James Mackintosh's *Vindiciae Gallicae* (1791).[38] Complimented by Fox in the Commons, it became the one response for which Burke, while first dismissing it as 'Paine at bottom',[39] was to acknowledge a grudging admiration, after Mackintosh had recanted his revolutionary enthusiasm in 1796, writing that 'it is on all hands allowed that you were the most able advocate for the cause which you supported'.[40] Disregarding the notion that Burke was an apostate Whig, Mackintosh proclaimed that 'An abhorrence for abstract politics, a predilection for aristocracy, and a dread of innovation, have ever been among the most sacred articles of his public creed.' The structure of the *Vindiciae* is otherwise similar to Christie's *Letters*, being divided into a justification for the necessity of the Revolution; an analysis of the composition and character of the National Assembly, a defence of the popular 'excesses' which had occurred as fuelled by the cruelties of the *ancien régime*; an account of the new French constitution; and a vindication of the British supporters of the cause and their fundamental allegiance to the principles of 1688, admiring but not wishing to imitate the French Revolution. Like most of Burke's antagonists, Mackintosh asserted centrally that the *ancien régime* had been an 'incorrigible' outmoded feudal despotism incapable of gradual and moderate reform by that enlightened commercial 'monied interest' or middle class which was the harbinger of

modern civilization and basis of modern Whiggism. As such it
was antithetical both to the British constitution and its Whiggish
underpinning, and to the doctrine of natural rights (to which
Mackintosh, while hostile to a titled aristocratic class, Burke's
'Corinthian capital of polished states', pays less heed than, for
instance, Paine or Wollstonecraft, by contrast to an argument for
rights based on utilitarian expediency).[41] On the issue of the
confiscation of Church lands and elimination of the 'sacerdotal
aristocracy' of great interest and importance to the *Reflections*,
Mackintosh was insistent that 'The lands of the Church possess
not the most simple and indispensable requisites of property.
They are not even pretended to be held for the benefit of those
who enjoy them.' As such they were not inalienable, but could be
disposed of for the public good without subverting the laws of
property as such or eradicating the spirit of true Christianity.
Against Burke's Gothic support for the ancient aristocracy and
its ethos, then, Mackintosh gave stress to the progressive aims of
an enlightened commercial society:

> commerce has overthrown that 'feudal and chivalrous system' under
> whose shade it first grew. In religion, learning has subverted the
> superstition whose opulent endowments had first fostered it.
> Peculiar circumstances softened the barbarism of the middle ages to
> a degree which favored the admission of commerce and the growth
> of knowledge.

The French Revolution, then, was linked to the cause of literary,
intellectual and commercial progress. It was Burke who promoted ignorance and barbarism, not the revolutionaries.

As might be expected from one of the leaders of the
Dissenting interest, Joseph Priestley's *Letters to the Right Hon.
Edmund Burke*[42] pays greater heed to the religious issues raised
by the Revolution than most responses to the *Reflections*. Other
readers of course also thought the religious issue crucial, if not
central, to Burke.[43] Much of Priestley's work, however, covers
similar ground to that of other respondents, examining the general
causes of the Revolution; the emergence of the new constitution
and popular character of the new form of government, whose
prepondence of lawyers paralleled that in America, and holds out
no dangers for Priestley; and doctrines of natural rights, which

along with utilitarian justifications are strenuously supported against the notions upheld by Burke of *'Passive obedience and non-resistance,'* peculiar to the Tories and the 'friends of arbitrary power'; and parallels with the events of 1688. Proportionately more effort, however, is devoted to the case for disestablishment in general, the dangers and corruptions of an established clergy maintained by public property, and the resulting inhibition of mental liberty, religious debate, and genuine religion, a Church establishment, which 'naturally tends to debase the minds of those who officiate in it,' being merely a specific instance of the interference of government where individual effort should be left to its own devices. Instead an elective clergy, parallel in its virtues to elected representatives compared to hereditary legislators, is given full support as a means of promoting a 'general enlargement of liberty,' when civil wars, colonies, grievous inequalities, and intolerance would be abolished.

The leading responses to the *Reflections* thus reveal both a consistency of argument, a concentration on half a dozen main themes in the text, and the general consensus that Burke had 'unwhigg'd' himself in departing so far from the established interpretation of the principles of 1688 with respect to natural rights and the popular nature of the British constitution in particular. While reactions to the *Reflections* reveal existing resentments and disagreements (Scott, Fox, Sheridan), Burke's critics, unlike many subsequent conservative commentators, did not on the whole understand him as defending the British constitution as such. Instead he was accused of bolstering monarchical absolutism, and an odious Catholic hierarchy to boot. We have focused here on the years 1790–92. The effect of Burke's critics in this period, and especially Paine, was considerable; as Romilly commented in May 1791: 'It is astonishing how Burke's book is fallen; though the tenth edition is now publishing, its warmest admirers at its first appearance begin to be ashamed of their admiration. Paine's book, on the other hand, has made converts of a great many persons; which, I confess, appears to me as wonderful as the success of Burke's.'[44] To examine the debate over the next two years would reveal a very different public conception of Burke's strengths and weaknesses. With the outbreak of war with France, and the loyalist onslaught against popular reformism which began in the spring of 1792, with the violent events of August and September 1792 and the growing movement towards social equality in France, and finally with the guillotining of Louis and Marie Antoinette, then still further with the Terror, Burke's critics were silenced, either by judicial and social pressure, or by the growing realization that Burke's warnings now seemed unusually prescient.

Aftermath: Burke on his critics; and some critics on Burke, revisited

This view, of course, would dominate much subsequent writing about the *Reflections*. Most nineteenth-century Whigs echoed George Canning's view that virtually all of the *Reflections* 'has been justified by the course of subsequent events; and almost every prophecy has been strictly fulfilled',[45] and took up the line adopted by Henry Brougham, that

> For nearly the whole period during which he survived the commencement of the revolution, – for five of those seven years – all his predictions, save one momentary expression, had been more than fulfilled: anarchy and bloodshed had borne sway in France; conquest and convulsion had desolated Europe ... The providence of mortals is not often able to penetrate so far as this into futurity.[46]

Burke may thus have been inconsistent in writing that he was 'no friend' (in 1770) 'to aristocracy, in the sense at least in which that word is usually understood' by contrast with 'the high monarchical tone of his latter writings'.[47] The popular radical view was certainly, as Hazlitt put it, that Burke had by 1790 'abandoned not only all his practical conclusions, but all the principles on which they were founded. He proscribed all his former sentiments, denounced all his former friends, rejected and reviled all the maxims to which he had formerly appealed as incontestable.'[48]

Burke himself, however, regarded his efforts as protecting Whiggery – a view his biographers have often taken[49] – and thought some of his leading critics were temporarily deluded rather than constitutionally at variance with his views. This was not of course true for Paine.[50] But it was for Fox, of whom he was fond of saying that their opinions were in fact quite similar,[51] despite the Foxites' industrious attempts to disseminate contrary principles.[52]

The most important of the leading critics to re-enter the Whig fold as defined by Burke was James Mackintosh, of whom it was said (by Sidmouth, among others) that, humble and penitent, he 'received absolution from the Pope at Beaconsfield' at the end of 1796.[53] The conversion was very complete; by mid–1799 Mackintosh was speaking of Burke 'with rapture, declaring that he was, in his estimation, without any parallel, in any age or country, except, perhaps, Lord Bacon and Cicero; that his works contained an ampler store of political and moral wisdom than could be found in any other writer whatever'.[54] Yet if here the conversion was obvious and public, elsewhere it was reflective and private: Godwin, too, the author of the *Enquiry Concerning Political Justice*, in its own way the most philosophic response to the *Reflections,* moved sharply away from the rationalism of the high Enlightenment and towards Burkean sentimentalism in *The Enquirer* (1797). A friend neither to popular tumult nor natural rights ideas, Godwin clearly shared some common ground with Burke before this shift. A vast distance, however, separated them in 1793. By 1797, however, Godwin had moved sharply away from the overtly rationalistic strategy of the first edition of *Political Justice*. In his opposition to enthusiasm he came to agree that 'politeness' and 'refinement' needed to be seen not in narrow, moralistic terms, but as a civilized discourse adverse to the ferocity the Revolution had sparked, and hostile in an important degree to that 'sincerity' of which Godwin had been such an outstanding apostle in 1793. Famously, he conceded substantial ground to Burke in moving from a reliance upon reason as the basis for voluntary action to the feelings. He also turned markedly away from pleading for a substantially simpler society, altering his views on luxury, now associated with refinement and the progress of knowledge, to emphasize the degenerative effects of the inequality it entailed rather than the evils of wealth or splendour as such. And perhaps most importantly, with respect to his sense of Burke's accomplishment, Godwin admitted, against the doctrine of universal benevolence preached in 1793, that 'we appreciate persons and things, not by an impartial standard, but from their nearness to ourselves', admitting thus, that if 'benevolence is the love of my neighbour, the domestic, private and local sphere was to be given priority over any conception of benevolence based upon our ability to contribute to the good of the species as a whole'.[55]

Godwin felt no less a Whig for these changes, and was wont to insist, indeed, that if his politics remained republican in principle, they were Whig in practice. His willingness to acknowledge not merely Burke's prescience, but the underlying and philosophic emphasis on sentiment, localism, and gradual, organic development which was central to Burke, indicate, however, how broad the Whig tradition indeed was. Burke, thus, here seen *philosophically* as a Whig by Godwin even if his practical politics were less easily so defined, could still legitimately claim to represent that tradition, in part by having himself redefined it in the *Reflections*.

Notes

1 Burke, *Speeches* (4 vols, 1816), vol. 3, p. 455. For previous accounts of the reception of the *Reflections* see especially Carl B. Cone, 'Pamphlet Replies to Burke's *Reflections*', *The Southwestern Social Science Quarterly*, 26 (1945), pp. 22–34.

2 Burke later wrote that:

> I do not recollect, that previous to my declaring my thoughts in my place upon occasion of the Army debate, I had spoken to one French person except to one French Gentleman, with some of whose family I had an acquaintance. This Gentleman was not a Refugee, but had come hither upon business, wholly unrelated to Politicks. On the subject of that business alone, as well as I can remember, I had conversed with him at that time.
>
> I had then scarcely read any thing upon the subject, except the general Instruction given to the Representatives; and the proceedings of the National Assembly, extremely at variance with those instructions; and some pieces supposed to be written by the Comte de Mirabeau; together with the fact which appeared uncontradicted in some foreign and domestick papers. From them I had formed my opinions. (*Correspondence*, vol. VI, p. 105)

3 In June 1792 Burke opposed this strenuously, and with success. See: *Memorials and Correspondence of Charles James Fox*, 4 vols (London: R. Bentley, 1853–57), ed. Lord John Russell, vol. 3, p. 12.

4 In August 1789 he wrote that: 'The spirit it is impossible not to admire', but added that 'but the old Parisian ferocity has broken out in a shocking

manner. It is true, that this may be no more than a sudden explosion: If so no indication can be taken from it. But if it should be character rather than accident, then that people are not fit for Liberty, and must have a Strong hand like that of their former masters to coerce them. Men must have a certain fund of natural moderation to qualifye them for Freedom, else it become noxious to themselves and a perfect Nuisance to every body else' (*Correspondence*, vol. VI, p. 10).

5 *The Windham Papers* (2 vols, 1913), vol. 1, pp. 93–4. He also wrote to Francis in early 1790 that 'the composition you say is loose; and I am quite sure it is. I never intended it should be otherwise; for purporting to be, what in Truth it originally was, a Letter to a friend, I had no Idea of digesting it in a Systematick order. The Style is open to correction, and wants it. My natural Style of writing is somewhat careless; and I should be happy in receiving your advice towards making it as little viscious as such a Style is capable of being made (*Correspondence*, vol. VI, p. 89).

6 See Thomas Moore, *Memoirs of the Life of the Right Honourable Richard Brinsley Sheridan* (London: Longman, Hurst, Rees, Orme, Brown and Green; 4th edn, 1826), vol. 2, pp. 91–140. On Sheridan's side, there was both 'hatred and envy' of Burke (*Memoir, Journal and Correspondence of Thomas Moore*, 8 vols (London: Longman, Brown, Green and Longmans, 1853–56), vol. 2, p. 186).

7 Lord Holland related that Sir Phillip Francis thought that 'the arrow was sped long before the French principle became the test of morality and virtue. They were a popular ground for attack, and upon them that venom burst, which had been rankling in his breast since the Regency; for at that period, in the partition of offices, etc., it appears Burke asked something, either for himself or son, which Fox denied him. From thence the enmity sprung, and was constantly fomented by a jealousy of Sheridan and various other trivial occurrences that would have passed unnoticed between sound friends, but were treasured up'. See *The Journal of Elizabeth Lady Holland,* ed. The Earl of Ilchester, 2 vols (London: Longmans, 1908), vol. 1, p. 269. Gilbert Elliot also reported that 'Burke tells me that Fox disapproves in the most unqualified manner his work on the French Revolution, both as to matter and composition. As I differ so entirely with Fox on this subject, I cannot help apprehending that his opinion is influenced in some degree by a leaning toward Sheridan in his difference with Burke, and that his professing these opinions unreservedly is an indication of his intention to take part openly with Sheridan on this occasion' (*Life and Letters of Sir Gilbert Elliot*, ed. Countess of Minto, 3 vols (London: Longmans, 1874), vol. 1, pp. 364–5, 369–70.

8 *The Journal and Correspondence of William, Lord Auckland*, 2 vols (London: R. Bentley, 1861), vol. 2, p. 291.

9 The story is told that when Pitt first invited Burke to dine with him in September 1791, with Grenville and Addington, Burke warned the party after dinner of the continuing threat of French principles. Pitt's response was: 'Never fear, Mr. Burke: depend upon it we shall go on as we are, until

the day of judgment', to which Burke retorted 'Very likely, Sir ... it is the day of judgment that I am afraid of' (George Pellew, *The Life and Correspondence of the Right Hon. Henry Addington*, 3 vols (London: J. Murray, 1847), vol. I, p. 72. It is clear, however, that Pitt had certainly not courted Burke directly after the *Reflections* was published. Burke wrote in August 1791: 'I told you, that the Ministers had taken no Notice of my Book. It was then true. But this day I have had the enclosed civil Note from Dundas – The success of this last Pamphlet is great indeed. Every one tells me, that it is thought much better than the former. I have no Objection to their thinking so – but it is not my opinion. It may however be more useful. Not one word from one of our party. They are secretly galled. They agree with me to a tittle – but they dare not speak out for fear of hurting Fox' (*Correspondence*, vol. VI, p. 360).

10   Berry says two weeks, but errs by a week in the first day the *Reflections* appeared.

11   George Croly, *A Memoir of the Political Life and the Right Honourable Edmund Burke*, 2 vols (Edinburgh: Blackwood and Sons, 1840), vol. I, p. 292. Joseph Farington estimated sales of 17,000 by 1797. See *The Farington Diary*, 8 vols (London: Hutchinson and Co., 1923–28), vol. I, p. 201.

12   At a levée on 3 February 1791 which Burke attended with the Duke of Portland, the King complimented him highly on the work.

13   *Correspondence*, vol. VI, pp. 155–6.

14   James Prior, *Life of the Right Honourable Edmund Burke* (London: Bohn's Classics, 1854), p. 315.

15   Ibid. p. 316.

16   *The Journal and Correspondence of William, Lord Auckland* (1861), vol. 2, pp. 377–8.

17   *Extracts of the Journal and Correspondence of Miss Berry*, 3 vols (London: Longmans, Green, 1865), vol. I, p. 251 (8 November 1790). Miss Berry agreed that 'To do the book full justice, it is not necessary to agree with it in all points. To say nothing of its eloquence, it has that merit in a sovereign degree without which no book can thoroughly charm me, that of making me love the author. His ideas on religion I did really take notice of, as being finely expressed.' See *The Berry Papers*, ed. Lewis Melville (London: John Lane, 1914), p. 35.

18   He added that 'One would think that the author of such a work would be called to the government of his country by the combined voice of every man in it. What shall be said of the state of thing when it is remembered that the writer is a man decried, persecuted and proscribed; not being much valued even by his own party, and by half the nation considered a little better than an ingenious madman!' (*Correspondence*, vol. VI, p. 23).

19   *Correspondence*, vol. VI, p. 193n.

20   *The Autobiography of Edward Gibbon* (London: Macmillan, 1930) p. 178; *The Letters of Edward Gibbon*, 3 vols (London: Cassell, 1956), vol. 3, p. 216.

21 *The Farington Diary* (1922), vol. 4, p. 22.

22 Francis and Windham both received advance copies from Burke on 27 October.

23 *Correspondence*, vol. VI, p. 89. Privately Francis said that 'Burke, was a man who truly & prophetically foresaw all the consequences which would rise from the adoption of the French principles, – but said Sir Francis, Burke wrote with so much passion, so much vehemence, that instead of convincing He created doubts in the minds of his readers, who hesitated to believe a man so carried away by his feelings' (*The Farington Diary*, 1922, vol. I, p. 271).

24 Burke's retort on this point (20 February 1790) was: 'I really am perfectly astonish'd how you could dream, with my paper in your hand – that I found no other Cause than the Beauty of the Queen of France (now I suppose pretty much faded) for disapproving the Conduct which has been held towards her, and for expressing my own particular feelings. I am not to order the Natural Sympathies of my own Breast, and of every honest breast to wait until all the jokes of all the anecdotes of the Coffee houses of Paris and of the dissenting meeting-houses of London are scoured of all slander of those who calumniate persons, that afterwards they may murder them with impunity?' And further: 'I tell you again, that the recollection of the manner in which I saw the Queen of France in the year 1774 and the contrast between that brilliancy, Splendour, and beauty, with the prostrate Homage of a Nation to her, compared with the abominable scene of 1789 which I was describing did draw Tears from me and wetted my paper. These Tears came again into my Eyes, almost as often as I lookd at the description. They may again' (*Correspondence*, vol. VI, pp. 89–91).

25 Burke's response was to write Francis that he was

> the only friend I have who will dare to give me advice. I must have, then, something terrible in me, which intimidates all others who know me from giving me the only unequivocal mark of regard. Whatever their rough and menacing manner may be, I must search myself upon it; and when I discover it, old as I am, I must endeavour to correct it. I flattered myself, however, that you at least would not have thought my other friends altogether justified in withholding from me their services of this kind. You certainly do not always convey to me your opinion with the greatest possible tenderness and management, and yet I do not recollect, since I had the pleasure of your acquaintance, that there has been a heat or a coolness of a single day's duration on my side during that whole time. I believe your memory cannot present to you an instance of it. I ill deserve friends if I throw them away on account of their candour, and simplicity of their good nature. In particular, you know that you have in some instance favoured me with your instructions relative to things I was preparing for the public. If I did not in every instance agree with you, I think you had on the whole sufficient proofs of my docility to make you believe that I received your corrections not only without offence,

but with no small degree of gratitude. (*Memoirs of Sir Philip Francis with Correspondence and Journals*, ed. J. Parkes and H. Merivale, 2 vols (London, 1867), vol. 2, pp. 282–3)

26 *The Speeches of the Right Honourable Charles James Fox*, 6 vols (London: Longman, Hurst, Rees, Orme and Brown, 1815), vol. 4, pp. 221–2.

27 For Burke's own response to the charge, see Burke, *Speeches* (4 vols, 1816), vol. 4, pp. 15–28.

28 In Parliament he 'added some warm compliments to Mr. Burke's general principles; but said that he could not conceive how it was possible for a person of such principles, or for any man who valued our own constitution, and revered the Revolution that obtained it for us, to unite with such feelings in indignant and unqualified abhorrence of all the proceedings of the patriotic party in France. He conceived their's to be as just a Revolution as ours, proceeding upon sound principle and a greater provocation. He vehemently defended the general view and conduct of the National Assembly' (*Speeches of the Late Right Honourable Richard Brinsley Sheridan*, 1816, vol. 2, p. 242, February 1790).

29 *Correspondence*, vol. VI, p. 160n. This occasioned Tooke's toast, 'If Mr Burke be ever prosecuted for such a libel on the Constitution, may his impeachment last as long as that of Mr Hastings', which was withdrawn after much opposition. But Lord John Russell was so incensed at this, and a second toast, 'May the Parliament of Great Britain become a National Assembly,' that he reportedly cut his name out of the membership book of the Club, from which Lord Stanhope also withdrew (*Life and Letters of Sir Gilbert Elliot*, vol. 1, pp. 364–5).

30 Reprinted in my *Political Writings of the 1790s*, 8 vols (London: Pickering and Chatto, 1995), vol. 1, pp. 11–58.

31 Mary Wollstonecraft, *Vindication of the Rights of Men*, in *The Works of Mary Wollstonecraft*, ed. Marilyn Butler and Janet Todd, 7 vols (London: Pickering and Chatto, 1989), vol. 5, pp. 14–15.

32 Reprinted in my *Political Writings of the 1790s*, vol. 1, pp. 121–54.

33 Ibid. pp. 2–39.

34 Published anonymously. Scott was Warren Hastings's political agent, and this work, among others, doubtless helped to cement in Burke's mind an association between the 'Revolution Society,' and 'their allies, the Indian delinquents' (*Correspondence*, vol. VI, p. 140). The story is still more complex, however; some, like Cornwallis, thought that Hastings 'in a great measure owes his misfortunes to the mistaken zeal of his friend Major Scott, who bullied Burke into the persecution' (*Correspondence of Charles, First Marquis. Cornwallis*, 3 vols (London: J. Murray, 1859), vol. 1, p. 376).

35 That is, Samuel Romilly, who said that 'It is written in his own wild but forcible style; inaccurate in point of grammar, flat where he attempts wit, and often ridiculous when he indulges himself in metaphors; but, with all that, full of spirit and energy, and likely to produce a very great effect'

(*The Life of Sir Samuel Romilly*, 2 vols (London: J. Murray, 1840), vol. 1, pp. 415–16).

36 *Thomas Paine: Social and Political Thought* (Boston and London: Unwin Hyman, 1989).

37 Burke's response on this theme was that: 'It is not calling the landed estates, possessed by old *prescriptive right*, the "accumulations of ignorance and superstition", that can support me in shaking that grand title, which supersedes all other title, and which all my studies of general jurisprudence have taught me to consider as one principal cause of the formation of states; I mean the ascertaining and securing *prescription*. But these are donations made in "ages of ignorance and superstition". Be it so. It proves that these donations were made long ago; and this is *prescription*; and this gives right and title' (*Correspondence*, vol. VI, p. 95).

38 Reprinted in *Political Writings of the 1790s*, vol. 1, pp. 270–386.

39 *Correspondence*, vol. VI, p. 311.

40 Burke to Mackintosh, 23 December 1796, *Correspondence*, vol. IX, p. 194.

41 Bentham is in fact cited by Mackintosh.

42 Reprinted in *Political Writings of the 1790s,* vol. 2, pp. 316–85.

43 Lord Holland later wrote:

> Till the ecclesiastical revenues were suppressed, Burke was far from disapproving the French Revolution. But what conclusion, against the sincerity of his opinions, is to be drawn from the fact? An extravagant veneration for all established rites and ceremonies in religion appear to have been a sentiment long and deeply rooted in his mind. It arose, indeed, from a conviction of the necessity of some establishment to the preservation of society, and the necessity of some outward show and pomp to the maintenance of that establishment, rather than from any strong predilection for particular tenets. Mr. Fox has on more than once assured me, that in his invectives against Mr. Hastings' indignities to the Indian Priesthood, he spoke of the piety of the Hindoos with admiration, and of their holy religion and sacred function with an awe bordering on devotion. The seizure of the property of the Clergy, in France, might then excite alarm in breasts less predisposed to sensibility on such subjects. It was, in the judgment of many, an outrageous violation of property; when, therefore, it professed to be the result of a philosophy which denied the usefulness of all ecclesiastical institutions, rather than the desperate resource of an exhausted exchequer, it suggested a train of apprehensions in the mind of Mr. Burke, who, from the habitual tenor of his opinions, was prepared to receive such impressions. (Henry Holland, *Memoirs of the Whig Party*, 2 vols (London: Longmans, 1862), vol. 1, p. 6)

44 *The Life of Sir Samuel Romilly*, 1840, vol. 1, pp. 426–7.

45 *The Speeches of the Right Honourable George Canning*, 6 vols (London: J. Ridway, 1828), vol. 5, p. 451.

46 But Brougham continued: 'That Mr. Burke did, however, err, and err
    widely in the estimate which he formed of the merits of a restored
    Government, no one can now doubt. His mistake was in comparing the old
    regime with the anarchy of the Revolution; to which not only the
    monarchy of France but the despotism of Turkey was preferable. He never
    could get rid of the belief that because the change had been effected with a
    violence which produced, and inevitably produced, the consequences
    foreseen by himself; and by him alone, therefore the tree so planted must
    for ever prove incapable of bearing good fruit' (Henry Brougham,
    Contributions to the Edinburgh Review (1856), vol. 1, pp. 280–1).

47 Henry Brougham, *Historical Sketches of Statesmen who Flourished in the
    Time of George III* (1839), vol. 1, pp. 157, 160.

48 William Hazlitt, *Political Essays* (London: William Hone, 1819), p. 264.

49 Croly wrote that Burke was the 'restorer of Whiggism to the principles of
    its ancient and better days' (George Croly, *Memoir of the Political Life and
    the Right Honourable Edmund Burke* (1840), vol. 1, p. 291). Portland of
    course also said that when anyone criticized the *Reflections* to him, he told
    them that he had recommneded it to his sons as containing the true Whig
    creed (Portland to Dr French Laurence, 29 August 1791, Portland MSS, at
    Nottingham, quoted in *Correspondence*, vol. VI, p. 161n).

50 Of Paine he was scathing:

> You talk of Paine with more respect than he deserves: He is utterly
> incapable of comprehending his subject. He has not even a moderate
> portion of learning of any kind. He has learned the instrumental part
> of literature, a style, and a method of disposing his ideas, without
> having ever made a previous preparation of Study or thinking – for
> the use of it. Junius, and other sharply penn'd libels of our time have
> furnishd a stock to the adventurers in composition; which gives what
> they write an air, (and it is but an air) of art and skill; – but as to the
> rest, Payne possesses nothing more than what a man whose audacity
> makes him careless of logical consequences, and his total want of
> honour and morality make indifferent as to political consequences,
> may very easily write. They indeed who seriously write upon a
> principle of levelling ought to be answered by the Magistrate – and
> not by the Speculatist. The People whom he would corrupt, and who
> are very corruptible, can very readily comprehend what flatters their
> vices and falls in with their ignorance; but that process of reasoning,
> which would shew to the poorest, how much his poverty is
> comparative riches in his state of subordination, to what it could be in
> such an equality as is recommended to him, is quite out of his reach,
> even if it were pleasing to his pride; because it involves in it a long
> and labourd analysis of Society. If he will not receive it on authority
> he is incapable of receiving it at all; and where a man is incapable of
> receiving a Benefit through his reason, he must be made to receive it
> thro' his fears. Here the Magistrates must stand in the place of the
> Professor. They who cannot or will not be taught, must be coerced.
> (*Correspondence*, vol. VI, pp. 303–4)

51 Burke in August 1791 said that: 'I believd, as he did, that inwardly even Fox did not differ from me materially, if at all; and that I was sure the rest for the far greater Number heartily agreed and without any limitation. The misfortune was that so many good and weighty men, thinking the same way, should, upon grounds of mistaken prudence, suffer themselves to be added to the weight of a scale to which they did not belong' (*Correspondence*, vol. VI, p. 336). And there is evidence for this. Fox in 1790 denied that his view on France meant that he was a friend to democracy: 'He declared himself equally the enemy of all absolute forms of government, whether an absolute monarchy, an absolute aristocracy, or an absolute democracy. He was adverse to all extremes, and a friend only to a mixed government, like our own, in which, if the aristocracy, or indeed either of the three branches of the constitution, were destroyed, the good effect of the whole, and the happiness derived under it, would, in his mind, be at an end' (*The Speeches of the Right Honourable Charles James Fox*, vol. 4, p. 52).

52 In mid-1791 Burke commented that

> I found that great, and almost systematick pains were taken to discredit that work in the Party, to get its principles disclaimed; and of course (for medium there is none) to get the Principles of Paine, Priestley, Price, Rouse, Mackintosh, Christie &ca &ca &ca magnified and extolled, and in a sort of obscure and undefined manner to be adopted as the Creed of the party. The supper at Brookes's was a sort of Academy for these Doctrines. Individuals, little courted before, were separately talked over, and, as it were, canvassed. I found, that the Prince of Wales, to Whose very existence the principles of that Book were necessary, was very early led to take, and to express, no small dislike to them; and to abstain even from expressions of common politeness on the Pamphlets being presented to him. If I had not received very particular intelligence of all these manœuvres, to the moment of the explosion in Parliament, yet the face of things, and the extraordinary change in Persons, could have left no Doubt in my Mind upon the subject. (*Correspondence*, vol. VI, p. 273)

53 George Pellew, *The Life and Correspondence of the Right Hon. Henry Addington*, 3 vols (London: J. Murray, 1847), vol. 2, p. 241. See Burke's letter to Mackintosh, in *Memoir of the Life of the Right Honourable Sir James Mackintosh*, ed. Robert James Mackintosh, 2 vols (London: E. Moxon, 1836), vol. 1, pp. 88–90.

54 *Memoir of the Life of the Right Honourable Sir James Mackintosh* (1836), vol. 1, p. 91.

55 See my 'From True Virtue to Benevolent Politeness: Godwin and Godwinism Revisited', in Gordon Schochet, ed., *Empire and Revolutions. Papers Presented at the Folger Institute Seminar 'Political Thought in the English-Speaking Atlantic', 1760–1800* (Washington, DC: The Folger Library, 1993), pp. 187–226.

4

Between Burke and the union: reflections on PRO: CO 904/2

W. J. M c C O R M A C K

> A word has been lately struck in the mint of the Castle of Dublin ...
> Edmund Burke, 1792

The publication of Edmund Burke's *Reflections on the Revolution in France* (on 1 November 1790) was not exclusively a London event, even though the first editions reached the public through the good offices of Dodsley on Pall Mall. Not only was Burke's topic of such extensive concern that publication elsewhere became imperative, but the structure of the late eighteenth-century book trade was such that London editions would inevitably be followed by editions published in Dublin – the author's birth-place, and the focal point of political concerns scarcely less urgent than those deriving from the fall of the Bastille.

According to a recent historian, the book was well received in Ireland. Certainly, Burke was without delay awarded an honorary degree by his old university, having earlier been made an honorary fellow of the Royal Irish Academy.[1] But Trinity's provost of the day, John Hely Hutchinson, was hardly typical of the Protestant Establishment, and the Academy's signal gesture was made months before the publication of *Reflections*. It might be more accurate to say that reaction in the Irish capital was sharp, always allowing for sharpness of approval and condemnation alike. If the *Freeman's Journal*, *Dublin Journal*, and *Dublin Chronicle* all published excerpts from Burke's high invective, other papers responded with selections from Tom

Paine's *Rights of Man* when it appeared the following spring.[2] The Paine/Burke controversy was taken up in popular song, or at least in the printed broadsides which sought to condition public opinion. As late as 1798, a Dublin bookseller issued *Paddy's Resource: or the Harp of Erin Attuned to Freedom. Being a Collection of Patriotic Songs; Selected for Paddy's Amusement.* Here the emphasis fell more on support of Paine than close attention (whether hostile, or otherwise) to Burke. The passage of time had led not only to that preference but also to the convergence of radicalism and national sentiment in a manner which still exercises historians of the 1798 rebellion.[3]

But not all of this popular material was unsophisticated doggerel or common praise. One anonymous versifier took Burke's famous apostrophe to Marie Antoinette and transformed it in a stanza which packed a subtle punch in the grammar of its last line:

Ten thousand Dons and Cavaliers
Around her stand with swords and spears,
To be her slaves was all they sought,
Thus was 'The grace of life unbought.'[4]

The earlier publication of excerpts from the *Reflections* proper cannot be considered without reference to the extensive control of the papers concerned by government. And it is noteworthy that Burke did not retain this high profile with the agents of officially sanctioned press subversion in Dublin Castle. Between 1790 and 1800, his name disappears to a large extent from the increasingly heated debates on Irish affairs which culminated in the Union of 1801. Why this should have been the case is one theme of the present enquiry. If Dublin Castle was happy to see the Burke of 1790 feature in the *Freeman's Journal* – which it largely controlled through Francis Higgins – its attitude towards Burke altered as the decade unfolded. His *Letter to Sir Hercules Langrishe* of 1792 reminded the authorities in Dublin that Burke favoured a liberal policy towards Catholics which they could never approve without jeopardizing their own position. The appointment of his friend and patron, the Earl Fitzwilliam, as Lord Lieutenant in 1795, created a crisis only resolved when the reformer was recalled to London after a few months in office.

Thereafter Burke regarded Dublin as a bunker of extreme anti-Catholic prejudice, from which the deliberate provocation of revolt was to be more expected than conciliation in the face of France's revolutionary threat to both the British and Irish establishments. When French-led insurrection duly occurred in 1798, Burke was already dead. Yet some of the chief architects of repression were prepared to countenance Catholic Relief: Burke had not adequately distinguished between the petty jobbers and the great ones.

Out of the rapidly altering conditions of the 1790s emerged an old, but only intermittently heard theme – a union between Britain and Ireland. On this issue, Burke had been less than crystal clear. The eclipse of his powerful writings – whether on the Revolution or on Catholic Relief – towards the end of the decade is naturally related to his death and the arrangements thereafter planned for his copyrights, for collected editions of his works, and the proper management of a literary estate vulnerable to depredations like any other. But his disappearance from view also marks shifts in the configuration of a public sphere in Ireland at a time of bloody revolt and equally bloody repression.

More than thirty years ago, Jürgen Habermas declared that 'Edmund Burke, before the outbreak of the French Revolution ... finally made the needed distinctions' through which 'the liberal theory of virtual representation' could be articulated. In this connection, Habermas characterized Henry St John, Viscount Bolingbroke (1678–1751), as a 'critical *frondeur*' and hence 'the first opposition member in the sense of modern parliamentary tactics'.[5] In the *Reflections*, Burke had famously dismissed the memory of Swift's hero – enquiring rhetorically 'who now reads Bolingbroke?' And among the better and more distinctively local respondents to Burke after 1790, Dublin produced a pseudonymous 'Bolingbroke' who deplored Burke's 'inverted order' and 'mob of metaphors'.[6] Though the Irish capital did see its own editions of the *Reflections* into print, and the Paine/Burke controversy had its own Irish colouration, the battle to control public opinion shifted away from Burkean themes. Towards the end of 1798, Under-Secretary Edward Cooke in Dublin Castle declared of any campaign for a union, 'it must be written up, spoken up, intrigued up, drunk up, sung up, and bribed up.'[7]

Some evidence of how Cooke and his associates (high and low) went about this uplifting business is recorded in account books preserved in the Public Record Office (Kew).

Students of the period need not fear allegations of naive empiricism if they contemplate the exercise of annotating such sources. For the presence of booksellers' names, alongside details of payments surreptitiously for the distribution of pamphlets, can also be read as the eclipse of Burke, the challenge to theory by theory, the struggle for a specifically configured public sphere. It is of course, a sphere upon which Dublin is marked as well as London, one defined neither by metropolitan exclusivism nor by anachronistic nationalist introspection.[8] Excerpts from PRO: CO 904/2 are given in appendices below by way of example, with preliminary annotation. From these the contradictions of Burkean politics, and of imperial attempts to deal with the Irish question of the day, intriguingly emerge.

Burke's Irish Jacobins

The career and legacy of Edmund Burke are alike marked by irony, and by ambiguity also. It is not necessary to rehearse once again the circumstances in which one of the ablest MPs of his day failed to secure public office, nor to dwell on the fate of an Irishman of Catholic origins supporting British administrations which had little but contempt for his 'people': by the time of his death in 1797, despair had claimed him for her own. Burke loomed large in the late eighteenth century, but he also disappeared from view on unexpected occasions. That is to say, the influence of his writings and his thought must sometimes be traced in terms of non-citation. It may be useful therefore to consider in some local detail certain exercises in propaganda conducted by a political elite he despised (Dublin Castle) in favour of a measure (union between Britain and Ireland) he did not condemn out of hand.[9] The objectives of such an undertaking are not simply to fill in the Burke-shaped silence or absence of the years 1797–1800, but to raise theoretical issues relevant in other areas of study or research.

Dublin booksellers (by which term the modern notion of publisher is often absorbed) were in no doubt about the value of the many score pamphlets, tracts, speeches and lampoons which

constituted the paper debate on the Union between Great Britain
and Ireland. Despite this lucrative self-awareness on their part,
recent research into the Dublin book trade has paid scant
attention to the inky struggle for and against the Union. Detailed
studies by Mary Pollard (the unrivalled doyenne of Irish
bibliography) and the late James Phillips have provided access to
a previously untapped resource, with little reference to what was
the climactic 'paper war' of the Irish eighteenth century.[10] One
particular bookseller, John Milliken, gathered together sets of
Union pamphlets and sold them as intellectual furniture for post-
Union country-house libraries. The commercial basis of his
enterprise deserves attention but, in relation to Edmund Burke,
the background to these printings and publications finds a focal
point of disappearance in the non-republication of the *Reflections
on the Revolution in France*. It might seem at first glance that we
could 'get Burke's posthumous reputation into perspective' if we
were diligently to read all these pro- and anti-Union pamphlets,
and tabulate his citation score – as though he were an insecure
university professor. Perspective – a feature of those arts of
architecture, garden design, portraiture and painting generally
which Burke exploits so richly in the *Reflections* – is too often
casually used as if it were merely the equivalent of proportion:
'Let us get things into perspective.' But, more absolutely than
any mere chatter about the relative proportions of this to that,
perspective has its vanishing-point, its *ligne de fuite*. Indeed, as
the interlinguistic equation demonstrates, one man's point is
another *homme's* line. The absolutes and relatives of the 1790s
refuse to divide into neat categories, while also refusing to
converge in any negotiable middle ground.

In keeping with this troublesome history, the present essay
attempts to negotiate between theory and practice, and in two
distinct senses. First, it is argued (briefly, here and now in this
paragraph) that the course of the 1790s saw a decisive shift, in
anti-revolutionary discourse, from theoretical practice to the
practical enforcement of theory. By theoretical practice is meant
the dissemination of theory through various practices in which
printing played a major role. By the practical enforcement of
theory is meant a greater diversity of activities ranging from
flogging to the establishment of loyalist associations based in

taverns. Money naturally plays a part in this – 'naturally' in the sense that it is filthy lucre, the ink of economic activity. In the Burke-shaped absence of 1797–1800, we can chart this shift in several of its stages.

It hardly needs to be said that Burke's politics is a theory, even if he himself inveighs against theory as being abstract, innovative, destructive, and so forth. The shift within anti-revolutionary discourse could be illustrated by contrasting the stylistic complexity of – to take the obvious example – Burke's *Reflections* (1790) with the undistinguished language of virtually all the pamphlets dully listed (irrespective of political 'line') in *The Pamphlet Debate on the Union Between Great Britain and Ireland, 1797–1800*. The events of 1798 provided a pretext (in the strict sense) for a reformulation of anti-revolutionary theory as practice, events which Burke had predicted to some extent in his letters of 1796 to John Keogh, French Lawrence and others.[11] The obverse of this position is neatly summarized by Alexander Knox (1757–1831). Writing in the immediate aftermath of an insurrection in part at least inspired by the French example, but also in canny anticipation of the Union debates, Knox reflected on Irish Jacobinism:

> The melancholy events which have taken place of late, imply no advance in the *Theory*; they are no more than that theory reduced in a very trifling degree to *practice*.[12]

Burke's views on the possibility of a union between Britain and Ireland are almost impossible to summarize, partly because the topic was not out in the open during his closing years and partly because his closing years were marked by melancholia and digression. To an unidentified correspondent in February 1797, he wrote: 'My poor opinion is, that the closest connexion between Great Britain and Ireland, is essential to the well being, I had almost said, the very being, of the two Kingdoms.'[13] What worried him was not so much the degree of connection (which might even become union), but the risk of greater separation even to the extent of Ireland's becoming independent. While he detested the ruling junto in Dublin who had virtually coined the term 'protestant ascendancy' as their *beau ideal*, he also averred that 'there is, and ever has been, a strong Republican, Protestant

Faction in Ireland, which has persecuted the Catholicks as long as persecution would answer their purpose; and now the same faction would dupe them to become accomplices in effectuating the same purposes; and thus either by Tyranny or seduction would accomplish their ruin'.[14] The evidence of the *Reflections* would suggest that, in a peculiarly retrospective view of politics, Burke incorporated even the regicides into this conspiratorial, phantasmic history. For example, the early introduction of the Reverend Dr Richard Price (1723–91) as Burke's contemporary stalking-horse is subsequently absorbed into the allusive treatment of the Reverend Hugh Peters (1598–1660), who mocked King Charles I.[15] If these individuals seem remote from Burke's Irish concerns, note that Peters accompanied Oliver Cromwell to Ireland in 1649, and that a number of the regicides settled in Ireland.

The professed separatists of the 1790s, United Irishmen under the leadership of Theobald Wolfe Tone (1763–98) fully appreciated the contribution of Burke's *Reflections* to the complex political situation in which they strove, first as an open society and, after 1794, as a secret revolutionary organization. In his memoirs, Tone identified 'Mr Burke's famous invective' as a defining moment, while also pointing out that the two kingdoms stood very different in relation to France. But when Tone argued in the name of Ireland that 'we had not, like England, a prejudice rooted in our very nature against France', the terms he used were Burke's, those of prejudice and rootedness and nature.[16] This is an unwitting tribute, the compliment and complement earned by Burke's thoroughgoing stylistics of reversal by which he invents 'the illustrious Champion of the Protestant World', Bonaparte, and sets against him 'the Directory in Ireland'. This may seem remote from Tone's lighthearted intelligence. Yet on several occasions in his autobiographical writings Tone anticipates the rebellion planned for Ireland as resembling the Vendée or Chouan counter-revolutionary wars rather than the Revolution itself.[17] It may be, of course, that Tone meant no irony here, but merely foresaw what the displacement of republicanism by national and sectarian feeling would bring about.

Between Burke and Irish Jacobinism, there existed a curious mutual grudging respect. In the letter to the Reverend Thomas

Hussey just cited, he proceeded to describe the United Irishmen with mitigated hostility as 'that unwise body' who 'have had the folly to represent' the evils of Ireland as proceeding from England's deliberate purpose. In contrast it was Burke's view that England's 'chief guilt is in its total neglect, its utter oblivion, its shameful indifference and its entire ignorance, of Ireland and of every thing that relates to it.'[18] Writing up his journal in Parisian exile at the beginning of March 1797, Tone recorded a conversation with Tom Paine. 'I mentioned to him that I had known Burke in England, and spoke of the shattered state of his mind in consequence of the death of his only son Richard. Paine immediately said that it was the Rights of Man which had broke his heart ... Paine had no children!'[19]

Burke expired at Beaconsfield on 9 July 1797. Tone died of self-inflicted wounds in a Dublin prison on 19 November 1798. By that latter date, the pamphlet campaign in favour of a union between Britain and Ireland was under way. No one saw fit, no one thought it worth their while, to relaunch Burke in or for Ireland at what was, for his native land, a crisis no less demanding than that of the early part of the decade. In the definitive bibliography, W. B. Todd lists no Dublin edition of the *Reflections* later than 1791, and can provide details of only three in toto. During 1792–93 twelve Dublin booksellers came together jointly to publish the three early volumes of Burke's *Works*, but did not stay the course to take up subsequent volumes of the (admittedly) slow-emerging London edition. In 1796, the printer John Chambers issued *A Letter ... To a Noble Lord* in three states – (i) without edition statement, (ii) as a 'ninth edition' and (iii) as a 'tenth edition'. The following year, Chambers, who had pronounced sympathies with the United Irishmen, issued a Dublin edition of the *Observations ... on the Conduct of the Minority* which was an unauthorized publication (13 February 1797) on all counts. Later in the same year, Patrick Byrne published *Three Memorials on French Affairs*, deriving from the London publication authorized by Burke's executors. But, in 1798 (when the French finally did land and United Irishmen rose in three of Ireland's four provinces) Burke was not republished.[20]

To return to the issue of theory and practice, it will be suggested (in what follows) that Burke's eclipse is the measure of

Burke's concealed presence. That no writer, in favour of union or opposed to it, made extensive use of Burke is worth noting. That the great 'invective' against revolution was not mobilized to illustrate the danger of leaving Ireland at the mercy of another Jacobin rebellion is a measure of larger changes. On the whole, high theory played little or no part in the union debates. And some of the most famous rhetorical performances associated with the parliamentary opposition defeated in 1800 – Henry Grattan's 'Esto Perpetua', allegedly of 1782 – have been reliably dated to no earlier than 1822. [21]

Instead of high-profile oral performance, there was a vast amount of pamphlet-making: less rhetoric, more commerce. This is not to deny the theatricality of the Irish parliament's last days, but simply to insist that the instrument of bribery which determined the vote had its equivalent in printers' workrooms and the offices of state functionaries. The practice of inscribing facts – in 'secret service' accounts – has its own theoretical perspective, a line of convergence/disappearance. A specific objective of this present essay is to examine one such account book, and to 'reflect' upon it in the sense that Burke's *Reflections* shed light on bureaucratic procedure as well as statecraft and natural law. To list and examine details of payment is not to abandon some higher discourse, but rather to insist that the highs and lows are necessary to each other.

The Cooke who spoils the Burke

The publication of an anonymous pamphlet, *Arguments For and Against an Union*, at the end of 1798 has been long recognized as crucial in the propaganda war through which suppression of the insurrection the previous summer was reinterpreted as the launching pad for a campaign to unite the two kingdoms and to abolish the Dublin parliament. Its author, Edward Cooke (1755–1820), was Secretary for War in Dublin Castle, and sometime Under-Secretary for Ireland. Apart from that, little is generally known of him. Though he indulged in ink later to defend Protestant causes, his only other known intervention in the pamphlet battle preceding the Union was to write, and see into proof stage, a work called *A Review of the Question of Union in*

July 1799, which survives in a unique 'copy' in the Russell
Library, Saint Patrick's College, Maynooth, the Catholic seminary
whose foundation in 1795 owes much to Burke's diplomacy. *A
Review of the Question of Union* never reached the public, for
reasons not yet established.[22]

These non-appearances – Cooke's uncelebrated second pamphlet, the potentially decisive republication of Burke's *Reflections*
in the era of Irish Jacobinism – pose challenging questions to
students of the Irish 1790s. At one level, it is easy to advance
arguments as to why the Dublin regime did not ensure that 'the
great melody' was heard again in 1798/1800. Burke, after all, had
been an excoriating critic in 1792 of Dublin Castle and the
'ascendancy' faction. They were, in his tersest definition 'that
Junto of Jobbers'.[23] The antagonism was reciprocated and perpe-
tuated: in some eyes he was, as near as damn it, a Catholic, to be
caricatured as a whiskey-Jesuit. But the author of *Reflections* and
of the 'Letter to Richard Burke' (1792) had done more than just
offend by his pedigree the Protestant moguls of Irish administration; he had pulled the iron glove inside out to reveal a
regime Jacobinical or Bonapartist in practical essence which was
also as *ancien* in its religious prejudices and defences of privilege
as anything the Paris clubs could despise.[24] On the other hand,
Dublin Castle (or its London masters) needed to win over Irish
Catholic opinion in the general scramble to achieve a parliamentary vote for union in 1799 or 1800. If the government was
prepared to (half)promise Catholic emancipation in the event of
the Union being granted, why jib at employing the late Edmund
Burke's symphonic denunciation of such Jacobinism as recently
had manifested itself in Antrim, Down, Kildare, Longford, Mayo,
Wexford, Wicklow?

In this connection, it is as well to remember that even well
known, widely distributed and (occasionally, no doubt) pirated
works such as the *Reflections* remained the intellectual property
of someone, publisher, bookseller or whoever. Thus, Irish advocates (or for that matter opponents) of union were not in a
position after Burke's death simply to reprint his writings. In
February 1797, the ailing Burke's friends protected him from the
impact of illicit publication of a letter to the Duke of Portland (the
Observations ... on the Conduct of the Minority), and after his

death in July the executors were no less vigilant. It is worth considering whether Burke's political 'legacy' was not diminished in its effect by the rigour with which his *literary estate* as a property was protected. If the *Reflections* constituted the most eloquent and sumptuous condemnation of political change known to living men, to reissue it in specific, local, and hypersensitive circumstances involved risk. One risk might have been prosecution for breach of copyright; another, less formal but no less damaging, might have been the response that union constituted radical change rather than a status quo *ante bellum*. Not only did Dublin fail to see a redeployment of Burke's *Reflections* against the United Irish Jacobins, and against the 'Protestant Directory' (as Burke had labelled the Castle administration), it saw in 1797–1800 a veritable moratorium on the use of Burke's name in political argument.

Instead of mobilizing great names from the past, whether recent or remote, the propaganda campaign sponsored by Dublin Castle employed discretion and insinuation. Cooke's anonymous *Arguments For and Against an Union* is a challenge to bibliographers. The bookseller over whose name it appeared – John Milliken – was a major figure in the city's book trade. In the course of the pamphlet debate on the union between late 1797 and the early months of 1800, his name appears in the imprint of some sixty publications, or almost one-fifth of the total.[25] Despite the resources at the joint command of Cooke and Milliken, the printing and publication of *Arguments* were complicated exercises, involving no fewer than two distinct imprints (both with Milliken's name) and at least nine so-called 'editions' – not to mention a piracy and sundry Cork and London printings.[26] From the outset, it was taken as the opening shot in a serious pamphlet war, though earlier skirmishes had taken place.

Given the anonymous author's position at the heart of the administration, the unusual manner of the pamphlet's dissemination deserves attention. Dublin Castle was in the habit of paying large sums of money to subvert the city's newspapers, and the financing of an important pamphlet can hardly have been beyond its capabilities financial or managerial. Evidence of the Castle's concern with the print trade is not abundant, but neither is it negligible. Records of payment by the Castle to figures in the book trade, overlooked by researchers keener to trace spies and informers, open up further discussion.[27] Commencing in mid–1795, an account book preserved in the Public Record Office (Kew) records a multitude of payments, ranging from Christmas gratuities 'for sundry persons' and boxes at the theatre, to regular quarterly or half-yearly retainers for named individuals including John Giffard ('The Dog-in-Office') and Francis Higgins ('The Sham Squire').[28] There are more cheerful occasions: on 21 January 1797, £11: 7: 6 was expended to release Chevalier O'Gorman from confinement. Among these records, PRO: CO 904/2 also records numerous payments in connection with newspapers, booksellers, and the sponsors of pamphlets.[29] A select list is given in Appendix 2 below.

Cooke is a central figure in the accounts. Indeed, they initially revolve round him, and their gradually diminishing references to him should not be taken as evidence of his disappearance from the field of action. On the other hand, an analysis of payments in connection with pamphleteering might support the view that, in the course of the years covered by PRO: CO 904/2, Cooke lost out in an internal debate about methods of counter-insurgency. The accounts are both a record of deliberate interventions into a volatile political situation and a response (haphazard at times) to it. Appendix 1 lists the majority of occasions when Cooke's name is specified.

The motley assortment of payments, brought under the heading of Secret Service, may indicate a casual approach to accountancy in this connection, at least in the period covered by the early pages of PRO: CO 904/2. But it should not be assumed that the practice was in its infancy: secret service activity of a comparable kind can be traced continuously back to the years of Queen Elizabeth. Indeed, while it is clear that a far longer general history of such practices would extend back to Old Testament days, the relationship between printing and subversion – both subversion of the state and by the state – deserves close attention.

The miscellaneous payments recorded in PRO: CO 904/2 place the specific suborning of printers and newspapers in context. Though the accounts cover the period of the rebellion, there are few details of payments made in direct response to events – an exception not the entry for 7 June 1798 which records arrangements through La Touche's bank for payment of £110 (originating in London) to the Bishop of Ferns[30] 'for the relief of Clergymen fled from the Co. of Wexford to Wales from the rebels'. On 30 June £200 was paid to the Reverend Dean Bond 'for the relief of 105 of his Parishioners Emigrants from Wexford in great distress in Dublin'. Substantial allowances were made on the same day to various office holders in the city, amounting to £160, in response to the emergency: these included £40 for Mr Dejoncourt, clerk of the post office, who also features in the lists below. Two English sailors, who escaped from a French ship in Killala Bay, County Mayo, were paid £5: 13: 9 on 15 December. As the Union looms in sight, there is reference to fees paid in relation to appointments made 'for the accommodation of government', e.g. those of 11 April 1799 in connection with Richard Harding's arrangements.

Ideology; or, the Devil is in neglecting the data

In connection with the authorities' efforts to use the medium of printing for propagandist purposes the occurrence of Giffard and Higgins's names are significant, frequent, and unsurprising. These regular (quarterly, for the most part) payments signify the authorities' unwavering support for the suborning of the newspaper press, whereas the evidence in relation to book or pamphlet publishing is irregular, and seemingly unpatterned. Not only covert payment through Higgins and Giffard, but systematic distribution of the suborned press through the Post Office, constituted a major plant in the anti-subversion campaign. The entries in Appendix 2 have been selected with an additional view to investigating less well-known aspects of covert official payment in the area of the print medium. Commentary or analysis is provided in relation to some, but by no means all of the identifiable persons or publications.

From such accounts as these, a number of fundamental details about the organization of the Dublin book trade in the years of revolution can be deduced. Two highly contrasting cases of literary influence arise – the first contemporary, the second to become activated in the mid-nineteenth century. Among the entries listed below, we find the following: 8 July 1797, Mrs Battier on

Charity account, £1: 2: 9. Henrietta Battier (1751–1813) has been identified as the author of the comic *Address on the Subject of the Projected Union to the Illustrious Stephen III, King of Dalkey* (Dublin: printed for the author, 1799), one of the few amusing contributions to the paper war. A minor satirical writer in verse, she has also been credited with writing *The Lemon*, a spirited response to John Giffard's *Orange*. Her fortunes went into reverse after the death of her husband in 1794.[31] The extent to which she benefited in PRO: CO 904/2 is slight indeed, the extent to which she was influenced remains to be seen.

Three references to Bob Martin record payments within three months (March–May 1797) of £4: 9: 3, or almost four times what was paid to the distressed poetess. Bob Martin was a humble parish functionary in Chapelizod, whose use to Cooke lay in his closeness to the military establishment in the Phoenix Park. (We might presume that Martin was paid for little acts of surveillance, or the running of discreet errands.) Many years later, Martin unwittingly served as an informant for the novelist, Sheridan Le Fanu, whose 'Ghost Stories of Chapelizod' appeared in the *Dublin University Magazine* of January 1851 though drawing on the writer's recollections of thirty years earlier.[32] That great haunted historical fiction of the Irish eighteenth century – Le Fanu's *House by the Churchyard* (1863) – may be said to have been partially funded by Cooke through PRO: CO 904/2. Indeed the so-called Gothic tradition of Irish literature, from Maturin's comments on revolution in the footnotes of *Melmoth the Wanderer* (1820) through to Yeats's 'In Memory of Eva Gore-Booth and Con Markiewicz' (1927), refers not only to Burkean ideals of the state as tree but also to presumptions of radical guilt (as Yeats expresses it, 'They convicted us of guilt') which are not so much theological as administrative-bureaucratic in their origins. A new literary history, materialist rather than idealist, could be constructed from deeper enquiries into the 'Burke-shaped silence' referred to at the outset, and from similar repressed relations or perspectives traceable between – say – Jonathan Swift and J. M. Synge.

But, for the cultural historian specializing in book-trade matters as a significant index, the most valuable details in the accounts are those relating to print-runs, that is, the number of copies of a particular title run-off by the printer to constitute an 'edition'. Figures for Dublin are notoriously scarce, and PRO: CO 904/2 provides details under 2 June 1797, 26 August 1797 and 13 September 1797, and 10 October 1797. The first of these is particularly valuable because it specifies:

i) the printer/booksellers concerned (Mercier),
ii) the author and title of the publication, which can be inferred as,
    Speech of Robert Johnson, Esq., Member for Hillsborough, Delivered in the House of Commons, Monday the 4th May 1795 on the Motion, that the Bill entitled 'A Bill for the Further Relief of His Majesty's Popish or Roman Catholic Subjects' be Rejected. Dublin: printed for R E Mercier, 1795. 100pp.,
iii) the number of copies printed (1000),
iv) the purpose for which these were intended (distribution [free?] in the North of Ireland, doubtless in the Hillsborough constituency and environs, County Down)
v) the date on which this was effected (June 1795),
vi) the patron (Arthur Hill, 1753–1801, 2nd marquis of Downshire) responsible either for the distribution or payment,
vii) the payment, £10: 16: 8. which, though paid to the bookseller/publisher, can be related to printing costs.

Beyond these technical details, it is possible to cite Burke's opinion on the matter. In a letter to the Earl Fitzwilliam, briefly the reforming Lord Lieutenant, he quoted a Catholic delegation as naming a notable opponent – 'the Marquis of Downshire, who had written to his Members to oppose the Catholick Bill'.[33] To add to the marquis's contrary reputation, he opposed the Act of Union, and feuded bitterly with Castlereagh and his family. The payment in June 1797, of a small debt evidently run up two years earlier, suggests official efforts either to win the affection of Mercier (the bookseller/publisher) or to open amiable negotiations with the marquis (who lived mainly in England). The former would seem the more likely, but the episode as known does not stand up to political analysis.

In the list given above (pp. 184–8), Milliken features on a further seven occasions, in date ranging from 18 April 1798 to 1 February 1799. The two entries under 28 June 1798 specify such sums of pounds, shillings and pence as to indicate payment for particular print-runs, numbers or copies, etc. In contrast stand the sums of £30, £50, and £100 which appear to be advances – indeed the first (£50 on 18 April 1798) is specifically named as such. While it is possible that the payments of 28 June 1798 (£47: 7: 6 and £8: 6: 0) simply tidied up what was due to Milliken for work completed by that date, the occurrence of two distinct entries for that day should prompt caution in reaching this conclusion. The naming of Camden (Lord Lieutenant from 1795 to 20 June 1798), together with lesser but still major officials, Thomas Pelham (Secretary for Ireland until March 1798) and Cooke, in the second of the 28 June entries indicates a very high level of engagement with the Dublin bookseller. What one traces behind these payments to the bookseller is the replacement of one team (Camden/Pelham) by another (Cornwallis/Castlereagh). On the basis of this observation we may also detect a shift in attitudes towards the press, especially the book press. It was not a shift accomplished overnight. Pelham was temporarily replaced by Robert Stewart, Viscount Castlereagh, on 29 March: on 3 November, the latter's appointment was confirmed.

The round sums (£30–£100) constitute a substantial investment in a future project. While Milliken's name appears on many publications which the Castle doubtless approved, including the second edition of Knox's *Essays*,[34] the most notable in terms of responses citing it was Edward Cooke's *Arguments for and against an Union* appearing almost simultaneously with Knox's much longer *Essays*. Milliken advertised Cooke's *Arguments* on Saturday 1 December 1798 as 'at two o'clock this day will be published'. A contemporary note confirms that publication was effected no later than the following Monday. Though this date falls within the period of the accounts under examination, there are no entries in them from which to infer payment for this publication specifically. Yet it would be illogical to assume that this absence of evidence establishes an absence of financial connection between the Castle and the printer/bookseller – after all the anonymous author, Cooke, acted as the most essential

connection. As we can see from the payments listed in Appendix
I, Cooke's name had virtually disappeared from the secret
service and related accounts in PRO: CO 904/2 by the summer of
1798, though his involvement thereafter cannot be denied.

After 1 December 1798, numerous 'editions' of Cooke's *Arguments* appeared with Milliken's name as the publisher. (No printer is
ever named.) The complex title-page dating of editions would
suggest that the publication of *Arguments* was far from the
straightforward implementation of covert government policy
one might have supposed. Ideology, or the practical enforcement
of theory, had its own practical complications.

What follows in this present paragraph is necessarily hypo-
thetical in part.[35] An examination of PRO: CO 904/2, in the light
of the pamphlet debate about the Union, suggests that prior
arrangements were made between the Castle and Milliken for the
production of a pamphlet, with the printer/bookseller receiving
an initial payment as early as 18 April 1798.[36] Changes at the
highest level in the Castle, notably the consolidation of
Castlereagh and his 'hard line' in the course of the year, led to
reconsideration but not abandonment of these plans. The outbreak of rebellion – datable either to the official proclamation of
martial law (30 March), the arrest of Lord Edward Fitzgerald (19
May) or the commencement of hostilities in Leinster (23 May) –
'naturally' constitutes a further structuring element in the growing crisis. But if Cooke's *Arguments* had been contracted with its
printer before the fighting began, then its relative silence on the
rebellion as an argument in favour of Union is explicable. Castlereagh's growing influence may be a further cause for delay in
publication, together with the distractions of military repression.

The occurrence of Alexander Knox's name five time between
late August 1798 and the following May highlights inconsistencies in the language of the account-keeper while also drawing
attention to political contradictions. Knox was a forty-year-old
'Gentlemen of the North of Ireland' when these payments
occurred: he was neither a printer nor bookseller. Yet he features
as receiving money on 29 August 1798 in two distinct roles – 'Mr
Alexr Knox for Printing Pamphlets £67: 14: 2 … [Mr Alexr Knox]
for L'Derry Journal 1 Qtr to 1 August £25'. Knox, however, is an
anomalous figure, given his subsequent career as a liberal lay

theologian and his support for Catholic Emancipation. His *Essays* demonstrate how thoroughly the United Irishman rebellion had shaken him, and in this one sees both a vindication of Burke's fears and neglect of Burke's advice. A similar twist affects Dublin Castle's generous payment of importation charges on books for a Catholic archbishop. Augustin Barruel's work was well known to Burke; the two men corresponded in mutually flattering terms. John Thomas Troy (1739–1823), the Archbishop of Dublin, saw hopes of Catholic Emancipation behind the campaign for union. Burke thought Troy a 'most timid, passive, and inert man'.[37]

Entries relating to payment in connection with the workings of the House of Commons Secret Committee, together with the entry of 29 July 1799 – 'Alderman Exshaw for Printing work on account by order of Lord Castlereagh £331: 5: 8' – clearly indicate that the new Chief Secretary utilized the secret service funds to finance various clerical and print-medium activities. The entry for 29 June exemplifies in a striking fashion the accuracy of Edmund Burke's dictum of seven years earlier:

> A word has been lately struck in the mint of the Castle of Dublin; thence it was conveyed to the Tholsel, or City-hall, where, having passed the touch of the corporation, – so respectably stamped and vouched, it soon became current in Parliament ...[38]

Money and printing become images of each other in Burke's analysis, with the physical 'coinage' constituting a central fulcrum in the ideological transformation. Exshaw is both bookseller/printer and alderman/middleman. In terms of a later dialectic, one could describe this as the reconstitution of quality as quantity; and see the third resultant term of the dialectic as a synthesis of ideology and brutality, spirit and body. One might even go further and analyse Castlereagh's activities as the Theoretical Practice of Filthy Lucre (TPFL) with its formal (or complementary) poles of insinuation and extortion. The insinuation of bribes and titles is exemplified in the cases of Richard Harding (11 April 1799 for the accommodation of government) or the much better known Sir Hercules Langrishe (£50 by Mr Cooke, 1 June 1797): the extortion of data concerning rebels might be decoded from the language of TPFL simply as beating the shite out of suspects, by Mr Giffard amongst others.

Burke's *Reflections* hover in the background, not so much out of sight as out of print. Whatever his attitude to the Union might have been in 1799 or 1800, it is neither his orotund defence of Marie Antoinette nor his vision of society as 'a partnership ... between those who are living, those who are dead, and those who are to be born' which springs to mind in this context. Rather it is the language of magic which Burke in the later pages of the *Reflections* applied to the fiscal arrangements of revolutionary France. The assignats were, in his view, 'paper amulets'.[39] This inversion or paradox is taken further in the 'Letter to Richard Burke' of 1792 already cited: there, words with a previously normative usage are shown to become 'this spell of potency, this abracadabra hung about the necks of the unhappy, not to heal, but to communicate disease'. The procedures adopted by Cooke in favour of union, and recorded in PRO: CO 904/2 as funded by the secret service, represent the application of a theory which Burke had detected in the radical practices of a revolutionary government. But these procedures were in turn superseded, as the failure of Cooke's *A Review of the Question of Union* to be published in July 1799 demonstrated.

There is a sentence in the *Reflections*, which the too-easily discredited Cruise O'Brien has found to exemplify Burke's furious irony. In its two-stage compacted survey of political discourse in 1790, it might be taken as also describing Cooke's use of print and Castlereagh's preference for violence in 1798 – 'That argument will do very well, with a lamp-post for its second ...'.[40] It is futile to ransack the *Reflections* for clues indicating Burke's likely opinion on the substantive events of eight or ten years later, but futility on those grounds does not rule out other benefits to be derived from reading 'the great melody' of 1790 in a context where it signally failed to remain a text, failed to be in print. Burke's demonstration of the indissoluble relations between substance and style, between political change and linguistic innovation compromises the propaganda of 1798–1800. It does so, not because the *Reflections* embodies some eternally valid doctrine of ideology, but because its specific ironies are complemented in the Irish political situation of 1798–1800. Dublin Castle in the 1790s was not the bastille of an Irish *ancien régime*; it was a bureaucracy of interest and self-interest, implementing thoroughgoing change in defence of the status quo, and effecting its own defence by a series of aggressive and subversive initiatives with printers' ink and boiling pitch. Or, TPFL.

'Hints on the Employment of Writers in Favour of a Union'

The Burke-shaped silence of 1797–1800 has now been considered in sufficient detail to confirm the hypothesis that a shift in Dublin Castle's policy, in relation to propaganda and counter-insurgency, can not only be detected but described in several of its stages. Castlereagh's lamp-posts may constitute the ultimate point of sophistication, but the transition from work through pamphlets to a confirmed policy of infiltrating the newspaper press is further illustrated in a remarkable document published in Castlereagh's correspondence.[41] The author was Thomas Lewis O'Beirne (1748?–1823) who had already benefited from the subvention of pamphlets by having his sermon circulated to the Lords and Commons (see the entry for 23 March 1798 in Appendix 2 below.) The text follows:

Hints on the Employment of Writers in Favour of a Union.
By the Bishop of Meath.

Secret.

It is much better to employ those who are to write in favour of the Union, in composing short essays than pamphlets.

As the appeal in favour of the Union must be to the reason and sound sense of the Nation, and not to its passions or its prejudices, the style of those should be plain, simple, and level to the understanding of plain, honest men. They must be directed to detect the fallacies and misrepresentations by which the public have been led away from the consideration of the subject itself to things totally foreign to its object. Wit may do great things against it, but nothing for it; yet, at the same time, those whose talent lies that way may do some service, and particularly in writing songs, and I understand the [sic] G. N – R – is very well disposed to exert his talents that way, provided that he were enabled to discharge some small debts, which force him now to confine himself.[42]

It is absolutely essential that some persons, on whom the

Government can rely, should be supplied with proper materials, by official communications respecting the state of the revenues, the amount of the customs and excise compared with those of England, what changes are proposed to take place, in what articles England is willing to consult the comparative inferiority of Irish manufacture by granting indulgences, as was done in many articles in Scotland; and every other subject that may enable them to satisfy the public mind on the various points on which they may wish to meet the objections of the opposers of the measure.

With respect to the mode of giving circulation to the different publications, it is perfectly nugatory to publish *merely* in the Dublin Journal. They should be inserted, if possible, in the Dublin Evening Post; but, in whatever paper they may be originally published, measures ought to be taken to get them immediately republished in the different county papers, and in small pamphlets to be dispersed through the country.[43] The usual mode of doing this, is by sending the pamphlets to the different post-offices; but as every one knows that this has not answered any adequate end, as the postmasters content themselves with giving them to those who come to their offices; and there is not one of these offices in which hundred of such pamphlets are not lying at this moment unopened.

I could recommend the appointment of some particular person to superintend this essential business; and Mr. M'Kenna, who, in the time of the Roman Catholic Committee, to which he acted as their secretary, and conveyed their publications through channels by which they were but too generally and too successfully disseminated, tells me he has no objection to undertake this or any thing else in which he can be of service.[44] In England, at the time of the Irish propositions, a committee of gentlemen was formed for that purpose among the Opposition.

I can only add that there is not a moment to be lost, and that, perhaps, it may be even now too late.

As O'Beirne's own efforts demonstrated, it was not too late to effect the Union. There was something to be gained by learning from the practices of the Catholic Committee once effectively led by Burke's friend John Keogh (patron of the United Irishmen) and the Dublin Catholic bookseller Patrick Byrne. A bureaucracy of post offices was already in place, only a lack of zeal on the part of postmasters frustrated its becoming the engine of all desired change.

But the methods recommended by the bishop once again oddly echoed Burke's *Reflections*. Suggesting to his correspondent of 1790 that French ideas of Britain were flawed in being based on 'certain publications', he inveighed against 'the vanity, restlessness, petulance, and spirit of intrigue of several petty cabals' who engaged 'in bustle and noise, and puffing, and mutual quotation of each other'. Against such 'literary men and ... politicians', he argued for the virtue, if not necessarily the efficacy, of silence:

> Because half a dozen grasshoppers under a fern make the field ring with their importunate chink, whilst thousands of great cattle, reposed beneath the shadow of the British oak, chew the cud and are silent, pray do not imagine, that those who make the noise are the only inhabitants of the field; ... or that, after all, they are other than the little shrivelled, meagre, hopping, though loud and troublesome insects of the hour.[45]

In PRO: CO 904/2 we trace how the grasshoppers of the Irish Directory organized their revolutionary Union so that a Junto of Jobbers might move into an imperial theatre of action. Castlereagh became Foreign Secretary in 1812, and acted as the chief 'British' plenipotentiary at the Congress of Vienna (1814–15) which concluded the Napoleonic Wars. With Arthur Wellesley (born Trim, County Meath) as the field-marshall who won Waterloo, and John Wilson Croker (born Dublin) as Secretary to the Admiralty from 1810 onwards, Castlereagh formed part of a crucial Irish component in the imperial leadership. When Wellington became Prime Minister in 1828, he succeed George Canning who, though not Irish born, came from an Irish background. When Croker retired from parliament in 1832, he had already coined the term 'conservatives' by which such politicians might be known for the future. Though acute on matters of linguistic innovation, Burke's irony did not quite anticipate for the grasshoppers success on such a scale. And, in any case, some of the principal figures in Dublin Castle (Castlereagh among them) had been prepared to concede Catholic Emancipation, though for reasons less noble-minded than Burke could have approved.

In terms of Habermas's account of the bourgeois public

sphere, it is necessary to balance his emphasis on virtual representation with some attention to the growth of 'bureaucracy', a
term introduced into English during this period. The careers of
Burke's Junto of Jobbers after 1800 would suggest that they
traded local parliamentary power for control of wider areas of
administrative influence. In fact, a reading of Burke's *Reflections*
on the growth of French systems of fiscal and political activity
might confirm the view that representation and bureaucracy
emerge as the twin terms of a bourgeois dialectic no less rightly
so described in its Dublin manifestation than in the Parisian.
Control of print, of newspapers and booksellers, song sheets and
even of wit itself would determine how the public sphere spun
between the poles of that dialectic.

Among the hundreds of publications debating in 1798–1800
the proposed union between Britain and Ireland, the name of
Burke is not often cited. Neither is the medium of fiction often
resorted to. But Maria Edgeworth's *Castle Rackrent*, published
anonymously in January 1800 by Joseph Johnson of London,
was read within that extended debate, as notes to subsequent
editions clearly indicated. The still unattributed *Letter from
Darby Tracy, Chairman in London, to Mr Denis Feagan, Breeches-
maker at Edenderry* (1799) may rank lower as fiction than *Castle
Rackrent* but it anticipates narrative strategies employed by
Edgeworth in *The Absentee* (1812), a novel in which an errant
family of Irish landlords is faithfully served by an agent simply
named, Mr Burke.[46] This nominal re-emergence of the author of
the *Reflections* could itself be read as dialogic, with the novel and
political discourse taking the main speaking parts. In *Patronage*
(published in 1814 after a long gestation), Edgeworth probed
dangerous political themes in the character of Lord Oldborough
in whom (it was suspected) she represented Castlereagh, Foreign
Secretary at the time of the novel's controversial publication. But
by 1817, in *Ormond* she had turned to late eighteenth-century
history and to a hero's character woven of both Irish and French
material. As Nicola Watson has carefully noted, the enterprise is
shot through with buried 'ominous and reiterated quotations
from Burke's *Reflections*'.[47] The Burke-shaped absence was gradually filling, at least as much with literary work as with political
acknowledgement.

A perspective on Burke's posthumous reputation cannot sensibly be taken from – say – W. B. Yeats's tributes in *The Tower* (1928) or elsewhere, no more than one can confidently assume that certain resemblances between the 'hands-on' politics of Lord Castlereagh and Gerry Adams will confirm the latter's seat in the imperial parliament at Westminster. Metaphors derived from the visual sense, as well Burke knew when he employed them, lock their beholders into a quasi-territorial model of temporal process. The preceding examination of PRO: CO 904/2, conceived as the obverse of Burke's *Reflections*, is intended to recommend the historical method. By it, evidence and interpretation are brought into effective mutual definition, hypothesis and text employed to test each other. These procedures give promise of rescuing us from a dictatorship of the contemporary (no more than a black-cartoon of Marx's 'dictatorship of the proletariat') too long propagated by the Cookes, Millikens and O'Beirnes of post-moderno-colonialism.

Appendix 1: Cooke in the books

Edward Cooke's name appears first on 5 September 1795 when he is paid £50 'account SS' (i.e. secret service). From March 1796 onwards it recurs frequently, often with additional details of the ultimate beneficiary. Given Cooke's activities in relation to the press (e.g. *The Derry Journal*) and (later) booksellers, it seems useful to tabulate payments made to him during this period. From these (essentially secret service) funds he received: on 17 March 1796 (£200), 14 May (£50), 9 June (£50), 18 June (for Mr Godfrey, £50), 20 June (and Secret Service, £50) 21 June (£10), 30 June (for Mr Hamilton £5: 13: 9, and do. for going to Belfast £50), 2 July (£8: 2: 6), 13 July (£5: 13: 9) 14 July (Mr D T [?] Ryan by Mr Cookes direction £56: 5: 0), 22 July (£50), 23 July (£6: 16: 6, £6: 16: 6, and £11: 7: 6), 28 July (£30), 29 July (£3: 8: 3, and £30), 6 August (£50), 11 August (£5: 13: 9), 13 August (£50), 16 August (£22: 15: 0), 22 August (£5: 13: 9), 5 September (in discharge of James Jones bill, £30), 7 September (£20), 12 September (£5: 13: 9), 2 October (£39: 16: 3), 12 October (for G … S Service £5: 13: 9), 17 October (for B £10), 19 October (for McNeil £11: 7: 6), 2 November (£20 and £5: 13: 9), 3 November (for Smith £20, and for Gray £5: 13: 9), 5 November (for Stewart £40), 7 November (for Collins … £54: 12: 6), 16 November (for Mitchel [?] £3: 8; 3), 19 November (for Gray £5: 13: 9), 30 November (on his own account £20), 6 December (for Mitchel & Gray £5: 13: 9), 9 December (for B £50), 10 December (for M £2: 5: 6), 12 December (on his own account £5: 13: 9, and for [blank] £5: 13: 9 and for Gray £2: 5: 6), 17 December (for Nicholson £5: 13: 9), 21 December (for Gray £3: 8: 3), 22 December (for Smith £20), 24 December (for B S £11: 7: 6 and for Mitchel £2: 5: 6), 31 December (for Mitchel & Gray £2: 5: 6).

In 1797, payments to Cooke were as follows: 2 January 1797 (for M £50), 3 January (for [?Cornelius] Clancy £5: 13: 9), 18 January (£30), 4 February (for N £5: 13: 9), 7 February (for Mr Tisdall £5: 13: 9), 20 February (for B £3: 8: 3), 21 February (for Serjeant Hart £1: 2: 9), 4 March (for Bob Martin £2: 5: 6), 7 March (£11: 7: 6), 12 April (for Miller £11: 7: 6), 15 April (for B Martin 1G, N3, B3, Murdoch 10, £19: 6: 9), 26 April (for Gray £3: 8: 3), 2 May (for his expenses to London & back in March ... £200), 10 May (for Newell £10), 13 May (for [blank] £5: 13: 9), 15 May (for Boyle, Kean, Dowling, £12: 16: 10½), 17 May (for ??, £50), 20 May (to Mr Annesley for D £10, for Murphy 5G), 26 May (for Hugh £30, for Bob Martin £1: 2: 9), 29 May (for Miller & Delany £2: 5: 6), 30 May (John Claudius Beresford by dir. of Mr Cooke £1: 9: 3), 1 June (Mr Newell by direction of Mr Cooke £11: 7: 6, Sir Hercules Langrishe by do. £50), 3 June (for the two Doyles £11: 7: 6), 10 June (for Dutton £45: 10: 0, for [two names illegible] £11: 7: 6), 16 June (for Mr Featherstone 14G & Mr Burdon 5G), 22 June (for M £60), 24 June (for a poor woman Charity account £1: 2: 9), 27 June (James Dawson by direction of Mr Cooke, £60), 3 August (for Mclean £10), 12 August (for N £10), 8 September (Mr D. T. Ryan by order of Mr Cooke £37: 10: 0), 10 October (for Miss Delahide £2: 5: 6), 24 November (for Lieut. Young £20), 12 December (for the Rev W Archer £100), 23 December (Mr Ryan by desire of Mr Cooke £37: 10: 0).

In the fatal year of 1798, we have the following details of payment to or through Cooke – 19 February (James Dawson £50), 3 March (£100), 6 March (Mr Swan by warrant of Mr Cooke £17: 1: 3), 7 April (Mr Ryan by direction of Mr Cooke £50), 3 May (Mr Isaac Heron of Waterford £20[48]), 23 July (£337: 10: 0), 1 August (Mr Giffard by direction of Mr Cooke £48), 20 August (Dr Chls Fletcher by direction of Mr Cooke £54: 3: 4).

The fall off in explicit references to Cooke, which is noticeable in 1798, continues in the following year – 31 January 1799 (£10), 27 September (expenses going to London £91), 6 December (£109).

Appendix 2: he who pays the printer

20 February 1796

T (?) Ryan for printing Pamphlets State of the War Oct O95 H. D.[49]   £27: 1: 8.

11 November 1796

Mr D. T. Ryan for Derry Journal, half year to Nov   £50.

13 December 1796

Mr Higgins for writers Freemans Journals from 16 April to 15 Oct   £88: 14: 6.

19 January 1797

Mr Ryan advance on Account of Printing Work   £40.

11 February 1797

Mr Cole Printer for Abstract of Insurrection Offers [?] for the
Commander in Chief[50] £4: 11: 0.

16 February 1797
Mr Ryan for Derry Journal 1 Qr to 1 Feb £25.

20 May 1797
Mr Ryan for Derry Journal 1 Qr to 1 May £25.

[To Mr Arnitt] for Dublin Journals sent to County Postmasters
1/2 year to 14 March £11.

2 June 1797
R & E Mercier for 1000 Copies of Mr Johnson's Speech
distributed in the North in June 1795 [acc.?] Lord Downshire[51] £10: 16: 8.

7 June 1797
Mr Ryan account of Printing Work £50.

8 July 1797
Mrs Battier on Charity account[52] £1: 2: 9.

4 August 1797
Mr Ryan for Derry Journal Qr to 1 Aug £25.

14 August 1797
Mr DeJoncourt, expenses of printing in the different
newspapers etc. £94: 13: 7.

26 August 1797
J. Milliken for 400 of Mr Sheridan's Pamphlet[53] £21: 13: 4.

7 September 1797
To [F. Higgins] for Writers & Note Takers from 15 Oct 96 to
3 July 97 £163: 8: 0.

13 September 1797
J. Milliken for 200 more of Mr Sheridan's Pamphlet £10: 16: 8.

10 October 1797
J. Milliken for 200 of Vindicators Remarks[54] £10: 16: 8.

3 November 1797

Mr. Ryan Derry Journal 1 Qr to 1 Nov   £25.

16 December 1797

[F. Higgins] for writers from 3 July 11 Dec 97, 23 weeks @ 3G   £78: 9: 9.

6 February 1798

[Mr W. Arnitt] for Irish news papers sent to the county Postmasters
to 20 Nov 97   £230.

Mr Ryan for Derry paper 1 qr to 1 Nov   £25.

23 March 1798

Bishop of Ossory his Sermon sent to the Members of both Houses[55] £22: 15: 0.

18 April 1798

Mr. Milliken on advance for Pamphlets   £50.

John Lees Esq Repayment of what he paid for Pamphlets   £7: 19: 3.

20 April 1798

Wm Arnitt Esq for News Papers distributed in the Country
[illegible] to 20 Feb   £123: 15: 0.

24 April 1798

[F. Higgins] for writers & Note Takers to [25 March]   £62: 8: 0.

25 April 1798

Alderman Exshaw[56] for Pamphlets   £66: 2: 6.

2 May 1798

Mr. Milliken on further account for Pamphlets   £100.

5 May 1798

Mr Robert Allen Belfast Paper to 25 March 97[57]   £200.

Mr Ryan for Derry Paper to 1 May 98   £25.

2 June 1798

J. Milliken on further account for Pamphlets   £50.

9 June 1798

Mr. Milliken on further account for Pamphlets   £30.

28 June 1798

Mr. Milliken Balance of account for Pamphlets certified &t
Mr Lees[58]   £47: 7: 6.

[Mr. Milliken] on act of Dn for Lord Camden, Mr Pelham &
Mr Cooke –   £8: 6: 10.

5 July 1798

Mr Wm Arnitt for News papers sent to Postmasters in the
Country from 20 Feb to 20 May   £225.

3 August 1798

Alderman Exshaw for Pamphlets sent by Post Office   £106; 5: 9.

17 August 1798

[Fr Higgins] Writers & Note Takers 13 weeks from 25 March
to 24 June   £59: 3: 0.

29 August 1798

Mr Alexr Knox for Printing Pamphlets[59]   £67: 14: 2.

[Mr Alexr Knox] for L'Derry Journal 1 Qtr to 1 August   £25.

23 October 1798

Mr Wm Arnitt General Post Office for Irish News Papers sent
to County Postmasters from 20 May to 20 Aug 98   £214: 12: 2.

5 November 1798

Mr Schoales for Derry Journal 1 Qtr to 1 Nov   £25.

7 November 1798

Mr Knox for printing work   £11: 7: 6.

27 November 1798

[F. Higgins] writers & Note Takers from 24 June to 29 Sept
14 weeks @ £4.0   £63: 14: 0.

30 November 1798

Cork Herald by J Lees Esq to be remitted to Cork[60]   £100.

8 December 1798

Sergeant John Henderson for Copying Papers for the Secret
Committee by direction of Lrd Castlereagh   £11: 7: 6.

30 January 1799

Mr Shaw of Cork for Cork News Papers[61]   £100.

1 February 1799

Mr Milliken on account of Pamphlets   £50.

Mr A Knox for R Comet to be repaid by Consideration   £20.

13 February 1799

Mr W Arnitt for News Papers sent to County Postmasters
from 20 Aug to 21 November 98   £204: 15: 0.

16 February 1799

[F. Higgins] Writers & Note Takers [1 qtr to 25 December 98]   £43: 15: 10½.

5 April 1799

Mr Roberts for copying Papers for the Secret Committee   £5: 13: 9.

5 May 1799

Mr Knox for Londonderry Journal half year to 1 May   £50.

Mr Allen for Belfast Paper 1 year   £200.

29 July 1799

Alderman Exshaw for Printing work on account by order
of Lord Castlereagh   £331: 5: 8.

6 August 1799

Dublin Evening Post for publishing Dissenters Address
in June 1798   £3: 19: 7½.

[F. Higgins] Writers & Note Takers on account 25 March
to 24 June   £56: 7: 9.

4 October 1799

Duty & Charges on Barruel's Memoirs of Jacobinism, sent from
England to Doctor Troy, to dispose[62]   £11: 7: 4.

4 November 1799

Lord Roscommon by direction of the Lord Lieutenant   £500.

Mr Schoales[63] for Derry paper ½ year to 4 November   £50.

18 December 1799

R. G. Hill Esq for sundry Publications in the Derry Paper ...
in 1796 7 & 8 by desire of Government   £69: 11: 0.

Notes

1 Edmund Burke to John Hely Hutchinson [provost of Trinity College, Dublin], 18 December 1790, Alfred Cobban and Robert A. Smith, eds, *Correspondence*, vol. VI, pp. 192–3. See Jacqueline Hill, *From Patriots to Unionists: Dublin Civic Politics and Irish Protestant Patriotism 1660–1840* (Oxford: Clarendon Press, 1997), pp. 212–13.

2 See for details R. B. McDowell, *Irish Public Opinion 1750–1800* (London: Faber, 1944), p. 164.

3 In recent years, some historians have stressed the early 'politicization' of groups previously thought to be essentially sectarian or agrarian secret societies with little by way of ideological sophistication in their arsenal. In a few instances such an emphasis echoes rather the politicization of the historian, relative to the 'national question' in late twentieth-century Ireland. For an example of how such tactics reverse historical chronology, see comments on the impact of the French Revolution and Burke's *Reflections* in Jim Smyth, *The Men of No Property: Irish Radicals and Popular Politics in the Late Eighteenth Century* (Dublin: Gill and Macmillan, 1992), pp. 91–3.

4 See Ray B. Browne 'The Paine–Burke Controversy in Eighteenth-century Irish Popular Songs', in Browne *et al.*, eds, *The Celtic Cross: Studies in Irish Culture and Literature* ([n. p.] Purdue University Studies, 1964), pp. 80–97. The stanza quoted is taken from a Philadelphia publication of 1796. Links between Dublin booksellers and Philadelphia were close, and false imprints were not uncommon.

5 Jürgen Habermas, *The Structural Transformation of the Public Sphere: An Inquiry into a Category of Bourgeois Society*, trans. Thomas Burger from the German edition of 1962 (Cambridge: Polity Press, 1989), p. 93.

6 *A Letter Addressed to a Noble Lord by Way of a Reply to that of the Right Honourable Edmund Burke*, by Bolingbroke (Dublin: printed for G. Folingsby, 1796), p. 2.

7 Edward Cooke to William Eden, 27 October 1798. I am grateful to Ruan O'Donnell for this reference.

8 Marilyn Butler, ed., *Burke, Paine, Godwin and the Revolution Controversy* (Cambridge: Cambridge University Press, 1984) exemplifies a scholarly tendency to regard London as both the centre and circumference of publishing – and of responses to publishing – during these years of widespread and pervasive controversy.

9 See G. C. Bolton, *The Passing of the Irish Act of Union* (Oxford: Clarendon Press, 1966) for a study of the parliamentary scene; the classic nationalist account of activities relevant to the present enquiry, W. J. Fitzpatrick, *Secret Service Under Pitt* (London: Longmans, 1892) is still valuable.

10 M. Pollard, *Dublin's Trade in Books 1550–1800* (Oxford: Clarendon Press, 1989). James W. Phillips, *Printing and Bookselling in Dublin 1670–1800: A Bibliographical Enquiry* (Dublin: Irish Academic Press, 1998). The latter

was completed in 1952 as a doctoral thesis, but retains its magisterial status after half a century of cherry-picking by readers of many kinds.

11 See Burke to John Keogh, 17 November, and to French Lawrence, 18 November and [23] November, all 1796. *Correspondence,* vol. IX, pp. 112–27.

12 [Alexander Knox], *Essays on the Political Circumstances of Ireland Written During the Administration of Earl Camden* (Dublin: printed by Graisberry & Campbell, 1798), p. 156. For Knox on Union, see pp. 136–67.

13 See *Correspondence,* vol. IX, p. 257.

14 Edmund Burke to John Keogh, 17 November [1796], *Correspondence,* vol. IX, pp. 114–15. It is ironic that Keogh, a leading and wealthy Catholic, was bank-rolling the United Irishmen whose schemes Burke here deplores.

15 See W. J. Mc Cormack, *From Burke to Beckett: Ascendancy, Tradition, and Betrayal in Literary History* (Cork: Cork University Press, 1994), pp. 31–2 for comment on the resemblance of Burke's writing strategies to those of the historical novelist.

16 *Life of Theobald Wolfe Tone,* ed. Tom Bartlett (Dublin: Lilliput Press, 1998), pp. 38–9, 734.

17 'I cannot blame France for wishing to retaliate on England the abominations of La Vendée and the Chouans, but it is hard that it should be at the expense of poor Ireland. It will be she and not England that will suffer' (*Journals,* 2 April 1796), *Life of Tone,* p. 523 (see also p. 626).

18 Edmund Burke to Thomas Hussey [post 9 December 1796], *Correspondence,* vol. IX, pp. 164–5.

19 *Life of Tone,* p. 734.

20 William B. Todd, *A Bibliography of Edmund Burke* (2nd edn, London: St Paul's Bibliographies, 1982). Augmented with data derived from the *Eighteenth-Century Short-Title Catalogue.*

21 See Gerard O'Brien, 'The Grattan Mystique', *Eighteenth-Century Ireland/ Iris an Dá Chultúir,* vol. 1 (1986), pp. 177–94.

22 See Michael MacDonagh, ed., *The Viceroy's Postbag; Correspondence Hitherto Unpublished of the Earl of Hardwicke, First Lord Lieutenant of Ireland After the Union* (London: Murray, 1904), pp. 365–7 for a short account of some alleged short-comings of Cooke's in the management of these accounts.

23 Edmund Burke to Richard Burke, Jnr [18 November 1792], *Correspondence,* vol. VII, p. 290.

24 The conception of early-to-mid-eighteenth-century Ireland as an *ancien régime,* not greatly different from European kingdoms of the era and so not be treated as a colony, has been worked out at length in S. J. Connolly, *Religion, Law and Power: The Making of Protestant Ireland, 1660–1760* (Oxford: Oxford University Press, 1992).

25 See W. J. Mc Cormack, *The Pamphlet Debate on the Union Between Great Britain and Ireland, 1797–1800* (Dublin: Irish Academic Press, 1996), p. [115].

26 See Mc Cormack, *Pamphlet Debate*, pp. 29–31 for a list of these.

27 But see R. B. McDowell 'The Personnel of the Dublin Society of United Irishmen', *Irish Historical Studies*, vol. 2 (1940/1), pp. 12–53 for a valuable analysis of material dating from the years immediately preceding the period treated here.

28 Giffard was a member of Dublin Corporation's Common Council who played an active, if inglorious, part in suppressing the United Irishmen in 1798: see W. J. Mc Cormack, *Ascendancy and Tradition in Anglo-Irish Literary History from 1789 to 1939* (Oxford: Clarendon Press, 1985), pp. 402–4; and, for his financial plight in 1795, see Edward Cooke to Earl of Westmorland, 2/2/1795.

29 PRO: CO 904/2. The volume bears no initial title or description, though the first text page (listing receipts) refers to £500 'account of secret service'; its successor in the series as preserved (PRO: CO 904/3 is more explicitly described as including secret service accounts.

30 Euseby Cleaver.

31 See Andrew Carpenter, ed., *Verse in English from Eighteenth-Century Ireland* (Cork: Cork University Press, 1998), p. 464.

32 For Le Fanu's comment on his debt to Bob Martin, see W. J. Mc Cormack, *Sheridan Le Fanu* (3rd edn, Stroud: Sutton, 1997), p. 120.

33 Edmund Burke to Earl Fitzwilliam [13] March 1795, *Correspondence*, vol. VIII, p. 193. Hillsborough was controlled by Downshire. The three other entries providing print-run evidence are far less complete. No uncertainty as to the bookseller/publisher arises – this is John Milliken, later to issue Cooke's *Arguments*. The figure of £21 : 13 : 4 for four hundred copies of a pamphlet, followed the next month by payment of £10 : 16 : 8 for two hundred indicates that payment was based on cost calculations, rather than on any rounded up sum agreed between the parties. Here one sees the Castle's committed opposition to Henry Grattan, who had introduced the bill opposed by Johnson of Hillsborough.

34 The first edition title page declared the work 'printed by Graisberry & Campbell'; the second 'printed for J. Milliken, 1799'; there was also a London issue 'Dublin: printed by Graisberry & Campbell, and sold by J. Wright, London, 1799'.

35 Unfortunately, neither Phillips nor Pollard pays any attention to Milliken's career, nor to the topic of pamphlet wars.

36 Milliken was basically a bookseller/publisher, but his name does feature occasionally as printer: see, for example, *An Appeal to the Loyal Citizens of Dublin. By a Freeman of Dublin* (Dublin: printed by John Milliken, 1800, 42pp.). The author of this was Thomas L. O'Beirne.

37 Edmund Burke to Walter King, 16 May 1797, *Correspondence*, vol. IX, p. 345.

38 'Letter to Richard Burke', *Writings and Speeches of Edmund Burke*, vol. IX, pp. 632–3.

39 *Reflections*, pp. 126–7, 146–7, 286.

40 See *Reflections on the Revolution in France*, ed. Conor Cruise O'Brien, pp. 43–4. But what Burke actually wrote was 'This sort of discourse does well enough with the lamp-post for its second' (*Reflections*, p. 103).

41 Charles Vane, ed., *The Memoirs and Correspondence of Castlereagh* (London, 1848), vol. 3, pp. 26–7.

42 George Nugent Reynolds (1770?–1802), a poet but a man of some spirit; he had been dismissed from his magistracy by John Fitzgibbon (the Lord Chancellor). O'Beirne's proposal involves minor reconciliations in the higher cause of supporting the Union. Reynolds had already shown his loyalty by writing 'Bantry Bay' which, like O'Beirne's sermon, celebrated the dispersion of the French fleet; see Mc Cormack, *Ascendancy and Tradition*, pp. 150–2.

43 *An Appeal to the Loyal Citizens of Dublin* (attributed to O'Beirne on a copy in Trinity College Dublin Library) was printed by Milliken; a further and even shorter (12pp) pamphlet, *A Hint to the Inhabitants of Ireland* (no imprint, but with a date-line on p. 11 reading 'February 1800') may also be by O'Beirne.

44 Theobald M'Kenna (died 1808), a figure of inconstant positions.

45 *Reflections*, p. 136.

46 See Mc Cormack, *Pamphlet Debate*, Items A15, L6 and L7 for the Darby Tracy/Denis Feagan material which took up three pamphlets, one of them running to three editions.

47 Nicola J. Watson, *Revolution and the Form of the Novel, 1790–1825* (Oxford: Clarendon Press, 1994), p. 125.

48 One of the proprietors of the *Waterford Herald*.

49 'H. D.': Probably Henry Dundas (1742–1811).

50 Mr Cole is probably R. Cole, who (with V. Dowling) printed *The Trial at Large of Samuel Busby and Judith His Wife* [1793]: not a prolific printer. The project referred to here remains unidentified.

51 For a detailed account of this project, see p. 74 above. For an account of Richard Edward Mercier, see Phillips, p. 76.

52 See pp. 72–3 above.

53 This was Charles Francis Sheridan's anonymous, *Some Observations on a Late Address to the Citizens of Dublin, with Thoughts on the Present Crisis* (Dublin: Milliken, 1798) which ran to three editions. Its target was Henry Grattan, recently re-elected an MP for the city.

54 This was *Vindicators Remarks on Sarsfield's Letters, which Appeared in Four Numbers of the Dublin Evening Post, Beginning 26th August and Ending 2nd of September* (Dublin: J. Milliken, 1797), 40pp.

55 Thomas Lewis O'Beirne (1748?–1823), a Catholic by birth but converted to the Established Church; Bishop of Ossory from 1795 until his translation to Meath in 1798. See *A Sermon … on the Providential Dispersion of the*

Enemy's Fleet (Dublin: printed by W. Watson, 1797). O'Beirne had preached in Kilkenny, and the title-page of his sermon declared it 'Published at the desire of the Recorders, Mayor, and Corporation of the City of Kilkenny, and of the Portrieve and Burgesses of Irishtown'.

56 John Exshaw was a long established bookseller/printer in Dublin (father, succeeded by son of the same name). Of the thirteen of the items listed in *The Pamphlet Debate on the Union* which carry the imprint, none dates from this period (the year 1798). As an alderman in the city's Corporation, John Exshaw Jnr had taken part in the 1792 resolution which launched 'Protestant ascendancy' as an ideological totem: see *From Burke to Beckett*, p. 70.

57 Robert Allan was one of two Scottish proprietors of the *Belfast Newsletter*; see A. Aspinall, *Politics and the Press c.1780–1850* (London: Home and Van Thal, 1949), pp. 110–11, etc.

58 John Lees was secretary of the Irish Post Office. On Lees's support in 1796 for expanded free distribution of newspapers supporting the government, see Aspinall, *Politics and the Press*, p. 1499.

59 Knox's *Essays on the Political Circumstances of Ireland* opens with a preface dated 23 November 1798, and thus cannot be the subject of payment here. Knox became private secretary to Robert, Lord Castlereagh.

60 Aspinall, *Politics and the Press* (p. 113) suggests that the young proprietor of the new *Cork Herald* received no support.

61 Bernard Shaw of Cork helped Edward Henry Morgan (whose *Cork Herald* had died quickly) to establish the *Cork Advertiser*.

62 This is a puzzling entry, from the point of view of book-trade history. Augustin Barruel (1741–1820) published *Mémoires pour servir à la historie du Jacobisme* in four parts, the first volume of which he forwarded to Burke who acknowledged it on 1 May 1797. A translation (part of vol. 1, but amounting to 388pp.) was published by Watson in Dublin in 1798, under the title *Memoirs Illustrating the Anti-Christian Conspiracy*.

63 John Schoales was a barrister-at-law, who also functioned as a publishing reporter of important trials, for example that of the Rev. Wm Jackson in 1795. In 1804, when the proprietors of the *Londonderry Journal* received their annual £100 allowance, the receipts were signed by Schoales; see Aspinall, *Politics and the Press*, p. 116, n6.

5

Burke, popular opinion, and the problem of a counter-revolutionary public sphere

KEVIN GILMARTIN

Except that a 'Burke problem' in several guises has haunted the revival of Burke studies in recent decades, it might seem perverse to question his role as the consummate British anti-radical and counter-revolutionary writer in the age of the French Revolution.[1] For Romantic-period literary scholarship especially, his name and the *Reflections on the Revolution in France* (1790) seem to stand for the conservative reaction to revolution as fully as Tom Paine and the *Rights of Man* stand for its defence; subsequent conservative ideologists can be described as assuming 'the Burkean role as public critic of radicalism'.[2] Yet questions do arise about the typicality of this 'Burkean role', and recent scholarship has intensified them. Revisionist treatments of the range and character of conservative movements in Britain can make Burke seem a less central figure. Linda Colley's account of the pivotal role of mass ritual and spectacle, and above all public displays of royal splendour, in the consolidation of popular loyalist opinion suggests that the stridently anti-theatrical politics of the *Reflections* – Burke's contempt for 'magnificent stage effect', 'grand spectacle', and 'all the arts of quackish parade'[3] – may have been out of step with key features of the British national rejection of revolutionary energy.[4] A broader and deeper familiarity with the whole range of the printed debate triggered by events in France makes it more difficult to treat the 'Burke–Paine controversy' as a synonym for the whole

Revolution controversy, let alone for the broad contours of a contest between radical and conservative positions in Britain. Gregory Claeys has recently made this point in a survey of the literature, concluding that 'for most of its participants, neither Burke nor Paine defined the British response to the French revolution'; H. T. Dickinson agrees that, while 'Burke's fears and prophecies won him many admirers and adherents', it would be a 'mistake to think that all the leading conservative writers of the age were simply repeating or embellishing Burke's original arguments'.[5] And in a useful meditation on what we mean when we term the *Reflections* a 'classic', J. G. A. Pocock has suggested that 'the counter-revolutionary associations which were formed in and after 1793 seemed to have relied less on Burke for their polemics than on William Paley, Hannah More, and other authoritarian elements lying deep in Whig and Tory tradition'.[6]

Yet to problematize Burke in this way is not simply to shift attention from one writer or one political language to others. The central place accorded to the *Reflections* by literary romanticism has, I would argue, limited and attenuated our understanding of anti-revolutionary culture in Britain, foregrounding a limited set of rhetorical, philosophical, and aesthetic issues, and shifting attention away from questions of political organization and agency, the production and distribution of texts and other modes of public discourse, and the assembly of reading audiences and popular reading practices, to say nothing of the repressive exercise of state power and violence. In a challenge to what he considers 'the recent over-emphasis' among some historians on 'the intellectual vigour of conservative doctrine and the natural loyalty of the British people', Mark Philp has issued what may be the most trenchant challenge yet to Burke's hold upon the construction of Romantic-period conservatism. According to Philp, the 'multi-dimensional and complex' reaction of British loyalists to the challenge of revolution abroad and unrest at home precipitated a '"vulgar" conservatism', which necessarily rejected the Burkean view that 'the vulgar were the objects of conservative thinking, not intended participants in it'. Writers like Hannah More and John Bowles, and counter-revolutionary organizations like John Reeves's Association for the Preservation of Liberty and Property against Republicans and Levellers, quickly recognized that they could not ignore or wish away the increasingly restive audiences addressed and constituted by Paine and others sympathetic to the French; in so doing, they necessarily 'advanced a process of mass participation which they had come into existence to prevent', and transformed the premises of emergent conservative movements. If, as Philp argues, 'to pursue this course was to transcend Burke', then Burke's own course, in the *Reflections* and the series of anti-revolutionary polemics he produced up until his death in 1797, can be seen to have resisted the pragmatic and potentially transgressive energies of a '"vulgar" conservatism' in Britain, especially its efforts to reach and organize lower-class reading audiences.[7] To recommend this approach to Burke is to suggest not that we ignore him, but rather that we continue rethinking his work and his counter-revolutionary career.

I want to begin such a rereading by way of William Hazlitt, arguably the first sustained critic of Burke to have perceived a problem. As he came in the aftermath of the Congress of Vienna and Waterloo to position himself on the far side of the triumph of counter-revolution throughout Europe, Hazlitt employed a series of dialectical procedures, chiastic terms, and paradoxical formulations to disrupt ever-hardening assumptions about the structure of British politics: Sir Walter Scott, for example, is said to have founded his loyalty 'on *would-be* treason: he props the actual throne by the shadow of rebellion', and Robert Owen's *New View of Society* is dismissed as a 'species of matter of fact hallucination', so far from novelty that it 'is as old as ... the "Utopia" of Sir Thomas More, as the "Republic" of Plato; it is as old as society itself'.[8] At the centre of all these political contradictions stood the troubling figure of Edmund Burke. As John Whale has shown, Hazlitt's profound ambivalence about the author of the *Reflections* hinged on a 'conflict between aesthetic and political power': 'When Hazlitt considers the combination of imagination and politics to be found in Burke's prose from a literary point of view ... his response is dominantly celebratory. But when he adopts the alternative stance of political and social commentator he is scathing where before he had been eulogistic.'[9] This last point is important, since romanticist treatments of Hazlitt have too often privileged aesthetic considerations. Confronted with the question of Burke's political impact, Hazlitt's ambivalence fell away, and the late Romantic essayist could take up the terse idiom and unequivocal judgement of English radical discourse: 'I should not differ from any one who may be disposed to contend that the consequences of his writings as instruments of political power have been tremendous, fatal, such as no exertion of wit or knowledge or genius can ever counteract or atone for.'[10] Yet where he was able to sustain the dialectical methods and dizzying antitheses that were more characteristic of his prose, a subtler account of Burke emerged, and the author of the *Reflections* remained a critical site upon which to complicate and challenge prevailing assumptions about British political life.

The essay 'On Court Influence', which appeared immediately after the 'Character of Burke' in Hazlitt's 1819 volume, *Political Essays,* opens with a counter-intuitive proposition in the spirit of Hume – 'It is not interest alone, but prejudice or fashion that sways mankind. Opinion governs opinion.'[11] – which is then illustrated with an anecdote from the career of Burke:

It is usually supposed by those who make no distinction between the highest point of integrity and the lowest mercenariness, that Mr. Burke changed his principles to gain a pension: and that this was the main-spring of his subsequent conduct. We do not think so; though this may have been one motive, and a strong one to a needy and extravagant man. But the pension which he received was something more than a mere grant of money — it was a mark of royal favour, it was a tax upon public opinion. If any thing were wanting to fix his veering loyalty, it was the circumstance of the king's having his 'Reflections on the French Revolution' bound in morocco (not an unsuitable binding), and giving it to all his particular friends, saying, 'It was a book which every gentleman ought to read!' This praise would go as far with a vain man as a pension with a needy one; and we may be sure, that if there were any lurking seeds of a leaning to the popular side remaining in the author's breast, he would after this lose no time in rooting them out of the soil, that his works might reflect the perfect image of his royal master's mind, and have no plebeian stains left to sully it. Kings are great critics: they are the fountain of honour; the judges of merit. After such an authority had pronounced it 'a book which every gentleman ought to read', what gentleman could refuse to read, or dare to differ with it? With what feelings a privy-

counsellor would open the leaves of a book, which the king had
had richly bound, and presented with his own hand! How lords of
the bed-chamber would wonder at the profound arguments! How
peeresses in their own right must simper over the beautiful similes!
How the judges must puzzle over it! How the bishops would bless
themselves at the number of fine things ...![12]

Now this anecdote, originating perhaps in a conversation in which
George III was reported to have offered Burke the compliment
'that there is no Man who calls himself a Gentleman that must not
think himself obliged to you',[13] had a complex political valence.
Having appeared first in January 1818 in John Hunt's *Yellow
Dwarf,*[14] it was securely embedded in the print culture of post-
war radicalism, and was in part a rebuke to what Hazlitt
perceived as the limited range of radical argument, especially its
tendency (under Cobbett's influence) to pursue a narrowly
economic case against ministerial corruption and predatory taxation as the roots of political injustice. As Hazlitt knew, Burke was
from the 1790s on a key figure in this critique. His name and the
names of his heirs and relatives continued to figure centrally in
radical catalogues of corruption right up through the period of
the appearance of 'On Court Influence' in *The Yellow Dwarf;* in
fact, one printed source offered George III's compliment to Burke
as ironic evidence that the anti-radical position 'was somewhat
more profitable than contending for REFORM'.[15] Hazlitt's notion
of 'a tax upon public opinion', exacted in a courtly economy
where financial interest mattered less than hierarchies of reputation and esteem, was an attempt to transform the framework in
which Burke's influence and capacity to be influenced was
understood. As usual, the essayist was tilting on several fronts,
and the appearance of the morocco-bound volume as court fetish
was a way of sealing off the actual text of the *Reflections* from its
supposed advocates on the right, thereby denying them Hazlitt's
own cherished capacity to appreciate Burke's aesthetic power.

In placing the reception of the *Reflections* securely in an elite
social register, and in mischievously deriving the authority of
the printed text from the king rather than the author, Hazlitt's
anecdote carried with it specific implications about literary influence and authorial construction. The charmed circle of court
opinion, where 'kings are great critics' and 'judges of merit', was

the antithesis of the levelling republic of letters that was emerging, albeit fitfully, in Hazlitt's prose in this period.[16] As a writer whose work appeared in periodical venues ranging from William Cobbett's *Political Register* and Leigh Hunt's *Examiner* to the *London Magazine* and *Edinburgh Review,* Hazlitt was acutely aware of contemporary discriminations that made the print public sphere a sharply heterogeneous and discontinuous terrain. The atmosphere of court influence within which he situated the reception of the *Reflections* and the exercise of a Burke-effect was for him suffocating and destructive, a 'subtle poison, the least exhalation of which taints the vitals of its victims',[17] but it could by no means be easily dismissed as residual or irrelevant. Indeed, much of Hazlitt's post-Waterloo prose was founded on the claim that 'the old doctrine of Divine Right, new-vamped up under the style and title of Legitimacy',[18] was being mobilized in Britain and throughout Europe to root out the last vestiges of popular right. 'We are all of us more or less the slaves of opinion', he complained in the essay 'On Court Influence'; the inverted and anti-democratic order of a courtly political culture allowed influence and opinion to descend from the monarch through 'the Ministers to both Houses of Parliament, from Lords to Ladies, from the Clergy to the Laity, from the high to the low, from the rich to the poor', until at last 'the opinion of the King is the opinion of the nation'.[19]

While all of this may suggest tangled partisan motives and an eccentric historical sensibility on Hazlitt's part, the lineage of simpering peeresses and puzzled lords of the bedchamber does contain a perversely deployed Burkean logic (all the more perverse given the anti-court inflection of much of Burke's pre-Revolutionary career), and it challenges us to reconsider the location of the *Reflections* in the climate of Romantic-period political culture and opinion. Burke's notorious contempt for 'a swinish multitude',[20] which provided a generation of British radicals with a useful rallying cry and a furiously negative sense of their own political identity, achieved its sharpest focus when he was confronted with the introduction of ordinary people into the political life of the nation, and with the spectre of a plebeian public sphere that was both the antithesis of Hazlitt's court influence, and the region where conservative activists like

Hannah More and the Reevesite Associations were prepared to set about their work. In his *Thoughts on French Affairs* (1791), Burke contemptuously dismissed the activity of the 'Frith Street Alliance', a reforming organization reportedly composed of 'fifteen or sixteen journeymen Barbers, Bakers, and Carpenters',[21] as 'the delirium of a low, drunken, alehouse-club'. Claiming to be less offended by the danger than by 'the ridicule and absurdity' of their correspondence with the French Assembly, he diminished the episode through a relentless insistence on the 'low and base' character of its participants: 'This address of the alehouse club was actually proposed and accepted by the Assembly as an *alliance*. The procedure was in my opinion a high misdemeanour in those who acted thus in England, if they were not so very low and so very base, that no acts of theirs can be called high, even as a description of criminality'.[22] The very capacity for seditious criminal responsibility, let alone legitimate political participation, was in Burke's account beyond the political reach of the lower orders.

If to disdain the exercise of plebeian opinion in this way was at least to acknowledge its emergence, then a more interesting and complicated problem in Burke's post-revolutionary political thought was the way he resisted and repressed such an acknowledgement altogether, by restricting, in sharply deline-ated class terms, the sphere within which political opinion might legitimately find form and expression. In this sense, Burke could not participate in a conservative project to manage and direct the popular response to French revolutionary principles because he did not readily acknowledge the emergence of a plebeian counter-public sphere in Britain.[23] In a cogent account of the theory of political representation that takes shape in the *Reflections,* James Chandler has shown how an 'adequate repre-sentation' consistent with British tradition, as compared with Richard Price's alien standard of '*a pure and equal representation*',[24] depended for Burke first upon 'prerogatives of property' that were 'inherently incompatible with the principle of equality', but also upon a less explicitly political, but still *representational,* system of chivalric manners, which negotiated and enforced the uneven social consequences of an unequal distribution of property.[25] The 'pleasing illusions' of chivalry consolidated the

stratification of wealth and privilege even as they blunted its
social and psychic impact, yielding that consummate Burkean
paradox, hierarchy experienced as equality: 'without confounding ranks', the 'mixed system of opinion and sentiment' that 'had
its origin in the antient chivalry' yielded 'a noble equality and
handed it down through all the gradations of social life'.[26] Similar
structures of feeling determined the hierarchical formation and
distribution of political opinion. In Burke's reversal of a Scottish
Enlightenment derivation of manners and culture from
commerce,[27] opinion shared with 'modern letters' an unacknow-
ledged debt to 'antient manners'.[28] Far from acceding to Enlightenment fantasies about an egalitarian republic of letters, Burke
considered levelling opinion a contradiction in terms, a product
of the unholy artifice of those who 'change and pervert the
natural order of things'.[29] Public sentiment required for its very
existence a system of manners in which individuals deferred to
their superiors in wealth, privilege, and merit. After repudiating
Rousseau in *A Letter to a Member of the National Assembly* (1791),
Burke offered his own version of a social contract, according to
which 'men are qualified for civil liberty, in exact proportion to
their disposition to put moral chains upon their own appetites',
and 'in proportion as they are more disposed to listen to the
counsels of the wise and good, in preference to the flattery of
knaves'.[30] The political opinions of most people are legitimate
only if they are formed and acquired at second hand, through the
benign ministrations of an economic and social elite. In the
Reflections, the revolutionary interruption or failure of this
process of deference as socialization led, predictably, to the
dissolution of 'the whole chain and continuity of the commonwealth', as collective social structures were 'disconnected into
the dust and powder of individuality, and at length dispersed to
all the winds of heaven'.[31] Far from emerging in the period of the
French Revolution as a legitimate protest against ancient
privilege and present injustice, 'all this violent cry against the
nobility' was 'a mere work of art', the conspiratorial design of
Jacobin factions rather than a genuine expression of public
feeling. 'To be honoured and even privileged by the laws,
opinions, and inveterate usages of our country, growing out of
the prejudice of ages, has nothing to provoke horror and

indignation in any man', Burke maintained, not only because 'nobility is a graceful ornament to the civil order', but because that order, and with it the very capacity to form and hold opinions about social and political affairs, had as its precondition the unequal formations of a hierarchical society: 'He feels no ennobling principle in his own heart who wishes to level all the artificial institutions which have been adopted for giving a body to opinion, and permanence to fugitive esteem'.[32] This last term is crucial: it is not going too far to say that for Burke public political opinion was essentially a matter of socially orchestrated esteem, an esteem that helped negotiate the transition from a state of nature to civil society, and carried with it an implicit consent to inequitable social and economic arrangements. Public opinion is embodied ('giving a body to opinion'), and achieves its actual form in social life, only through institutions and practices that are inherently 'artificial' and unequal. To revise and complicate Hazlitt's circular formula ('opinion governs opinion'): property arranges esteem, esteem governs opinion, and opinion secures property.

This position was reinforced in *An Appeal from the New to the Old Whigs* (1791), where Burke extended his version of a social contract by insisting that 'the idea of a people' is a 'wholly artificial' idea of 'a corporation', made 'like all other legal fictions by common agreement': 'the particular nature of that agreement ... is collected from the form into which the particular society has been cast', with its full array of social and economic arrangements. Without that agreement men lose their 'corporate existence' as a people, and dissolve back into 'a number of vague loose individuals, and nothing more'; under the original agreement, by contrast, they assent to 'a true natural aristocracy', which 'is not a separate interest in the state, or separable from it', but 'an essential integrant part of any large people rightly constituted'. It is crucial to see that this 'natural aristocracy', which must in Burke's terms also be *artificial,* for 'art is man's nature', is both the subject and object of public opinion properly understood:

> To be bred in a place of estimation; To see nothing low and sordid from one's infancy; To be taught to respect one's self; To be habituated to the censorial inspection of the public eye; To look

early to public opinion; To stand upon such elevated ground as to be enabled to take a large view of the wide-spread and infinitely diversified combinations of men and affairs in a large society; To have leisure to read, to reflect, to converse ... To be led to a guarded and regulated conduct, from a sense that you are considered as an instructor of your fellow-citizens in their highest concerns ... These are the circumstances of men, that form what I should call a *natural* aristocracy, without which there is no nation.[33]

By the end of the *Appeal,* this highly rhetorical movement, via elevated perspective, leisured literacy, and social influence, from a class formed by the opinion of others ('the censorial inspection of the public eye'), to a class in which authoritative opinion forms ('leisure to read, to reflect, to converse') and is then transmitted to others ('an instructor of your fellow-citizens in their highest concerns'), underwrote not only the 'legitimate presumptions'[34] of a socially integrated elite, but also the range and deliberate exclusions of Burke's own argument. The Burkean defence of constitutional government precludes the claims of 'a low, drunken, alehouse-club', and cannot by definition be addressed to the members of that club:

The British constitution may have its advantages pointed out to wise and reflecting minds; but it is of too high an order of excellence to be adapted to those which are common. It takes in too many views, it makes too many combinations, to be so much as comprehended by shallow and superficial understandings. Profound thinkers will know it in its reason and spirit. The less enquiring will recognize it in their feelings and their experience.[35]

If Hazlitt exaggerated for his own purposes the precise region in which opinion circulated for Burke, he did not exaggerate the rigidity of its boundaries. The excellence of 'wise and reflecting minds' was displayed in their recognition of the excellence of the constitution; the 'less enquiring', endowed at best with the 'principles of natural subordination'[36] that were the mirror image of 'natural aristocracy', could legitimately participate only by consenting to their own exclusion. To do anything else would be to fall outside the scope of civil society, where opinion dissolved with the commonwealth into 'the dust and powder of individuality'.

How, then, did Burke account for the fact of popular agitation against the exclusions of the British constitution, the fact, that is, of an emerging plebeian counter-public sphere? He himself estimated that fully 'one fifth' of the British population were 'pure Jacobins', though he characteristically denied this portion the deliberative capacities required for participation in public life: 'On these, no reason, no argument, no example, no venerable authority, can have the slightest influence'.[37] The existence of the revolutionary fifth in Britain registered a perversion of the natural order of things. It was only 'by art', and here Burke is thinking of what he termed 'extraordinary and unnatural' rather than natural artifice, that 'the body of the people' could ever have 'the principles of natural subordination … rooted out of their minds' in matters of property, privilege, and opinion.[38] Yet the precise source of this unhallowed art remained obscure. French influence was of course a leading candidate, though on this question Burke was curiously unclear. His *Appeal* followed the *Reflections* in attacking a 'French faction in England', whose Jacobin principles were 'imported from France, and disseminated in this country' through the corrupting instruments of a political public sphere detached from hierarchy and property: 'dissenting pulpits … federation societies, and … pamphlets'.[39] Yet the *First Letter on a Regicide Peace* (1796) offered a more balanced treatment of the problem when it described a Jacobin 'Colossus which bestrides our channel', with 'one foot on a foreign shore, the other upon the British soil', and the *Fourth Letter on a Regicide Peace* (1795) went further still, suggesting that 'it was in this Country, and from English Writers and English Caballers, that France herself was instituted in this revolutionary fury'.[40] This problem of the national derivation of Jacobin arts becomes still more complicated if we consider Burke's account of two further sources of subversive influence, political writers and their clubs and academies. J. G. A. Pocock has usefully insisted upon the specific economic context in France for Burke's critique of 'the political Men of Letters', above all, the separation of literature from property through the decline of patronage, and the unleashing of literary energy in alliance with a similarly disaffected and anchorless 'monied interest'.[41] Such conditions did not precisely obtain in Britain, where the spectre of revolution tended to appear to Burke as a cause rather than an effect of the redistribution of property. Here again, though, he was not wholly consistent, sometimes insisting that the French revolution in property did not obtain in England even in its effects upon the political exercise of literary influence. The *Reflections* could discover 'no party in England, literary or political', to compare with the cabal of French atheists; free-thinkers and infidels existed, 'but whatever they were, or are, with us, they were and are wholly unconnected individuals ... They never acted in corps, nor were known as a faction in the state'.[42] Where he did discern correlative Jacobin developments outside France, Burke tended to trace them not to broad historical movements but to yet another artifice, the 'hollow murmuring' and 'confused movement' of conspiracy,[43] or to the overweening ambition of individuals and groups who made representative claims without having achieved genuine repre-sentative status. Thus Jacobin interests threatened 'to incorporate themselves for the subversion of nothing short of the whole constitution of this kingdom',[44] and Price and the Revolution Society would 'erect themselves into an electoral college', and issue 'in the name of the whole people' a 'new, and hitherto unheard-of bill of rights'.[45] Part of the logic of Burke's sustained outrage at the 'formal public correspondence'[46] between Britain's self-constituted societies and the French Revolutionary govern-ment was his keen sense of the lack of correspondence between the two parties in question, and he could restore an ironic symmetry to the proceedings only by calling into question the French as well as the British side of the equation: having abandoned legality and property, the National Assembly reduced itself to 'a voluntary association of men, who ... availed themselves of circumstances, to seize upon the power of the state',[47] and therefore became the fit correspondents of Britain's self-incorporated Jacobin factions.

Burke's contempt for the political men of letters as 'semi-detached writers bent on innovation'[48] helps account for his calculated diffidence about his own authorial voice, particularly his staging of the anti-revolutionary tracts of the 1790s as a series of private letters in which he spoke only for himself, without public political authority. Insofar as his complaints about communication between British political clubs and the French National Assembly were motivated by the asymmetry of the correspondence, he introduced the terms of the problem in the opening sentence of the *Reflections,* where he absolved himself of such hubris by tracing *'the following Reflections'* to *'their origin in a correspondence between the Author and a very young gentleman at Paris'*.[49] Presumably, the scale of the claims that follow will correspond to the scale of the communication. Yet any potential reticence about the scope of the *Reflections* soon dissolves in what James Chandler has termed Burke's 'recurring resort to the first-person plural in the context of invidious comparisons between the English and the French',[50] and in a series of tendentious political claims and calculations about British opinion: 'the body of the people of England', 'not one in a hundred amongst us', 'the majority of the people of England', 'not *one* public man in this kingdom'.[51] The justification for this kind of collective phrasing comes after Burke's repudiation of the proceedings of the Revolution Society, and immediately before his long, first-person plural account of national character:

> I have no man's proxy. I speak only from myself; when I disclaim, as I do with all possible earnestness, all communion with the actors in that triumph, or with the admirers of it. When I assert any thing else, as concerning the people of England, I speak from observation not from authority; but I speak from the experience I have had in a pretty extensive and mixed communication with the inhabitants of this kingdom, of all descriptions and ranks, and after a course of attentive observations, begun early in life, and continued for nearly forty years.[52]

The spatial and temporal perspective ('observation' and 'experience') provided by Burke's immediate occupation in the social medium of British manners and habits ('mixed communication') authorizes his collective voice. Experience in effect becomes authority, and Burke takes his stand here on the 'elevated ground' of 'natural aristocracy' that he mapped in the *Appeal,* with its 'large view of the … diversified combinations of men and affairs'. The hybrid discourse of the *Reflections,* its miscellaneous response to the equally miscellaneous threat of a 'monstrous medley of all conditions, tongues, and nations',[53] is in part a function of the range of the author, as he manages, paradoxically, 'to communicate more largely' by exercising the private 'freedom of epistolary discourse' in order to move away from private communication, and towards a collective though not exactly public form of expression.

Burke famously refused to identify the mode of the *Reflections* and of his other anti-revolutionary works, falling back instead on a diffidence about unsystematic prose and 'my own loose, general ideas'.[54] His rhetorical procedures are probably best understood in relation to the many discourses they repudiate, as a series of feints and counter-feints against 'the mazes of metaphysic sophistry', 'the farce of deliberation' 'in 'riotous' clubs and societies, the 'formal public correspondence' of unauthorized factions, and the explosive 'pulpit style' of 'political theologians, and theological politicians'.[55] I would argue that periodical discourse, considered in broadly modal rather than merely formal terms, and epitomized for Burke by its least stable newspaper form, provides another crucial if implicit counterpoint to Burke's own enlarged mode of private expression. His *Fourth Letter on a Regicide Peace,* itself framed in manuscript as a letter to the Earl Fitzwilliam, was launched with an assault on Auckland's pamphlet, *Some Remarks on the Apparent Circumstances of the War in the Fourth Week of October 1795.* For Burke, such a title could only signal the shift to a transitory and therefore diminished mode of political expression:

> The very title seemed to me striking and peculiar, and to announce something uncommon. In the time I have lived to, I always seem to walk on enchanted ground. Every thing is new, and according to the fashionable phrase, revolutionary. In former days authors valued themselves upon the maturity and fullness of their deliberations. Accordingly they predicted (perhaps with more arrogance than reason) an eternal duration to their works. The quite contrary is our present fashion. Writers value themselves now on the instability of their opinions and the transitory life of their productions.[56]

After contrasting 'the sportive variability of these weekly, daily, or hourly speculators' with the enlarged views of the 'great politician', whose 'opinions ought not to be diurnal, or even weekly', Burke once again slipped into the first-person plural, and invoked with mock humility the 'slow and coarse understandings' of 'us simple country folk' as a counterpoint to the 'fugitive' race of cosmopolitan public life in print.[57] Having recovered from his initial estrangement in the face of this 'transitory' mode of writing, Burke unfolded his critical response in an appropriately measured, even leisurely fashion, as he pursued through the pages of an almanac his notion of a more permanent, or at least more broadly historicized, *ancien régime* discourse. As it turns out, this humble, archaic, and to all appearances eminently time-bound print form contains an unlikely residue of discursive stability. Burke consults its forecast of *'foggy weather'* – and here he exploits the ironic convergence of 'the haze and mist ... of that changeable week' with a textual regime that 'is not only fugitive in its duration, but is slippery, in the extreme, while it lasts' – in order to discover just what it was about 'the last week of October' that struck the fugitive pamphleteer as significant. 'Here I have fallen into an unintentional mistake', he comments in a mocking footnote, for 'Rider's Almanack for 1794 lay before me; and, in truth, I then had no other. For variety that sage astrologer has made some small changes on the weather side of 1795; but the caution is the same on the opposite page of instruction'.[58] The textual register of a gentlemen farmer turns out to be as 'coarse' and secure as his understanding, barely perceiving the lapse of a year, let alone the fleeting shifts in a week or month that mark 'our present fashion'.

More direct encounters with the revolutionary impact of periodical discourse left Burke little room for this kind of satirical play. His *Thoughts on French Affairs* blamed 'newspaper circulations', now 'infinitely more efficacious and extensive than ever they were', for the rise of 'the French spirit of proselytism'. The 'contempt' in which newspaper writers were once held prevented them from disrupting 'a permanent landed interest' as effectively as the elite 'men of letters' (who were typically 'courted', 'caressed', and in Burke's crucial term, 'esteemed'), but with the rapid erosion of this contempt, newspaper men were incorporated in the growing Burkean catalogue of disaffected interests, which now included 'tradesmen, bankers, and voluntary clubs of bold, presuming young persons; – advocates, attornies, notaries, managers of newspapers, and those cabals of literary men, called academies'. Advances in commercial society increasingly mingled and empowered economic currency, political discourse, and the individuals who controlled them: 'As money increases and circulates, and as the circulation of news, in politicks and letters, becomes more and more diffused, the persons who diffuse this money, and this intelligence, become more and more important.' Even without this explosive combination, newspaper writers managed to achieve their ends through the sheer force of periodical repetition. The result was an enervating and attenuated but no less pervasive version of Burke's own dense medium of prejudice and manners: 'They are like a battery in which the stroke of any one ball produces no great effect, but the amount of continual repetition is decisive. Let us suffer any person to tell us his story, morning and evening, but for one twelvemonth, and he will become our master'.[59] By 1796 and the *Second Letter on a Regicide Peace,* affairs had advanced and deteriorated still further, and newspaper culture acquired priority rather than mere parity in the determination of revolutionary events. The tragic flaw of Louis XVI was, according to Burke, a historical sense so profound that it 'blinded him' to a 'silent revolution in the moral world', brought about by 'the correspondence of the monied and the mercantile world, the literary intercourse of the academies', and 'above all' by 'the press', which 'made a kind of electrick communication every where', assisting the erosion of 'the chain of subordination', and dissolving hierarchically organized opinion into its monstrous other, a revolutionary rage for equality. Confronted with these deep structural transformations in civil society and public communication, Burke's own historical sense seemed as futile as Louis XVI's, though he hedged the concession with an awkward string of qualifications: 'The press, in reality, has made every Government, in it's spirit, almost democratick'.[60]

Having appealed throughout his anti-revolutionary prose to personal experience as a source of authority and a counterweight to revolution, Burke could not entirely suppress from consideration his own experience as a writer in a rapidly changing political public sphere. 'His own position was', as Tom Furniss has observed, 'not so different from that of the writers he criticizes.'[61] Although Burke's case for the foundation of 'modern letters' and commerce on 'antient manners' rested in part on a recognition that clerical and aristocratic patronage had 'kept learning in existence',[62] there was no real nostalgia on his part for monastic existence,[63] nor for its attendant modes of literary patronage and production. Here lay some of the polemical force behind Hazlitt's anecdote about the reception of the *Reflections* in an anachronistic circuit of court opinion. The critical text for Burke's sometimes vexed sense of his authorial identity, the point at which he dramatically marked the limit of his courtly and aristocratic commitments, was *A Letter to a Noble Lord* (1796).[64] In responding to attacks upon him in the House of Lords by the Duke of Bedford and the Earl of Lauderdale, Burke insisted that his pension 'was the fruit of no bargain; the production of no intrigue', thereby distinguishing himself on two critical points, conspiratorial design and monied connections, from the political men of letters in France. His 'exertions' as an anti-revolutionary ideologist were wholly disengaged from the cash nexus, 'such as no hopes of pecuniary reward could possibly excite; and no pecuniary compensation can possibly reward'.[65] Yet as the *Letter* turned from economic to personal considerations, and to an invidious comparison between the author's own 'original and personal' merits and the 'derivative' merits of Bedford,[66] Burke returned to the issue of personal experience as a source of quasi-public authority, this time acknowledging his potential implication in a Jacobin energy that he himself defined as 'the revolt of the enterprising talents of a country against it's property':[67]

> I am better able to enter into the character of this description of men [the Jacobin philosophers] than the noble Duke can be. I have lived long and variously in the World. Without any considerable pretensions to literature myself, I have aspired to the love of letters. I have lived for a great many years in habitudes with those who professed them. I can form a tolerable estimate of what is likely to happen from a character, chiefly dependent for fame and fortune, on knowledge and talent, as well in it's morbid and perverted state, as in that which is sound and natural.[68]

In contrasting the 'morbid and perverted' talents of a revolutionary intelligentsia with his own 'sound and natural' exertions, Burke very nearly converted his rage into a threat, particularly if we recall the notice given earlier in the *Letter* that his own talent had been mobilized in defence of 'those old prejudices which buoy up the ponderous mass of [Bedford's] nobility, wealth, and titles'.[69] The warning to his critics was clear: talent becomes morbid, esteem is corroded, and levelling opinion becomes dominant when the manners that facilitate reciprocal obligation in a stratified society are neglected, and when property forgets its responsibility to men of talent and to the 'higher oeconomy' and 'distributive virtue'[70] that yielded Burke's own pension. The warrant for such a caution could only be an acknowledgement that subordination was neither given nor wholly 'natural', but instead required for its support the active exercise of literary authority. Ironically, it was Burke's steady insistence that subordination was and should remain natural, an inherent feature of a given social order rather than the result of artificial literary intervention, that prevented him from throwing his own authority into the service of counter-revolution in those restive sectors of political opinion where deference was in fact eroding.

Notes

1 For 'the Burke problem', see Isaac Kramnick, *The Rage of Edmund Burke: Portrait of an Ambivalent Conservative* (New York: Basic Books, 1977), pp. 3–11; C. B. Macpherson, *Burke*, Past Masters series (Oxford: Oxford University Press, 1980), pp. 1–7; and Tom Furniss, *Edmund Burke's Aesthetic Ideology: Language, Gender, and Political Economy in Revolution* (Cambridge: Cambridge University Press, 1993), pp. 3–8. In part because there is no one historically faithful and precise alternative, I have throughout this essay used terms like 'conservative', 'reactionary', 'counter-revolutionary', and 'anti-revolutionary' to describe positions critical of the French Revolution and domestic British radicalism; for an effective survey of this 'semantic problem' in describing conservative movements, see Robert Hole, *From Jacobite to Conservative: Reaction and Orthodoxy in Britain, c.1760–1832* (Cambridge: Cambridge University Press, 1993), pp. 1–7 .

2 See Mark Parker, 'The Institutionalization of a Burkean–Coleridgean Literary Culture', *Studies in English Literature*, 31 (1991), p. 695.

3 *Reflections*, pp. 115, 183.

4 Linda Colley, *Britons: Forging the Nation, 1707–1837* (New Haven: Yale University Press, 1992), pp. 195–236.

5 Gregory Claeys, 'Republicanism Versus Commercial Society: Paine, Burke and the French Revolution Debate', *History of European Ideas*, 11 (1989), p. 313, and H. T. Dickinson, 'Popular Conservatism and Militant Loyalism, 1789–1815', in H. T. Dickinson, ed., *Britain and the French Revolution, 1789–1815* (Basingstoke: Macmillan, 1989), pp. 104–5.

6   J. G. A. Pocock, Introduction, *Reflections on the Revolution in France* (Indianapolis, Indiana: Hackett, 1987), p. xl.

7   Mark Philp, 'Vulgar Conservatism, 1792–3', *English Historical Review*, 110 (1995), pp. 44–5.

8   William Hazlitt, *The Complete Works of William Hazlitt*, ed. P. P. Howe, 21 vols (London: J. M. Dent and Sons, 1930–1934), vol. 11, pp. 65; vol. 19, p. 159; vol. 7, p. 98.

9   John Whale, 'Hazlitt on Burke: The Ambivalent Position of a Radical Essayist', *Studies in Romanticism*, 25 (1986), pp. 465, 472. For a related distinction between Hazlitt's sympathy for a democratized 'political republic' and his more aristocratic construction of the 'republic of taste', see John Barrell, *The Political Theory of Painting from Reynolds to Hazlitt* (New Haven: Yale University Press, 1986), p. 337.

10 Hazlitt, *Complete Works*, vol. 7, pp. 308–9.

11 For a similar formulation in Hume, see the essay 'Whether the British Government Inclines More to Absolute Monarchy, or to a Republic', in *Essays, Moral, Political, and Literary*, ed. Eugene F. Miller (Indianapolis, Indiana: Liberty Classics, 1985), p. 51: 'It may farther be said, that, though men be much governed by interest; yet even interest itself, and all human affairs, are entirely governed by *opinion.*'

12 Hazlitt, *Complete Works*, vol. 7, p. 231.

13 *Correspondence*, vol. VI, p. 239.

14 *Yellow Dwarf*, no. 1 (3 January 1818), pp. 5–6.

15 *The Extraordinary Red Book* (4th edn, London: J. Johnston and W. Clarke, 1821), p. 82; see also John Wade's *The Black Book; or, Corruption Unmasked* (London: John Fairburn, 1820), p. 23. For a modern account, and defence, of the circumstances surrounding Burke's pension, see Carl B. Cone, *Burke and the Nature of Politics: The Age of the French Revolution* (Lexington: University of Kentucky Press, 1964), pp. 446–53, and for a nuanced rhetorical exploration of the problem of patronage in Burke's prose, see Christopher Reid, *Edmund Burke and the Practice of Political Writing* (Dublin: Gill and Macmillan, 1985), pp. 79–92.

16 Not of course without the same ambivalence that surrounded the figure of Burke. The best evidence for this comes in the 'Project for a New Theory of Civil and Criminal Legislation', where, after complaining that 'the author of the *Sublime and Beautiful* would have … an empty title, a bloated privilege, or a grievous wrong overturn the entire mass of truth and justice', Hazlitt comes out securely on the side of 'the principle of universal suffrage', and invokes the example of the republic of letters against the objection that 'by this means property is not represented'. As it turns out, what finally interests him in literary practice is a combination of democracy and hierarchy, levelling energy and habitual deference: 'Literature is at present pretty nearly on the footing of universal suffrage, yet the public defer sufficiently to the critics; and when no party bias interferes, and the government do not make a point of running a writer

down, the verdict is tolerably fair and just' (*Complete Works*, vol. 19, pp. 307–8).

17 Hazlitt, *Complete Works*, vol. 7, pp. 235–6.

18 Ibid. p. 260.

19 Ibid. pp. 235–6.

20 *Reflections*, p. 130.

21 See *Correspondence*, vol. VI, p. 465, n. 4.

22 *Reflections*, pp. 380–1.

23 For the vexed position of popular or plebeian politics in theories of the public sphere, and for revisionist accounts of rifts within the public sphere that open up the possibility of a counter-public or publics, see my 'Popular Radicalism and the Public Sphere', *Studies in Romanticism*, 33 (1994), pp. 549–57, and *Print Politics: ThePress and Radical Opposition in Early Nineteenth-Century England* (Cambridge: Cambridge University Press, 1996), pp. 1–10.

24 *Reflections*, pp. 102, 106.

25 James K. Chandler, 'Poetical Liberties: Burke's France and the "Adequate Representation" of the English', in *The French Revolution and the Creation of Modern Political Culture*, vol. 3, *The Transformation of the Political Culture, 1789–1848*, ed. François Furet and Mona Ozouf (New York: Pergamon Press, 1987–94), pp. 49, 51–2.

26 *Reflections*, pp. 127–8.

27 J. G. A. Pocock, 'The Political Economy of Burke's Analysis of the French Revolution', in *Virtue, Commerce, and History: Essays on Political Thought and History, Chiefly in the Eighteenth Century* (Cambridge: Cambridge University Press, 1985), pp. 199, 210.

28 *Reflections*, p. 130.

29 Ibid. p. 100.

30 Ibid. p. 332.

31 Ibid. pp. 145–6 .

32 Ibid. pp. 187–8.

33 Edmund Burke, *Further Reflections on the Revolution in France*, ed. Daniel E. Ritchie (Indianapolis, Indiana: Liberty Fund, 1992), pp. 163–4, 168–9.

34 Burke, *Further Reflections*, p. 168.

35 Ibid. pp. 196–7.

36 *Reflections*, p. 290.

37 *Writings and Speeches*, vol. 9, p. 224.

38 *Reflections*, pp. 162, 290.

39 Burke, *Further Reflections*, pp. 96, 123.

40 *Writings and Speeches*, vol. 9, pp. 84, 199.

41 *Reflections*, p. 160. Pocock, 'Political Economy', pp. 201–2, and Introduction,

Reflections, pp. xxx, xxxiv. For a perceptive treatment of the 'Political Men of Letters' along deconstructive lines, see Furniss, *Burke's Aesthetic Ideology*, pp. 251–7.

42 *Reflections*, p. 140.

43 Ibid. p. 205. For Burke and a conspiratorial account of the French Revolution and its prehistory in the Enlightenment, see Seamus Deane, *The French Revolution and Enlightenment in England, 1789–1832* (Cambridge, MA: Harvard University Press, 1988), pp. 7, 10–11.

44 Burke, *Further Reflections*, p. 81.

45 *Reflections*, pp. 65–6.

46 Ibid. p. 56.

47 Ibid. p. 213.

48 Furniss, *Burke's Aesthetic Ideology*, p. 251.

49 *Reflections*, p. 53.

50 Chandler, 'Poetical Liberties', pp. 46–7.

51 *Reflections*, pp. 66, 136, 149, 154.

52 Ibid. p. 136.

53 Ibid. p. 118.

54 Ibid. p. 326.

55 Ibid. pp. 56, 61–2, 72, 119.

56 *Writings and Speeches*, vol. 9, pp. 45–6.

57 Ibid. pp. 48–9.

58 Ibid. pp. 46–7, 49.

59 *Reflections*, pp. 344–8.

60 *Writings and Speeches*, vol. 9, pp. 291–2.

61 Furniss, *Burke's Aesthetic Ideology*, p. 256.

62 *Reflections*, p. 130.

63 See Pocock, Introduction, *Reflections*, p. xxxv.

64 See Kramnick, *The Rage of Edmund Burke*, pp. 5–7, for a treatment of the *Letter* as the primary site for the 'ambivalence' at the heart of a 'Burke problem', and for 'Burke's Rhetorical Problem' in the *Letter*, see Stephen H. Browne, *Edmund Burke and the Discourse of Virtue* (Tuscaloosa: The University of Alabama Press, 1993), pp. 106–8.

65 *Writings and Speeches*, vol. 9, pp. 148, 150.

66 Ibid. p.165.

67 Ibid. p. 241.

68 Ibid. p. 176.

69 Ibid. p. 162.

70 Ibid.

6

Cementing the nation: Burke's *Reflections* on nationalism and national identity

TOM FURNISS

Recent historians and theorists have argued that nationalism is primarily a modern phenomenon fundamentally connected, at least in its early phases, with the emergence of modern nation states. There are considerable differences about the definitions of nationalism, nation states, and even nations themselves, and little consensus about when these phenomena begin to emerge.[1] Yet there is general agreement that the American and French Revolutions were path-breaking episodes which ushered in the era of nationalism and nation states that reshaped the world in the nineteenth and twentieth centuries.[2] This assumption often leads to the claim that nationalism in Britain was a belated phenomenon emerging only in a reactionary form in the face of threats from revolutionary and Napoleonic France.[3] Burke's response to the French Revolution is often seen as a founding moment in the development of this reactionary nationalism in Britain, although Cobban argues that Burke was a pioneer in the development of nationalism in Britain from the 1760s onwards.[4] Yet, as several recent historians have shown, there were in fact a number of nationalist movements in eighteenth-century Britain, some of which were backed by fully articulated nationalist ideologies.[5] This has allowed critics to argue that Burke's conservative nationalism was developed through appropriating and reorientating the assumptions of an already flourishing radical English nationalism.[6] In what follows, I will argue that the nationalist ideology that Burke develops in his *Reflections on the Revolution in France* (1790) was shaped not only in reaction to the radical nationalism being instituted in France but also in response to the radical British nationalism articulated in Richard Price's 'A Discourse on the Love of our Country' of 1789.

As is often the case with nationalist ideologies, Burke's English nationalism identifies internal as well as external enemies. As its subtitle suggests, the *Reflections on the Revolution in France and on the Proceedings in Certain Societies in London Relative to that Event* is as much concerned with reflecting upon particular responses in London to the French Revolution as it is with reflecting on the event itself. Burke's title refers to the 'proceedings' of 'two clubs of gentlemen in London, called the Constitutional Society, and the Revolution Society'.[7] Burke dismisses the Constitutional Society as a charitable organization that distributes radical books that no one would otherwise bother to buy or read. The Revolution Society, which had been created to celebrate the centenary of the 'Glorious Revolution' of 1688, is a much more serious threat in Burke's eyes. At its meeting on the fourth of November 1789, Price had delivered his 'Discourse on the Love of our Country' in which he celebrated the French Revolution and appeared to suggest that those who really loved Britain ought to follow the French example. In the 'Discourse', Price offers a radical reinterpretation of the British constitution and of the duties entailed on citizens who love their country.

Price's sermon of 1789 was not the first occasion he had reflected on questions of national identity and the duties of those who love their country. His great contribution to the discourse on nationalism in the eighteenth century was to combine Puritan and Whig traditions, the political theories of Locke, Milton, and Rousseau, civic humanism and Dissenting millennialist doctrine, into a radical Enlightenment version of nationalism. As D. O. Thomas has argued, Price's 'defence of religious liberty, of the freedom of enquiry, of the right to participate in the process of government, of national autonomy ... above all, his concept of patriotism, deserve to be celebrated as an enduring contribution to the thought that has shaped our political traditions'.[8] Beginning in 1759 with a sermon called 'Britain's Happiness, and the Proper Improvement of it', Price's contributions to the discourse of nationalism are powerful instantiations of Linda Colley's thesis: taking full account of the implications of the Revolution of 1688 and the Act of Union of 1707, Price's imagined nation is emphatically Protestant and British. In this early sermon, Price lists the peculiar qualities and advantages of the British nation and suggests that these are signs that Britain is the Jerusalem of the modern world and that the British are God's chosen people.[9] As the chosen people, however, the British have to remain vigilant against encroachments on national virtue, since only virtue guarantees liberty and God's continued approbation. Nationalism is rarely purely celebratory: one of its defining characteristics is a critical alertness to the potential corruption of the nation. In his *Two Tracts on Civil Liberty, the War with America, and The Debts and Finances of the Kingdom* (1778), Price suggests that Britain's attempt to force its will on the American colonies reveals a potential for tyranny akin to that which the Catholic Church exercised over peoples all over the world. Price implies that the baton of liberty is passing from Britain to America, where he imagines an ideal republican society is already being established 'without bishops, without nobles, and without kings'.[10] By 1785, in his *Observations on the Importance of the American Revolution*, Price argues that America has displaced Britain as the most politically advanced nation in the world and it is now the Americans who appear to be God's chosen people.[11]

In the sermon of 1789 Price is less idealistic about Britain than in the sermon of 1759. He celebrates the British constitution for its potential rather than for what it has become; yet he also suggests that the virtuous struggle to realize that potential is one of the principal duties of those who love their country. Price describes the love of country as 'a noble passion' which, 'like all other passions ... requires regulation and direction'. In order to regulate and direct this passion, Price begins by defining what is meant by 'country'. He sets out by stressing that he is referring to a civil and political society rather than a piece of land or geographical area: 'by our country is meant, in this case, not the soil or the spot of earth on which we happen to have been born, not the forests and fields, but that community of which we are members ... under the same constitution of government, protected by the same laws, and bound together by the same civil polity'.

Price's nationalism, then, is a civic nationalism. Although loving our country in this sense is a primary obligation, this 'does not imply any conviction of the superior value of it to other countries'. Price therefore urges his listeners and readers 'to distinguish between the love of our country and that spirit of rivalship and ambition which has been common among nations'. This is to distinguish between blind patriotism and an enlightened nationalism compatible with the general love of humanity that Christianity inculcates. A proper love of our country should be ardent but not exclusive; it should lead us to strive for our country's good, but allow us at the same time to 'consider ourselves as citizens of the world, and take care to maintain a just regard to the rights of other countries'.[12]

Price argues that the love of one's country ought to manifest itself in efforts to promote truth, virtue, and liberty in that country. According to Price, 'our whole duty to our country' is included in these three aims: 'for by endeavouring to liberalize and enlighten it, to discourage vice and to promote virtue in it, and to assert and support its liberties, we shall endeavour to do all that is necessary to make it great and happy'.[13] Yet since nationalism often depends on the identification of internal and external enemies (identity, or sameness, being formed through a staged encounter with otherness), Price stresses that the love of one's country involves being prepared to defend it against 'enemies ... of two sorts; internal and external, or domestic and foreign'.[14] Price indicates that the people ought to be ready, if need be, to die fighting against their country's external aggressors.[15] Internal threats frequently come from rulers attempting to extend their power and it is thus the duty of citizens always to be ready to resist such encroachments on their rights. Yet there are other, more intangible but equally dangerous, threats which come from within. Since virtue is the origin and sign of a nation's liberty, internal corruption and luxury is perhaps the greatest threat of all.

According to Price, the 'Glorious Revolution' of 1688 was a response to both kinds of internal threat. In effect, it was an example of the people successfully resisting a ruler (James II and VII) who had become an internal enemy by posing threats to religious and civil rights. The Revolution delivered the people from 'the infamy and misery of popery and slavery' and established various principles which, Price stresses, need to be adhered to and improved:

> First, the right to liberty of conscience in religious matters.
> Secondly, the right to resist power when abused. And
> Thirdly, the right to chuse our own governors, to cashier them for misconduct, and to frame a government for ourselves.[16]

Yet if these are the rights established by the Revolution, Price nonetheless urges his readers 'to remember that, though the Revolution was a great work, it was by no means a perfect work'. The constitution that was set up by the Revolution is itself in need of reform, and efforts towards such reform are one of the duties involved in loving one's country. In the first place, the religious toleration obtained by the Revolution was 'imperfect' because it 'included only those who could declare their faith in the doctrinal articles of the Church of England'. Because such a declaration was necessary for obtaining civil posts, the Protestant dissenters (of which Price was one) were excluded from full citizenship (Price is not, of course, troubled by the similar exclusion of British Catholics). The most important defect of the constitution, however, 'is the inequality of our representation' – which is an evil in itself and leads to corruption.[17]

For Price and the Dissenters, then, the Revolution set up a constitutional pattern that was a first sketch, at least, of a radical nationalism. But if patriots had a duty to maintain and reform the constitution, an equally important duty was to sustain this patriotic zeal through moral virtue. Virtue and liberty together constitute the ethical 'cement' of radical, Protestant nationalism in eighteenth-century England. This assumption allows Price to mobilize the characteristic nationalist claim that internal elements of moral corruption are threatening the country's well-being:

> It is too evident that the state of this country is such as renders it an object of concern and anxiety. It wants (I have shewn you) the grand security of public liberty. Increasing luxury has multiplied abuses in it. A monstrous weight of debt is crippling it. Vice and venality are bringing down upon it God's displeasure. That spirit to which it owes its distinction is declining, and some late events seem to prove that it is becoming every day more reconcilable to

> encroachments on the securities of its liberties. It wants, therefore,
> your patriotic services and ... we ought to do our utmost to save it
> from the dangers that threaten it.[18]

One of the recent events that Price alludes to here is the response
of the people to George III's recovery from a bout of 'madness' in
1788, in which 'we have appeared more like a herd crawling at
the feet of a master than like enlightened and manly citizens
rejoicing with a beloved sovereign, but at the same time conscious that he derives all his consequence from themselves'.[19]
Price stresses that the people need to realize that they are themselves the source of majesty and sovereignty and that they confer
these upon their civil governors and kings:

> Civil governors are properly the servants of the public and a King
> is no more than the first servant of the public, created by it,
> maintained by it, and responsible to it; and all the homage paid him
> is due to him on no other account than his relation to the public.
> His sacredness is the sacredness of the community. His authority is
> the authority of the community, and the term *Majesty*, which it is
> usual to apply to him, is by no means his own majesty, but the
> majesty of the people.[20]

Price, then, measures Britain at the end of the eighteenth century
against the nationalist ideals that he claims are at least implicit in
its constitution. Behaving according to the duties entailed in his
own account of what it means to love one's country, Price calls
on his readers to rectify a number of defects in the political
system and to resist the encroachment of internal corruption. By
going on to claim that the example of the French Revolution has
made the 'present times' particularly favourable 'to all exertions
in the cause of public liberty',[21] Price almost seems to imply that
it is the duty of patriotic Britons to try to emulate the French
example. Certainly, his rapturous greeting of the French Revolution at the end of his sermon presents it as the triumph of the
French nation over the *ancien régime*. Yet we should remember
that Price is celebrating the English as well as the French
Revolution. Since he thanks God for having allowed him to share
'in the benefits of one Revolution', and for having 'spared [him]
to be a witness to two other Revolutions, both glorious',[22] it
would appear that he sees the English Revolution as the first of a

series of similar, though perhaps more progressively radical, revolutions. Hence Price is not calling for the British to imitate the French Revolution but rather for British patriots to renew their efforts to complete the work begun in 1688 so that Britain might realize the full potential and promise of its own revolution. That he sees Britain and the new France as essentially similar to one another is brought out in a footnote that looks forward to the two 'kingdoms' working in harmony together to bring about world peace and liberty.[23]

As well as providing a platform for Price's sermon, the Revolution Society sent a congratulatory address to the National Assembly and received a grateful response. The Revolution Society had then published Price's 'Discourse' along with the congratulatory address and the National Assembly's reply. In the *Reflections*, Burke suggests that, by taking it upon itself to address the government of another country, the Revolution Society had seemed to assume a representative status – or, as Burke puts it, 'a sort of public capacity'.[24] By receiving an address by a group of private individuals, most of whose names were not attached to the document, the National Assembly had revealed its own political inexperience and conferred an inappropriate importance on the Revolution Society:

> the house of Commons would reject the most sneaking petition for the most trifling object, under that mode of signature to which you have thrown open the folding-doors of your presence chamber, and have ushered into your National Assembly, with as much ceremony and parade, and with as great a bustle of applause, as if you had been visited by the whole representative majesty of the whole English nation.[25]

Burke, then, seeks to impress on his readers the difference between the representations of the Revolution Society and 'the whole representative majesty of the whole English nation'. Each element in this phrase – 'whole', 'representative', 'majesty', 'English', and 'nation' – carries an impressive weight, and the phrase apparently adds up to a powerful conception of the nation. While Price invokes the majesty of the people, and while the Revolution Society might claim to represent English opinion, only Parliament (presumably) could properly represent the whole majesty of the English nation. Yet Burke's phrase is more ambiguous than this makes it sound. The ambiguity arises over the problem of deciding whether 'majesty' is attached to the visiting representation or to the English nation that is being represented. Is Burke invoking the majesty of Parliament or the majesty of the people?

Burke counters the Revolution Society's illegitimate ambassadorial status by dwelling on the implications of writing and publishing his own *Reflections* on the French Revolution. One of the original stimulants for the *Reflections* was a private letter from a French correspondent asking Burke to comment on, and give his seal of approval to, the doings of the National Assembly. Although the *Reflections* outgrew Burke's original reply, it retains the rhetorical form of a private letter between an individual British subject and a French citizen. This appears to allow the *Reflections* to avoid the issues about improper representation that Burke claims are raised by the exchange between the Revolution Society and the National Assembly. In the opening paragraph, he tells his correspondent that in his original letter 'I wrote neither for nor from any description of men; nor shall I in this'.[26] A few paragraphs later he seeks to distinguish his own action in publishing the *Reflections* from the actions of the Revolution Society:

> I certainly take my full share, along with the rest of the world, in my individual and private capacity, in speculating on what has been done, or is doing, on the public stage; ... but having no general apostolical mission, being a citizen of a particular state, and being bound up in a considerable degree, by its public will, I should think it, at least improper and irregular, for me to open a formal public correspondence with the actual government of a foreign nation, without the express authority of the government under which I live.[27]

Burke, then, refuses any suggestion that he might be writing in an official representative capacity. Yet the question of representation is continually at issue throughout the *Reflections*. Burke repeatedly brings into question Price's claims to represent anything other than the opinions of an eccentric minority in England; and although he claims to speak only for himself, Burke frequently suggests that he is able nonetheless to speak for the people of England. Responding to what he took to be Price's celebration of the 'triumph' of the events at Versailles on 5–6 October 1789, Burke seeks to differentiate between Price's opinions and those of the majority of the people of England:

> To tell you the truth, my dear Sir, I think the honour of our nation to be somewhat concerned in the disclaimer of the proceedings of this society of the Old Jewry and the London Tavern. I have no man's proxy. I speak only from myself; when I disclaim, as I do with all possible earnestness, all communication with the actors in that triumph, or with the admirers of it. When I assert any thing else, as concerning the people of England, I speak from observation not from authority; but I speak from the experience I have had in a pretty extensive and mixed communication with the inhabitants of this kingdom, of all descriptions and ranks, and after a course of attentive observation, began early in life, and continued for near forty years.[28]

Burke, then, assumes that he can speak for the people of England on the basis of the long and extensive experience he claims to have of English people 'of all descriptions and ranks'. Although the opinions of Richard Price and the Revolution Society may have been thrust upon the attention of the French, Burke urges his reader not to take those opinions as representative. He claims to be surprised how little the French seem to know the English, and suggests that 'this is owing to your forming a judgment of this nation from certain publications, which do, very erroneously, if they do at all, represent the opinions and dispositions generally prevalent in England'. In fact, he will 'almost venture to affirm, that not one in a hundred amongst us participates in the "triumph" of the Revolution Society'.[29]

The *Reflections*, then, can be read as dramatizing a struggle over who and what represents authentic English opinion. In order to discredit Price and his cohorts, Burke foregrounds his own character as authentic and exemplary. A major task of the *Reflections* is to promote Burke himself as a man of extensive experience – as a practical politician, and as someone familiar with English feeling through long years of attentive observation and experience. But Burke presents himself as more than a mere observer of Englishness: instead, he becomes an *embodiment* of the English national character – despite the fact that politicians and journalists constantly harped on Burke's Irishness. Burke's assumed character includes being a man imbued with nationalist sentiment: he assures his correspondent that he is 'Sollicitous chiefly for the peace of my own country, but by no means unconcerned for your's'.[30] He describes himself as having demonstrated in his public career a love for liberty that can match that of anyone in the Revolution Society: 'I flatter myself that I love a manly, moral, regulated liberty as well as any gentleman of that society, be he who he will; and perhaps I have given as good proofs of my attachment to that cause, in the whole course of my public conduct. I think I envy liberty as little as they do, to any other nation'.[31] Burke also distinguishes himself from Price by posing as a practical politician not willing to praise liberty merely in the abstract: 'I should therefore suspend my congratulations on the new liberty of France, until I was informed how it had been combined with government; with public force; with the discipline and obedience of armies; with the collection of an effective and well-distributed revenue; with morality and religion; with the solidity of property; with peace and order; with civil and social manners'.[32] Burke is here sketching out the programme of the *Reflections*, but he is also implicitly pointing out what he considers to be the defining characteristics of the English constitution – which, as we will see, supposedly combines and balances these factors with a due degree of 'regulated liberty'.

As one of the leading Whig intellectuals of the second half of the eighteenth century, Burke spends a significant portion of the *Reflections* in attempting to show that Price's interpretation of the Glorious Revolution, and hence of the English constitution, is not only wrong but actually threatens the constitution in its essence:

> His doctrines affect our constitution in its vital parts. He tells the Revolution Society, in this political sermon, that his majesty 'is almost the *only* lawful king in the world, because the *only* one who owes his crown to the *choice of his people'* ...
>
> This doctrine, as applied to the prince now on the British throne, either is nonsense, and therefore neither true nor false, or it affirms a most unfounded, dangerous, illegal, and unconstitutional position.[33]

Countering Price's unconstitutional doctrine, Burke seeks to demonstrate that the monarchs of Great Britain hold their crown according to a fixed law of hereditary succession rather than to the choice or election of the people. He then quotes the three fundamental rights which Price claims the people of England acquired in 1688 (see above) and asserts that they add up to a 'new, and hitherto unheard-of bill of rights'. He goes on to suggest that 'the people of England' would be bound by law to reject such a bill of rights and, more revealingly, that they 'have no share in it. They utterly disclaim it. They will resist the practical assertion of it with their lives and fortunes'.[34] A few pages later, Burke asserts that 'The people of England ... look upon the legal hereditary succession of their crown as among their rights, not as among their wrongs ... as a security for their liberty, not as a badge of servitude.'[35] The claim to know and speak for what the English people think, feel and will do is repeated throughout the *Reflections*. But this is not simply an example of Burke taking it upon himself, legitimately or not, to speak for the English people. This act of supposed ventriloquism, along with Burke's own self-characterization, can be read as a process of *constructing* (or *reconstructing*) the English national character rather than simply reflecting a pre-existing character and set of opinions. Burke is not only reinventing the English constitution at a moment of impending crisis; he is also using that crisis as an occasion for coaxing the English people into reimagining who they are and what they ought to think and do.

But for all Burke's differences from Price, they both share the widespread eighteenth-century assumption that the well-being of states, like that of individuals, depends on their collective virtue. The claim to moral virtue is characteristic of almost all nationalist movements. Nationalists tend to represent their programme as a moral crusade devoted to re-establishing native virtues and to resisting the moral corruption of foreign nations or of 'alien' elements within the nation state.[36] Such assumptions can be seen in radical nationalism in Britain from Milton through to Price. In the *Reflections*, Burke is contending for the same high moral ground, using similar rhetorical strategies, on behalf of a different kind of nationalism. As part of his self-characterization as a generous nationalist, Burke represents himself as being prepared to admire a nation's efforts to regenerate itself. The very title and function of a National Assembly would normally have commanded his veneration: 'In that light the mind of an enquirer, subdued by such an awful image as that of the virtue and wisdom of a whole people collected into a focus, would pause and hesitate in condemning things even of the very worst aspect.'[37] Yet when Burke comes to examine the actual circumstances of the Assembly, especially its composition and actions, he represents himself as compelled to condemn what he was disposed to admire. One of the major problems, for Burke, arises from the fact that the Assembly is almost wholly composed of the Third Estate, with no counterbalancing powers in the monarch, nobility, or clergy. Burke assures his correspondent that his critique of the composition of the National Assembly does not mean that he would 'confine power, authority, and distinction to blood, and names, and titles'. Instead, he would make 'virtue and wisdom' the only qualifications for government: that country would bring woe upon itself 'which would madly and impiously reject the service of the talents and virtues, civil, military, or religious, that are given to grace and to serve it'.[38] Yet virtue and talent need to be tried and developed through difficulty and struggle: 'If rare merit be the rarest of all rare things, it ought to pass through some sort of probation ... let it be remembered too, that virtue is never tried but by some difficulty, and some struggle.'[39] Even then, the recruitment of proven ability and talent into government ought to be counterbalanced, in Burke's view, through the representation of landed property – as in the English constitution.[40]

Burke's emphasis on the link between proven virtue and political liberty within nation states is a characteristic nationalist assumption. It is also an indicator of how close some of Burke's positions are to those developed in Price's 'Discourse'. Conservative and radical nationalism can often seem awkwardly similar. In the *Reflections*, such similarities occur in part because Burke's nationalism is driven to appropriate and redeploy some of the central features of radical nationalism. This can be seen in those moments when Burke seeks most urgently to distance himself from Price's sermon:

> Before I read that sermon, I really thought I had lived in a free country; and it was an error I cherished, because it gave me a greater liking to the country I lived in. I was indeed aware, that a

> jealous, ever-waking vigilance, to guard the treasure of our liberty, not only from invasion, but from decay and corruption, was our best wisdom and our first duty. However, I considered that treasure rather as a possession to be secured than as a prize to be contended for.[41]

Burke paraphrases here those assumptions which he shares with Price: as nationalists, they both assume that their first duty as lovers of their country is an ever-waking vigilance to guard the treasure of Britain's liberty, not only from invasion, but from decay and corruption. But Burke's attempt to distinguish his position from Price's on the basis that he 'considered that treasure rather as a possession to be secured than as a prize to be contended for' is not wholly convincing. Price too claims that the Revolution of 1688 had put the people of Britain in possession of liberty; he also urges that that this possession needed to be secured against the threats imposed by current corruption. It is perhaps only in stressing that British liberty needed to be contended for once again that Price differs from Burke.

In order to prise apart conservative and radical nationalism, Burke presents exaggerated accounts of the problems emerging in France. While he claims that the version of English nationalism he is promoting is characterized by 'manly' virtue, he attempts to castigate the French Revolution for abandoning the basic principles of nationalist ideology. Instead of repudiating the tendency to licence that had marred the *ancien régime*, the French Revolution has allowed dissoluteness to spread like a disease through all the ranks of France:

> All other people have laid the foundations of civil freedom in severer manners, and a system of a more austere and masculine morality. France, when she let loose the reins of regal authority, doubled the licence, of a ferocious dissoluteness in manners, and of an insolent irreligion in opinions and practices; and has extended through all the ranks of life, as if she were communicating some privilege ... all the unhappy corruptions that usually were the disease of wealth and power.[42]

The ideological task of the 'centrepiece' of the *Reflections* – Burke's melodramatic account of the events at Versailles on 5–6 October 1789 – is to put as much distance as possible between English moral virtue and the ferocious moral dissoluteness of the

French Revolution. In Burke's version of these events, a 'mob' of Parisians march to Versailles, break into the royal apartments, and almost rape the queen. Behaving like 'American savages', the people force the king and queen to return to Paris and leave Versailles 'swimming in blood, polluted by massacre, and strewed with scattered limbs and mutilated carcases'. Two gentlemen of the royal guard are beheaded and their heads are 'stuck upon spears' and carried at the front of the procession. As the procession moves along, the monarchs are surrounded by 'horrid yells, and shrilling screams, and frantic dances'.[43] Through such lurid images, Burke is suggesting that the French Revolution is being carried out by a people who are destroying their own national character and common humanity in the process. Burke also uses this account to distance himself as far as possible from Price and to distinguish between their different versions of English nationalism. Although Price makes moral virtue the foundation of national liberty, Burke presents him as a minister capable of celebrating in the pulpit the events at Versailles as a 'triumph' of liberty. By claiming that these 'unmanly and irreligious' events filled 'our Preacher with ... unhallowed transports',[44] Burke attempts to bring into question the claim to virtue that is so central to Price's version of nationalist fervour.

Burke was mocked from the outset for suggesting that the events at Versailles marked the passing of the age of chivalry and its replacement by the age 'of sophisters, oeconomists, and calculators'.[45] Yet it is possible to suggest that he is making a sophisticated case for the integral role of culture in cementing and sustaining political systems. He is also implying that the French have embarked upon a revolution in their national character. According to Burke, the 'most important of all revolutions' which took place at Versailles was 'a revolution in sentiments, manners, and moral opinions'.[46] The behaviour towards the Queen of France at Versailles, together with the fact that no one seems to have attempted to defend her honour, is a sign that the French have abandoned a code of manners which had once distinguished them as a nation: 'little did I dream that I should have lived to see such disasters fallen upon her in a nation of gallant men, in a nation of men of honour and of cavaliers'.[47]

By saying that these events 'must shock, I believe, the moral taste of every well-born mind',[48] Burke begins to direct his reader to a 'proper' response. He is also reminding his readers that the 'French' cultural code of chivalry was not limited to France. It was a European-wide cultural system of the 'well-born' which, Burke claims, had distinguished modern Europe 'under all its forms of government, and distinguished it to its advantage, from the states of Asia, and possibly from those states which flourished in the most brilliant periods of the antique world'. The manly virtues of chivalry are now to be found only in England because the French, who once set the standards of European culture, have abandoned them. As Burke puts it, 'In England we are said to learn manners at second-hand from your side of the water, and that we dress our behaviour in the frippery of France. If so, we are still in the old cut.' By claiming that 'Several English were the stupified and indignant spectators of that triumph', Burke indicates that the English still know how to feel in response to such outrages.[49] Burke's display of sensibility over Marie Antoinette's treatment at Versailles bears witness to his own character, but it is also an attempt to provide an influential exemplification of Englishness. By contrast, the response of Price and his followers reveals their abandonment of English sensibility. (That Burke was Irish and Price was Welsh simply underlines the fact that the exchange between them involves ideological character positions rather than national provenance.)

While it might be said that the code of manners which Burke is referring to was limited to an elite, pan-European culture involving a relatively small number of people (the well-born), Burke claims that it also operated within nation states – as 'the cheap defence of nations'[50] – to harmonize and stabilize social and political relations across classes. In an extraordinarily revealing passage, Burke regrets that

> All the pleasing illusions, which made power gentle, and obedience liberal, which harmonized the different shades of life, and which, by a bland assimilation, incorporated into politics the sentiments which beautify and soften private society, are to be dissolved by this new conquering empire of light and reason.[51]

Although Burke may admit that the culture whose passing he laments may have been composed of a set of pleasing illusions, he nonetheless stresses that such illusions are a necessary means of cementing nations together. Suggesting that states are like poems in that they must charm, Burke counters Price's largely rationalist account of how we come to love our country: 'There ought to be a system of manners in every nation which a well-formed mind would be disposed to relish. To make us love our country, our country ought to be lovely.'[52] Burke, I suggest, is arguing that it is a shared culture rather than an over-arching political system that binds people together into a nation. One of the things he objects to about the Revolution is that its over-reliance on supposedly 'rational' calculation and economics seems to overlook the role that culture plays in creating emotional attachments to the nation state:

> On the scheme of this barbarous philosophy ... laws are to be supported only by their own terrors ... In the groves of *their* academy, at the end of every visto, you see nothing but the gallows. Nothing is left which engages the affections on the part of the commonwealth. On the principles of this mechanic philosophy, our institutions can never be embodied, if I may use the expression, in persons; so as to create in us love, veneration, admiration, or attachment.[53]

Burke is suggesting here that people can only be brought to love their nation through the symbolic activity of 'embodying' its institutions in 'persons'. Without such cultural and ideological processes, a state will have nothing but violence to motivate its people.

The *Reflections* is of particular interest, therefore, because it lays bare and seeks to justify the processes involved in constructing a cultural nationalism which is conservative in the sense that it claims that its assumptions are the only means by which nations can be bonded together and conserved. Faced with the collapse of the old order, Burke is driven to develop a cultural nationalism by powerfully reimagining the relation between culture and politics that had once sustained the European *ancien régime* as a whole. While Burke represents himself as having once been a good European, the French Revolution has forced him not into a revaluation of all values but to their relocation within the confines of the English (sometimes British) nation state. The Revolution's destruction of the 'chivalric' culture which had

once distinguished Europe above all other noble civilizations
means that, for Burke, England has become the last spot on earth
where the old humane values still reside.[54]

The geographical proximity of England and France, as well
as a long history of political and cultural interchange and enmity,
meant that the activities of the French revolutionaries had a
particular resonance for England. The France of the *ancien régime*
had operated as England's (and Britain's) constitutive 'other'
throughout the eighteenth century, not only in the radical
English nationalism traced by Gerald Newman,[55] but also in the
more widespread British nationalism which Linda Colley[56] has
drawn attention to. Yet we have seen that Burke's English
nationalism supposedly holds on to the manners and morals of
the *ancien régime* – tempered, of course by the English constitution and national character. The defining other for Burke is not
ancien régime France but a revolutionary France that has abandoned the established standards of humanity:

> Formerly your affairs were your own concern only. We felt for
> them as men; but we kept aloof from them, because we were not
> citizens of France. But when we see the model held up to ourselves,
> we must feel as Englishmen, and feeling, we must provide as
> Englishmen. Your affairs, in spite of us, are made a part of our
> interest; so far at least as to keep at a distance your panacea, or your
> plague. If it be a panacea, we do not want it. We know the
> consequences of unnecessary physic. If it be a plague; it is such a
> plague, that the precautions of the most severe quarantine ought to
> be established against it.[57]

Feeling and providing as an 'Englishman,' Burke works continually to protect the English national character from the plague of
revolutionary France. While the Revolution seems to have metamorphosed the character of the volatile French, Burke would have
it that the English remain steadfast to their essential character. The
difference in the way the two nations treat vulnerable kings
reveals a critical difference:

> We have formerly have had a king of France in that situation; you
> have read how he was treated by the victor in the field; and in what
> manner he was afterwards received in England. Four hundred years
> have gone over us; but I believe we are not materially changed since
> that period. Thanks to our sullen resistance to innovation, thanks

> to the cold sluggishness of our national character, we still bear the stamp of our forefathers. We have not (as I conceive) lost the generosity and dignity of thinking of the fourteenth century.[58]

The English national character is generous and dignified; its cold sluggishness is a virtue that expresses itself as a sullen resistance to innovation. The use of the first person plural here not only absorbs Burke himself into the general national character, but also tends to reinforce the claim that the English literally have not changed in any way since the fourteenth century. Indeed, this device is merely a foretaste of a passage in which its repeated use adds up to a powerful rhetorical delineation of the English national character:

> In England we have not yet been completely embowelled of our natural entrails; we still feel within us, and we cherish and culti-vate, those inbred sentiments which are the faithful guardians, the active monitors of our duty, the true supporters of all liberal and manly morals ... We preserve the whole of our feelings still native and entire, unsophisticated by pedantry and infidelity. We have real hearts of flesh and blood beating in our bosoms. We fear God; we look up with awe to kings; with affection to parliaments; with duty to magistrates; with reverence to priests; and with respect to nobility. Why? Because when such ideas are brought before our minds, it is natural to be so affected; because all other feelings are false and spurious, and tend to corrupt our minds, to vitiate our primary morals, to render us unfit for rational liberty ...[59]

English feelings remain native and natural; they ensure the maintenance of 'liberal and manly morals;' and the reverence of the English for God, kings, parliaments, magistrates, priests, and nobility is not a slavery, as the radicals would have it, but the basis of their fitness for 'rational liberty'. The English national character finds its authentic expression and counterpart in the English constitution:

> The whole [of the constitution] has emanated from the simplicity of our national character, and from a sort of native plainness and directness of understanding, which for a long time characterized those men who have successively obtained authority amongst us. This disposition still remains, at least in the great body of the people.[60]

For the English, then, to remain loyal to their constitution is to remain true to their essential national character. Indeed, as the last bastion of humanity, Burke confers enormous responsibilities on the English remaining true to themselves (or to his representation of them).

Burke embarks upon a powerful reimagining of the English nation in ways designed to cement it together in preparation for resisting the dissolving principles of radical nationalism. This involves Burke in developing a powerful articulation of the English (sometimes 'British') constitution. Figured, often, as a building whose foundations and fabric have been fashioned, preserved and added to over many generations, the constitution, as Burke represents it, binds the people by duty and sentiment to cherish and preserve what they have inherited – especially when they are called on to reform and restore it. The constitution is not changeless, but changes may be made only in order to preserve it:

> A state without the means of some change is without the means of its conservation ... The two principles of conservation and correction operated strongly at the two critical periods of the Restoration and Revolution, when England found itself without a king. At both those periods the nation had lost the bond of union in their antient edifice; they did not, however, dissolve the whole fabric. On the contrary, in both cases they regenerated the deficient part of the old constitution through the parts which were not impaired.[61]

Rather than making the English constitution continually vulnerable to revolution whenever the people felt aggrieved, Burke argues that the Revolution sought to protect the constitution from the incursion of kings so as to obviate the need for future revolutions. By limiting the powers of a constitutional monarchy, establishing the conditions of hereditary succession, and enhancing the controlling powers of both houses of Parliament, the Revolution had set up a balanced constitution able to secure 'the rights and liberties of the subject'.[62] Instead of breaking with the past or introducing new-fangled rights of men, 'The Revolution was made to preserve our antient indisputable laws and liberties, and that antient constitution of government which is our only security for law and liberty'.[63] Thus, in characteristic nationalist fashion, Burke assures his readers that the English constitution he is describing, perhaps partly inventing, has its roots deep in the past. English liberties are not a new invention but have been the central concern of the English constitution from time immemorial.

The continuity over time that characterizes English history and its constitution is not simply a formal or legal one. Burke figures England as a huge family which extends across time as well as space: 'We wished at the period of the Revolution, and do now wish, to derive all we possess as *an inheritance from our forefathers*'.[64] The use of the first person plural here – as elsewhere in the *Reflections* – allows Burke to be a constituent member of a nation whose consciousness and will seem to be unified in the present and through the past. By imaginatively and legalistically organizing the English people as a national family, the English constitution allows them to claim their 'franchises not on abstract principles "as the rights of men," but as the rights of Englishmen, and as a patrimony derived from their forefathers'.[65] In this way, the advantages of the constitution are 'locked fast as in a sort of family settlement':

> In this choice of inheritance we have given to our frame of polity the image of a relation in blood; binding up the constitution of our country with our dearest domestic ties; adopting our fundamental laws into the bosom of our family affections; keeping inseparable … our state, our hearths, our sepulchres, and our altars.[66]

Families are held together in the present through bonds of blood, love, and property relations, and to the past through memory and inherited property. Burke imagines the English nation as being locked together through analogous ties and affections. Yet the family Burke is imagining here is an aristocratic one with material and symbolic connections with its past: 'By this means our liberty becomes a noble freedom. It carries an imposing and majestic aspect. It has a pedigree and illustrating ancestors. It has its bearings and its ensigns armorial. It has its gallery of portraits; its monumental inscriptions; its records, evidences, and titles'.[67] Burke is here engaged in consecrating the nation though a kind of ancestor worship. He is also seeking to make the English aristocracy appear to be the custodians of the national family heritage rather than being alien to the national tradition (as radical nationalism asserted).

One of the crucial principles of the English constitution, for Burke, is the way it consecrates the state through connecting it with the established Church. Burke praises that sense which 'not only, like a wise architect, hath built up the august fabric of states, but like a provident proprietor, to preserve the structure from prophanation and ruin, as a sacred temple ... hath solemnly and for ever consecrated the commonwealth, and all that officiate in it'.[68] Treating the nation state as an object of worship is one of the defining characteristics of nationalist ideology. While Price argues for the disestablishment of the Anglican Church, he nonetheless conceives of Britain as consecrated by claiming, after the example of seventeenth-century Puritan republicans, that it is the Jerusalem of the modern world. Burke's metaphor of the state as a sacred temple, however, is designed to resist what he sees as the improvident desire on the part of radicals to tear down the fabric of the country in order to begin building again from nothing. The state is to be regarded as consecrated in order that we 'should approach [its] faults ... as to the wounds of a father, with pious awe and trembling solicitude'.[69] If the state were subject to being changed with every change of fashion, Burke says, 'the whole chain and continuity of the commonwealth would be broken. No one generation could link with the other. Men would become little better than the flies of a summer'.[70] Thus, for Burke, a nation or commonwealth has continuity not only across the space of the national territory, but also backwards through the nation's history. This prepares the way for one of Burke's most characteristic statements:

> Society is indeed a contract ... It is a partnership in all science; a partnership in all art; a partnership in every virtue, and in all perfection. As the ends of such a partnership cannot be obtained in many generations, it becomes a partnership not only between those who are living, but between those who are living, those who are dead, and those who are to be born.[71]

England is an exemplary case here, and the English are exemplary in having understood these principles across the generations: 'These ... are, were, and I think long will be the sentiments of not the least learned and reflecting part of this kingdom'. Both these and 'the less enquiring' section of the populace accept that the state is divinely ordained as the appropriate arena for human development: 'They conceive that He who gave our nature to be perfected by our virtue, willed also the necessary means of its perfection – He willed therefore the state'. Such a conception of the origins and purpose of the state justifies the fact that the 'oblation of the state itself, as a worthy offering on the high altar of universal praise, should be performed, as all publick solemn acts are performed, in buildings, in musick, in decoration, in speech, in the dignity of persons, according to the customs of mankind, taught by their nature'.[72] The primary focus of national culture, then, should be the pomp and circumstance of the state itself. As an embodiment of the national character, Burke assures his reader that he is speaking for 'the majority of the people of England':

> I assure you I do not aim at singularity. I give you opinions which have been accepted amongst us, from very early times to this moment, with a continued and general approbation, and which indeed are so worked into my mind, that I am unable to distinguish what I have learned from others from the results of my own meditation.[73]

Burke, then, claims that there is continuity between his own mind and the national mind as expressed in the national culture. Personal and national identities become impossible to disentangle. It is upon such a basis that Burke claims the authority to state that the English consider the Church as 'the foundation of their whole constitution, with which, and with every part of which, it holds an indissoluble union. Church and state are ideas inseparable in their minds'.[74]

A good deal of the last third of the *Reflections* is made up of a sustained analysis of the achievements of the revolutionary nation builders in France. The standard of comparison throughout is, of course, Burke's own imagining of the English constitution and of the statesmanship which shaped it over the centuries. Rather than following the sustained example of the wise architects of the English constitution, the new statesmen of the French Revolution behave as if a country were a kind of *tabula rasa* with no history, customs, or established institutions: 'I cannot conceive how any man can have brought himself to that

pitch of presumption, to consider his country as nothing but
carte blanche, upon which he may scribble whatever he pleases
… a good patriot and a true politician, always considers how he
shall make the most of the existing materials of his country'.[75]
Burke complains that 'The French builders, clearing away as
mere rubbish whatever they found, and, like their ornamental
gardeners, forming every thing into an exact level,' have
reorganized the country according to three supposedly rational
principles: territory, population, and contribution to the trea-
sury.[76] On the basis of the first principle, the country is divided
up into squares of eighteen leagues by eighteen leagues called
départments; these are then divided into squares called *communes*,
which are in turn divided up into squares called *cantons*. In other
words, the national map is redrawn according to geometrical
principles that literally cut through the circumstantial variations
of natural and human geography. Local allegiances and identities
are overridden supposedly in favour of national identifications.
Yet, for Burke, the inevitable result of these contrivances is to
divide the country into competing, irreconcilable units:

> In this whole contrivance of the three bases, consider it in any light
> you please, I do not see a variety of objects, reconciled in one
> consistent whole, but several contradictory principles reluctantly
> and irreconcilably brought and held together by your philo-
> sophers, like wild beasts shut up in a cage, to claw and bite each
> other to their mutual destruction.[77]

The internal divisions introduced by this spatial reorganization
of France are exacerbated, Burke complains, by the introduction
of a system of representation that severs all contact between the
members of the National Assembly and the general electorate
who vote within the cantons. As Burke explains it, voters elect
representatives to the cantons; these representatives, in turn,
elect deputies to the communes; the deputies of the communes
then elect deputies to the departments; and, finally, the deputies
in the departments elect deputies to the National Assembly. The
consequence of this system is that 'there is little, or rather no,
connection between the last representative and the first constituent. The member who goes to the national assembly is not
chosen by the people, nor accountable to them'.[78] Thus the

attempt to homogenise the nation leads instead to its internal fragmentation: 'They have attempted to confound all sorts of citizens, as well as they could, into one homogenous mass; and then they divided this their amalgama into a number of incoherent republics.'[79] Although the Revolution poses as a nationalist movement, it has acted as if it were a foreign invader seeking to destroy any possibility of national sentiment or unity:

> in the spirit of this geometrical distribution, and arithmetical arrangement, these pretended citizens treat France exactly like a country of conquest. Acting as conquerors, they have imitated the policy of the harshest of that harsh race. The policy of such barbarous victors, who contemn a subdued people, and insult their feelings, has ever been, as much as in them lay, to destroy all vestiges of the antient country, in religion, in polity, in laws, and in manners …[80]

Recent historians and theorists of nationalism tend to regard the theory and practice of the French Revolution as an exemplary case of modernizing nationalism that sought to replace local identities and differences with a homogenized national politics and culture.[81] Burke is suggesting here that this version of nationalism wages civil war on the populace. A 'modern' homogenous culture spreads out from the metropolitan centre and attempts to destroy the local identities and cultures of the regions and districts:

> It is boasted, that the geometrical policy has been adopted, that all local ideas should be sunk, and that the people should no longer be Gascons, Picards, Bretons, Normans, but Frenchmen, with one country, one heart, and one assembly. But instead of being all Frenchmen, the greater likelihood is, that the inhabitants of that region will shortly have no country. No man ever was attached by a sense of pride, partiality, or real affection, to a description of square measurement … We begin our public affections in our families … We pass on to our neighbourhoods, and our habitual provincial connections … Such divisions of our country as have been formed by habit, and not by a sudden jerk of authority, were so many little images of the great country in which the heart found something which it could fill. The love to the whole is not extinguished by this subordinate partiality. Perhaps it is a sort of elemental training to those higher and more large regards, by

which alone men come to be affected, as with their own concern, in the prosperity of a kingdom so extensive as that of France. In that general territory itself, as in the old name of provinces, the citizens are interested from old prejudices and unreasoned habits, and not on account of the geometric properties of its figure.[82]

Burke's nationalism, then, is at war with revolutionary nationalism – whose centrist and potentially totalitarian tendencies he represents as destructive of the sense of nation as he understands it. Burke's alternative to modernizing nationalism involves reinterpreting the relationship between local and national cultures and identifications. Instead of thinking of a country as a blank sheet of paper to be divided up into geometrical units, a nation state is refigured as an organic system made up of local identities that cohere into an imaginative whole. Burke presents a cultural and psychological account of how citizens come imaginatively to identify with the nation through extending their primary identifications with families, neighbourhoods, and provinces. In such a system, local attachments and identifications are not barriers to national ones but habits that prepare the mind for larger attachments: 'To be attached to the subdivision, to love the little platoon we belong to in society, is the first principle (the germ as it were) of public affections. It is the first link in the series by which we proceed towards a love to our country and to mankind'.[83]

According to Burke, then, the architects of the new France seem to be botching the job of building a nation. Their complicated and incoherent division of France into squares within squares promises to dismember their country. They have not left in place 'any principle by which any of their municipalities can be bound to obedience; or even conscientiously obliged not to separate from the whole, to become independent, or to connect itself with some other state'.[84] This would seem especially fatal given the fact that the Revolution has destroyed the cultural mores, or pleasing illusions, which had bonded civil society in the *ancien régime*. Burke dismisses the new cultural 'cement' which the National Assembly has provided as incapable of compensating for the loss of the old culture or of overcoming the incoherence introduced by the new political arrangements:

Finding no sort of principle of coherence with each other in the nature and constitution of the several new republics of France, I considered what cement the legislators had provided for them from any extraneous materials. Their confederations, their *spectacles*, their civic feasts, and their enthusiasm, I take no notice of, They are nothing but mere tricks.[85]

The only cementing principles which Burke takes notice of are the introduction of a paper currency based on the confiscation of the Church's property, the centralization of power in Paris, and the necessary recourse to the army. Burke predicts that each of these measures will in practice turn out to accelerate the dissolution of France.

For Burke, therefore, the French experiment is the very last example that Britain ought to follow. In fact, he advises the French to refashion their state on the British model. According to Burke, the political situation in France immediately before the Revolution was not so bad as the revolutionaries had claimed and the government simply needed to be reformed along the lines of the British constitution.[86] Even at this late stage, Burke recommends the British system of checks and balances as the only panacea that might save France from ruin.[87] Similarly, an authentic patriotism, a true love of country, would involve British subjects not in calling for a French Revolution in Britain but in protecting the British constitution from such a catastrophe: 'Our people will find employment enough for a truly patriotic, free, and independent spirit, in guarding what they possess, from violation. I would not exclude alteration neither; but even when I changed, it should be to preserve'.[88]

For Burke, the French Revolution constituted a radical break in the political world by destroying one of the old nations of Europe and attempting to replace it with a new nation state built on entirely new principles. Burke saw the Revolution as an experiment in nation making whose theory and practice would undermine the old nations without being able to construct stable nation states in their place. Yet Burke's reforming nationalism is designed primarily as a means of immunizing England against a revolutionary nationalism already at work in England and given new energy by the French Revolution. In response to Price's recommendation that Britain ought fully to adopt a modern civic nationalism, Burke claims that England already enjoys the benefits of a cultural nationalism that is the only means of cementing people into a nation.[89] The difference between Burke and Price is smaller than Burke would admit, but the difference is a critical one. Civic nationalism assumes that a nation can only be free, virtuous and fully coherent when all its citizens enjoy freedom of conscience and the right to participate in the political process. Burke's cultural nationalism assumes that a nation can only be free, virtuous and fully coherent through engaging the imaginative identifications of each citizen or subject. Both these competing accounts of nationalism suggest that the source of authority is the 'majesty' of the English nation. Yet the meaning and location of this is different in each case and depends on contending interpretations or constructions of the English (or British) constitution. Perhaps the central concern of this textual struggle is about what (and who) authentically represents the English people, English opinion, and the English national character. What Burke cannot admit is the degree to which the *Reflections* radically refashions, reinvents, the national character and constitution in response to an emergency which is largely of his own imagining.

Notes

1 See the extracts in John Hutchinson and Antony D. Smith, eds, *Nationalism* (Oxford and New York: Oxford University Press, 1994).

2 Ibid. pp. 3–10.

3 See Benedict Anderson, *Imagined Communities: Reflections on the Origins and Spread of Nationalism* (London and New York: Verso, 1991).

4 Alfred Cobban, *Edmund Burke and the Revolt Against the Eighteenth Century* (London: George Allen and Unwin, 1929), pp. 97–132.

5 See Gerald Newman, *The Rise of English Nationalism: A Cultural History, 1740–1830* (London: Weidenfeld and Nicolson, 1987) and Linda Colley, *Britons: Forging the Nation, 1707–1837* (London: Random House, 1994).

6 See Gerald Newman, *The Rise of English Nationalism*, pp. 228–9 and Anne Janowitz, *England's Ruins: Poetic Purpose and the Natural Landscape* (Oxford and Cambridge, MA: Basil Blackwell, 1990).

7 *Reflections*, p. 54.

8 Richard Price, *Political Writings*, ed. D. O. Thomas (Cambridge and New York, 1991), p. xxii.

9 Ibid. pp. 1–13.

10 Ibid. p. 19.

11 Ibid. pp. 116–51.

12 Ibid. pp. 178, 179, 181.

13 Ibid. p. 184.

14 Ibid. p. 187.

15 Ibid. p. 188.

16 Ibid. pp. 189–90.

17 Ibid. pp. 191–2.

18 Ibid. pp. 194–5.

19 Ibid. p. 185.

20 Ibid. pp. 185–6.

21 Ibid. p. 195.

22 Ibid.

23 Ibid. p. 188, n. 22.

24 *Reflections*, p. 56.

25 Ibid. p. 57.

26 Ibid. p. 54.

27 Ibid. pp. 56–7.

28 Ibid. p. 136.

29 Ibid.

30 Ibid. p. 60.

31 Ibid. pp. 57–8.

32 Ibid. pp. 58–9.

33 Ibid. p. 64.

34 Ibid. p. 66.

35 Ibid. p. 76.

36 See Newman, *The Rise of English Nationalism,* and Ernest Gellner, *Nationalism* (London: Weidenfeld and Nicolson, 1997), pp. 5–9.

37 *Reflections*, p. 91.

38 Ibid. p. 101.

39 Ibid.

40 Ibid. pp. 102–3.

41 Ibid. p. 105.

42 Ibid. pp. 88–9.

43 Ibid. pp. 117, 122.

44 Ibid. p. 117.

45 Ibid. p. 127.

46 Ibid. p. 131.

47 Ibid. p. 126.

48 Ibid. p. 117.

49 Ibid. pp. 127, 120, 117.

50 Ibid. p. 127.

51 Ibid. p. 128.

52 Ibid. p. 129.

53 Ibid. pp. 128–9.

54 For a similar argument, see Seamus Deane, *Strange Country: Modernity and Nationhood in Irish Writing since 1790* (Oxford: Clarendon Press, 1997), pp. 7–8, 14.

55 See Newman, *The Rise of English Nationalism*.

56 See Colley, *Britons*.

57 *Reflections*, p. 140.

58 Ibid. p. 137.

59 Ibid. pp. 137–8.

60 Ibid. p. 141.

61 Ibid. p. 72.

62 Ibid. p. 78.

63 Ibid. p. 81.

64 Ibid.

65 Ibid. p. 82.

66 Ibid. p. 84.

67 Ibid. p. 85.

68 Ibid. p. 143.

69 Ibid. p. 146.

70 Ibid. p. 145.

71 Ibid. pp. 146–7.

72 Ibid. pp. 147–8.

73 Ibid. p. 149.

74 Ibid.

75 Ibid. p. 206.

76 Ibid. pp. 220–1.

77 Ibid. p. 229.

78 Ibid. p. 235.

79 Ibid. p. 232.

80 Ibid. p. 230.

81 See Anderson, *Imagined Communities*, pp. 77–8, and Gellner, *Nations and Nationalism* (Oxford: Blackwell, 1983).

82 *Reflections*, p. 244.

83 Ibid. pp. 97–8.

84 Ibid. p. 272.

85 Ibid. p. 237.

86 Ibid. p. 180.

87 Ibid. p. 173.

88 Ibid. p. 292.

89 On the distinctions between civic and cultural nationalism, see John Hutchinson, *The Dynamics of Cultural Nationalism* (London: Allen and Unwin, 1987).

7

Burke, Toland, toleration: the politics of prejudice, speculation, and naturalization

SUSAN MANLY

In this essay I consider how Burke's *Reflections on the Revolution in France* and his writings on the subjects of religious freedom and toleration theorize the politics of prejudice, natural feeling, and family loyalty – the latter conceived as intimately connected to religious conviction. To do so I will examine the work of Toland, whom Burke uses to symbolize the moral bankruptcy of extreme Dissent. I then look at Maria Edgeworth's novel of 1817, *Harrington* which, I will argue, engages closely with the naturalization and toleration debates familiar to Burke, and examines the origin and force of anti-Semitic prejudice. Implicitly anti-Burkean even as it dwells on Burke's moral touchstones – family, inheritance, natural sympathies, and antipathies – *Harrington* is a critique of the Englishness that Burke opposes to French speculation and innovation.

Burke's interest in debates surrounding religious toleration was closely linked to his concern with the perpetuation of a political order which for him embodied moral value. But, even in the 1780s, he had already recorded his doubts regarding the Whig ascendancy's anti-Catholic policies in Ireland, and in public and private letters in the 1790s he would warn the Pitt ministry that continued disenfranchisement of Catholics was giving a legitimate complexion to a revolutionary movement.[1] An Irish Protestant by birth, Burke belonged neither to the Scottish-Irish Presbyterians of the north nor to the Anglo-Irish Protestant landowning

class of the Protestant Ascendancy. The name 'Burke' indicates
Old English or Norman-Irish descent, as does that of his wife Jane
Nugent, and it is probable that the families of both had only
recently converted from Catholicism.[2] The name 'Nugent' has
particularly strong Catholic resonances. So it seems probable that
there was a personal element as well as a political motivation
underpinning Burke's stance on anti-Catholic discrimination in
Ireland. Burke's doubts about government policy regarding free
religious expression complicated his own relationship to established political authority. As J. G. A. Pocock and James E. Bradley
have shown, those who dissented from the established Church in
eighteenth-century England were also implicitly questioning the
legitimacy of the civic order.[3] Some of this implicit critique had
its roots in Dissent's separation of religious practice and political
authority. If, as nonconformists believed, the Bible was an ultimate authority beyond the established Church hierarchy, then
the state's reliance on the Church for spiritual confirmation of its
legitimacy was undermined. But equally, the penalties of nonconformity alienated Dissenters from the polity and demonstrably
fostered their increased political radicalism in late eighteenth-
century England. James E. Bradley, for instance, sees the increasingly oppositional character of Protestant Dissent after the war
with the American colonies as stemming from the social and
political exclusion of Dissenters, which predisposed them to be
critical of their rulers. We can see a parallel here with the arguments Burke musters to attack the anti-Catholic penal code in
Ireland, which I'll discuss in some detail later in this essay. The
Dissenters' congregational polity, argues Bradley, provided a
longstanding and abiding orientation against a hierarchical conception of society; their more egalitarian religious practice
anticipated by many years their radical opposition to political
oppression. This sense of separateness and exclusion was shared
by other nonconforming groups, notably Catholics and Jews.
Like these latter groups, Dissenters increasingly came to be seen
in the late eighteenth century as dangerously alienated from the
state.

Like Bradley, J. G. A. Pocock also draws on English debates
about religious nonconformity and toleration in order to explain
Burke's analysis of revolution in 1790. In 1781, Josiah Tucker

had published an attack on the American Revolution, and on Price's support of it, as founded on a Lockean heresy of government.[4] By arguing for the legitimacy of the Americans' case, Burke risked being identified with such heretics, and we might speculate that the need to distance himself from pro-American Dissent is one of the motivating factors behind Burke's repudiation of 'rational Dissent' in the *Reflections* nine years after Tucker's polemic.

Why did the advocacy of toleration become such a problem for Burke in 1790? In this essay I suggest that Burke is partly prompted to take up the stance of religious conformity in the *Reflections* because of his involvement in the legislation which occasioned the politicized violence of the Gordon Riots in 1780. But, as Pocock points out, the revolution that is of more immediate importance to Burke in the *Reflections* is not that of 1789, but rather of 1688. The English Revolution of 1688 had been, fundamentally, a crisis in the history of the Church of England and the Anglican Church–state. This crisis had given rise to the Toleration Act of 1689, in which the Church–state had reluctantly agreed to cease regarding Dissenting worship as itself unlawful, while continuing to insist on the exclusion of Dissenters from crown office or membership in corporations. Catholics had been excluded from the Act's provisions, as had anti-trinitarians or those who denied the full divinity of Christ, and who therefore denied that the Church possessed authority as an extension of the divine body.

In the 1770s and 1780s, as the campaign for liberty of religious expression and full civic equality for Dissenters gathered pace, it became clear that true toleration, taken to its logical end, necessitated the complete separation of Church and state. Richard Price was among the leaders of this campaign, which included some dissenting Anglicans as well as other Protestant Dissenters, and Price was also among those who believed that this more radical understanding of toleration might be acted upon in the newly liberated America.

Like Bradley, Pocock lays great stress on the influence of Dissenting theology in the formation of political radicalism. He points out that for Unitarians, a consequence of their steady erosion of incarnationist theology was that religion came increasingly to be identified in their minds with enquiry. The separation of Church and state therefore rested less on the secularization of religion than on the identification of religion with the secular. If the religious spirit was one of free enquiry, the Church had to be free of its associations with secular authority, which resisted such enquiry. Unitarians wanted to deny the Church all partnership in the civil power so that the civil power would have the liberty to recognize that the liberty of reason – the free assent of the people – was the sole foundation on which it rested. For this reason, Pocock considers the campaign for freedom of religious expression and full civic equality regardless of religious affiliation to have been 'the most revolutionary programme … formulated by any organized group of Englishmen'. And this dissenting imperative is noted by Pocock as of crucial importance in the debates between Burke and Price over the interrelated meanings of 1688 and 1789.[5]

The connection that Burke makes in the *Reflections* between rational Dissent and the French revolutionaries is therefore by no means arbitrary. Indeed, as Pocock remarks: 'The verbal assaults on royal and aristocratic political power going on in the 1780s were launched largely by groups simultaneously engaged in the anti-trinitarian dissenters' campaign against religious establishments and the civil penalties which were the price of toleration; and it can be debated whether the religious or the secular aspect of their agitation had primacy over the other. The defence of the Whig political order therefore included a defence against enthusiasm.'[6] Turning to the work of John Toland, one of the rational Dissenters against whom Burke directs his contempt in the *Reflections*, we can immediately see the association of Protestant free-thinking and uncontrolled political speculation which so exercises Burke.

In the first of his *Letters to Serena* (1704), the Irish ex-Catholic turned deist John Toland seeks to explain the origin and force of prejudices, in the course of which he launches an attack on unquestioning loyalty to the 'little platoon' beloved of Burke, which, he considers, creates and strengthens false associations and error:

> We all partake but too much of the Inclinations of those that give us Life, and of the Passions that are predominant in the Blood of the

> Family ... The Temperament we receive in the first Formation, gives
> not only a Disposition to this or that particular Humor and Habit;
> but also a visible Bias to most Actions of our future Lives, which is
> not to be cur'd but by the utmost Efforts and Exercise of Reason.[7]

Superstitions and prejudices, argues Toland, are introduced to
the child so early in life that, 'not remembring when, or where,
or how he came by many of his Notions, he's tempted to believe
that they proceed from Nature it self ...'.[8] Children's nurses are
singled out for particular criticism, since they are prone to conjuring up frightening visions to ensure their charges' obedience
– and by so doing forever forge an unconscious link between
authority and its useful spectres. These apparently harmless
domestic strategies have public ramifications:

> What is thus invented at the beginning to keep Children under
> Government (a Government that indeed makes 'em miserable
> Slaves ever after) is believ'd by them in good earnest when they
> grow older, whereby the whole Generation and Country comes to
> be persuaded of it at last ...[9]

'[B]red in the same Persuasion' as those nearest and dearest to us,
we find it difficult, argues Toland, to disentangle our affections
from our opinions.[10] This readiness to identify right thinking
with those we love, and to whom we feel loyalty, produces party
spirit. The deep impressions made at an early age, Toland asserts,
acquire the authority of natural feelings, in comparison with
which rational enquiry seems perverse, and only *familiar* terms
carry conviction:

> Custom (which is not unfitly call'd a Second Nature) has imprest
> such a stamp on the very Language of the Society, that what is
> deliver'd in these or those Words, tho never so contradictory or
> abstruse, passes ordinarily for current Truth: but change your
> Terms, or use the Expressions of any other Party, and then if you
> speak Oracles, whatever you say is reputed false, or at best
> suspected.[11]

For Burke in the *Reflections*, the detached speculation and
rational enquiry that Toland would like to see applied to religious and political convictions is similarly contrasted with a
'sullen resistance to innovation'.[12] But Burke's argument is
explicitly anti-rationalist. According to Burke, the 'inbred senti-

ments' of which Toland complains should be – and in England are – reverenced as 'the faithful guardians, the active monitors of our duty, the true supporters of all liberal and manly morals'.[13] Such 'untaught feelings'[14] are based on the very prejudices that Toland interrogates.

Burke portrays prejudice as a kind of common capital, a sentimental economy which relieves the individual from having 'to live and trade each on his own private stock of reason'.[15] A sound common patrimony of 'wise prejudice'[16] is contrasted with the dangerously individualistic speculation of those who trust to their own inner light. Natural sympathies, Burke claims, instruct the English to eschew 'pedantry and infidelity'[17] – the destabilizing speculative tendencies of revolution. Furthermore, he argues, such sympathies ensure continuity between generations so that 'we still bear the stamp of our forefathers': 'our passions instruct our reason'[18] to this end, and this is natural and right.

Just after this emotional and emotive validation of prejudice, Burke contemptuously dismisses Toland and other leading Freethinkers as obscure but menacing 'Atheists and Infidels'.[19] This proximity of reference is far from accidental. As we have seen, Burke is deliberately picking up and inverting for his own purposes Toland's points about custom as second nature, prejudice as the servant of unquestionable authority, and affections or passions as the breeding-ground of fixed persuasions. 'Who,' Burke asks, 'born within the last forty years, has read one word of Collins, and Toland, and Tindal, and Chubb, and Morgan, and that whole race who called themselves Freethinkers?'[20] Although one would have to manipulate his birth-date a little, Burke's rhetorical question about the practical influence of Toland and his ilk is tacitly and ironically answered in the keywords of his own prose, which mirror those repeatedly used by Toland: authority, passion, government, inbred sentiments, natural feelings.

Like Burke, Toland consistently links civil liberties with theological concerns, connecting the health of the state and society at large with religion. But Toland delineates the origin and force of religious and political prejudice so as to demystify and explode it, with the aim of emancipating his reader from being 'led like a Beast by Authority or Passion', rather putting him in a position to give 'Law to his own Actions as a free and reasonable Man'.[21] Burke on the other hand argues that 'obstinacy and the blindest prejudice' is to be preferred to the 'inconstancy and versatility' of 'naked reason'.[22]

One reason for Burke's hostility in the *Reflections* towards rational Dissent is that he correctly saw how some prominent French 'men of speculation'[23] – Voltaire above all – had drawn on the extreme dissenting tradition of Deism, especially on Toland, to undermine the credibility of the Bible and of revealed religion and established authorities in general.[24] Dissenters had, by 1790, begun to look like the 'enemy within'.

Another linked explanation, as Iain McCalman has recently persuasively argued, is that Burke is polemically merging the beliefs of the rational Dissenter Richard Price with the 'bigoted enthusiast, enlightenment revolutionary, lunatic Jew, and libertine pornographer Lord George Gordon'.[25] Gordon was the instigator of the ultra-Protestant Gordon Riots, which wreaked havoc in London for over a week in June 1780 in a campaign of terror intended to force the Catholic Relief Act of 1778 off the statute books. He later converted to Judaism, which is why Burke calls him the 'protestant Rabbin'.[26] McCalman argues that Burke deliberately blurs the demarcations between the two men to suggest that there is a natural progression from rational Dissent to irrational revolution. Free rational speculation, implies Burke, inevitably degenerates into anarchic riot and the wholesale destruction of all cherished corrections and human ties, all revered establishments. McCalman suggests that Burke transfers Lord George Gordon's extremist tendencies to Price, making him embody Gordon's fanatical anti-popery and his reckless condonation of political violence, justified by theology. Later in this essay I'll look at how Burke links Jewishness and revolutionary theory in the attacks on speculation which pepper the *Reflections*, and I'll suggest that there is perhaps more to Burke's use of anti-Jewish slurs than a simple personal attack on Gordon and Price. But McCalman also notices the similarities between Burke and Gordon: that both were ethnic and social outsiders, both were intensely religious and emotional, both were visionary and extremist – and both were widely accused of being lunatics and latter-day Quixotes.[27]

What divided them was Protestant anti-popery. Superstition

– the target of revolutionary rhetoric and Deist dissent alike – for Burke carries resonances of the 'wise prejudice' which ensures that the 'paternal constitution'[28] of the state is treated with reverence and awe, not hacked apart in pursuit of a cure for its ills. But 'superstition' is also one of the watchwords of anti-Catholicism, which Burke had consistently denounced as a major cause of Ireland's failure to prosper. In the *Tract on the Popery Laws*, written in the early 1760s, he describes the penal code as 'one leading cause of the imbecility of the country'.[29] The danger if the laws penalizing Catholicism were not repealed, Burke was convinced, was revolutionary enthusiasm as opposed to the 'superstition' dreaded by Protestants. A people who had never experienced the benefits of full citizenship under the terms of the English constitution – who had never known the 'profit of the protection of a common father'[30] in the words of the 1792 *Letter to Sir Hercules Langrishe* – and who in fact could not help but associate it with daily persecutions, were much more likely to fall prey to the subversive persuasions of Protestant England's greatest enemy, France, and to react violently against their oppressors.

In line with the *Reflections'* concern with family and patrimony, in the *Tract on the Popery Laws*, it is the disordering of what he considers to be natural hierarchies and bonds which upsets Burke most about the penal code. The laws governing Catholics' rights to the ownership of land and education are primarily to be regarded as a contravention of natural justice because they destroy family connections and allegiances, potentially leading to 'the dominion of children [who conform] over their parents [who adhere to Catholicism]'.[31] These laws, Burke argues, literally estrange parents from children, wives from husbands, and alienate those who remain loyal to their ancestral faith from their own native towns.

To punish this fidelity to family is, argues Burke, to deprave society: 'you punish them for acting upon a principle, which, of all others, is perhaps the most necessary for preserving society, an implicit admiration and adherence to the establishment of their forefathers'.[32] Religion, in other words, is not reliant on and should not be bound by man-made laws. The Protestants who can alone be said to 'consent' to these laws contravene the deeper laws of nature: more able to sympathize with the sufferings of foreigners than with the persecution of those with whom they share a country, they 'transfer humanity from its natural basis, our legitimate and homebred connexions', and 'meretriciously ... hunt abroad after foreign affections'.[33]

Like the cosmopolitan men of speculation to whom the *Reflections* attributes the baseless prejudice against the old in favour of the new, those who uphold the penal code in Ireland betray the natural instructors of their reason, their 'homebred connexions'. This disapproval of purely elective affinities, which makes a good deal of sense in the context of Burke's arguments for Catholic Emancipation, is later important for the *Reflections*. But in contrast with the concrete social realities Burke brings to bear on the concept of natural feelings and native connexions in the early 1760s, by 1790 the influences of nature and nativity have a talismanic significance: powerful, authoritative, because inexplicit and inexplicable.

I want to turn at this point from Burke's annexing and inversion of Toland's language on the subject of prejudice, authority, and natural feeling to a novel written in 1817: *Harrington*, by Maria Edgeworth, which focuses on debates about toleration, social order, and naturalization. I'll argue that *Harrington* reflects on Burke's *Reflections*, although the novel's action is set at an apparently safe historical distance from the events of 1789.

Edgeworth's own experience of political violence, however, strikingly parallels Burke's during the Gordon Riots, a decade before he sat down to write his influential repudiation of revolution, when his life was threatened by a mob. Burke's experience at the hands of the Gordon rioters anticipates that of Edgeworth's father, Richard Lovell Edgeworth, who in 1798 was nearly lynched in an outbreak of 'popular phrenzy'[34] in the Protestant stronghold of Longford. Edgeworth, it was rumoured, was a French spy – possibly even a United Irishman. Although he was eventually left unharmed, enough suspicion existed about Edgeworth's political allegiances to cause applications to be made to Dublin to impeach his corps of yeomen, which included both Catholics and Protestants.[35] The impression this made on his daughter Maria Edgeworth can be measured by the power with which, two decades later, she depicted the Gordon Riots in *Harrington*.

In many respects analogous to the earlier Jewish Naturalization Act of 1753, the 1778 Catholic Relief Act, drafted by Burke,
was a small but significant gesture of amity to loyalist Catholics
living in England whose only dissent from the constituted
political order was one of conscience. The aim of the Act was to
reward and cement Catholic loyalties to the Crown – a project
which had gained urgency from the turn of events in America,
where France had just put its strength behind the American
rebels.

The riots which ensued – first in Scotland, and then in
London and other metropolitan centres – gave a new and lurid
salience to the well-established belief that the author of the
reviled Act, Burke, was a crypto-Catholic. Images of Burke in a
priest's black gown and biretta soon became a staple of carica-
tures.[36] The 'toleration of Popery' epitomized by the 1778 Act
was widely held to be part of a 'deep-laid ministerial plan' to
curtail the liberties of the English people.[37] What was felt by
Gordon and his fellow Protestant Association members to be an
un-English capitulation to papism, with all its associations of
foreignness, persecution and despotism, was countered with a
massive show of popular resistance, as Catholic churches and the
houses of wealthy Catholics and sympathizers were targeted,
torn down, and burned.

I want to argue that Maria Edgeworth's novel, *Harrington*
engages actively not only with the terms of Burke's pleas for
religious toleration, but also draws on other, more far-reaching
arguments about tolerance, prejudice, and integration, including
works by Toland, Richard Price and the German Jewish philosopher, Moses Mendelssohn.[38] As a consequence, Edgeworth
produces an interrogation of Englishness and English liberties far
less 'analgesic' than has recently been suggested.[39] Like Burke in
the *Tract on Popery* and in the *Reflections* Edgeworth links the
question of religious conviction to the theme of family lineage
and inheritance. But unlike Burke, Edgeworth's vision is consistently anti-aristocratic and cosmopolitan. Edgeworth, in short,
deliberately contests the discourse of nature, sentiment, and
authority deployed by Burke in the *Reflections*.

Harrington is explicitly offered to its readers as a revisionist
work of 'philosophical history':[40] an exploration of the origin and

force of anti-Semitic prejudice begun in response to the letter Edgeworth received in the summer of 1816 from a young American Jewish woman, Rachel Mordecai, who criticized the anti-Jewish stereotypes of several of Edgeworth's children's stories.[41] But as I've suggested, *Harrington* is not simply an act of personal 'atonement and reparation'.[42] It can usefully be compared to Burke's *Reflections*, which similarly philosophizes English history. Sentiment, as we have seen, plays an important role in Burke's moral economy, guaranteeing the authority of English political arrangements and the instinctively felt unnaturalness of French events. So much so that it dictates the form of the *Reflections*. Burke in his preamble 'beg[s] leave to throw out my thoughts, and express my feelings, just as they arise in my mind, with very little attention to formal method'.[43] This stress on the unconscious and unmethodical nature of the outgrowth of sentiment that Burke purports to represent, in other words, is in the spirit of the English constitution, an organic expression of shared values. Edgeworth, on the other hand, is anxious to foreground the philosophical and political influences which legitimize anti-Semitism in order to question so-called 'natural' sentiments – and in so doing aligns herself with the forces of speculation epitomized for Burke by Toland, whose psychopathology of prejudice echoes through her descriptions of the origin of her young hero's prejudice against Jews.

The story opens with Harrington, the narrator and hero, remembering the first occasion on which, as an excitable child of six, he sees an old Jewish clothes-man, whose appearance is seized on by his nurse, impatient to get her charge off to bed. She frightens him into obedience by telling him that 'Simon the Jew' is in the habit of carrying naughty boys away in his bag.[44] Struck by the disciplinary success of this ploy, she is quick to reinforce her authority by relating tales of abominations practised on children by Jews, until her charge is so traumatized that he succumbs to a nervousness which cannot be dispelled by any rational means. The child's fear, which he is too frightened to explain, is indulged and encouraged by his morbidly sensitive mother, so that he grows vain of what she regards as his 'positively natural antipathy to the sight or bare idea of a Jew'.[45] Although some of his nervousness is initially affected, he quickly becomes prey to night terrors caused by phobic fantasies of persecution which have gone 'beyond the power of [his] reason, or of [his] most strenuous voluntary exertion to control'.[46] This primal scene gives a visible bias, to paraphrase Toland, to most actions of Harrington's future life, a bias which is 'not to be cur'd but by the utmost Efforts and Exercise of Reason'.

Toland, we recall, had linked the 'Passions … predominant in the Blood of the Family' together with the spectres invented by children's nurses, to the erroneous persuasions of entire countries.[47] Edgeworth follows Toland's aetiology of prejudice, connecting Harrington's early fears with his mother's neurotic belief in 'natural antipathies', and then showing how this false association is reinforced by storybook legends about Jews and by Harrington senior's party spirit. Harrington's fear is thus shown to be the product not only of his nurse's government and his mother's enthusiastic indulgence of unconstrained sensibility, but of the superficially more rational public sphere of print culture and political debate.

It is Harrington's father who first introduces the anti-naturalization politics which form an apparently rational justification for what Harrington has been encouraged to consider his instinctive dislike of Jews. Irritated by his wife's superstitious credulousness in regard to her son's inexplicable terror of Jews, Harrington senior vows to conquer his son's fear with his more rational masculine influence: to make a man of him by involving him in his world of politicking. The date invoked in this scene of political dinner debate is 1754: the time of the fracas over the Jewish Naturalization Act (popularly known as the Jew Bill). We see the eight-year-old Harrington listening to his father, a country MP of the landed class, as he debates the extension of civil rights to Jews at a dinner party given for his constituents.[48] Bred up in his father's persuasion, the child by a 'metonymy of the passions' identifies those guests who are sympathetic to the Jews' cause as his father's enemies, for which he is pronounced by his father to be 'an honour to my country, my family, and my party': a true scion of his 'little platoon'.[49] He confirms that he has absorbed his lesson when, in response to a lady's questioning why the Jews should not be naturalized, he punningly replies: 'because the Jews are naturally an unnatural pack of people, and you can't naturalize what's naturally unnatural'.[50] In 1714, Toland had written a pamphlet, *Reasons for Naturalizing the Jews in Great Britain and Ireland*, which had denied any essential difference between Jews and natives of their adoptive countries: 'since their dispersion, they have no common or peculiar inclination distinguishing 'em from others; but visibly partake of the Nature of those nations among whom they live, and where they were bred'.[51] Jews were therefore, in Toland's eyes, already natural citizens. The uproar which followed the very limited provisions of the 1753 Naturalization Act provoked a flood of books and pamphlets about Jews and the rights and wrongs of the legal disabilities under which they were labouring – many of which cited Toland's earlier tract.[52] Those calling for the repeal of the Act frequently echo the sentiments of anti-popery advocates captured by Burke in the *Letter to Sir Hercules Langrishe*. Anti-Catholics, argues Burke, regarded the penal laws as 'pleasing and popular' insofar as they harassed 'a set of people, who were looked upon as enemies to God and man; and indeed as a race of bigotted savages who were a disgrace to human nature itself'.[53] Like the anti-Jewish party line adopted by Harrington senior, the anti-Catholic argument summarised by Burke constructs a definition of 'nature' which justifies legal exclusion and rationalizes prejudice. But this awareness that 'nature' can be polemically annexed to the cause of oppression is not a feature of the *Reflections*. For the sake of his argument, Burke has to disavow his analysis of the rhetorical abuses of nature which he knows underlie the opposition to religious and social integration in Ireland.

Instead, Burke himself exploits the idea of unnaturalness to attack 'men of speculation', 'literary caballers, and intriguing philosophers', whom he demonizes for their suspect intelligence activities and their unlimited exchange of ideas with 'political theologians, and theological politicians, both at home and [more to the point] abroad'.[54] Price, Gordon, and French speculators – Dissenting men of letters and Jewish stock-jobbers – all merge into one enemy with this formulation. For Burke, caballing is an illicit and sinister political scheming contrary to the established government ideology of constitution, law, and nation. But with its Jewish associations of 'cabbala', the rabbinical oral tradition of mystical interpretations from the scriptures, the word 'cabballing' immediately calls up the fears of inhumanity, vengefulness, and subversive foreignness linked in the public mind to Jews.

The phobic identification of Jews with dangerous speculation, financial and otherwise, also played a part in the Jew Bill uproar that Edgeworth focuses on. Since 1656, Jews had been tolerated in England for their commercial expertise. It was acknowledged that a rapid expansion of overseas trade was necessary for the health of the economy. At war with France for much of the late seventeenth and early eighteenth centuries in a bitter struggle for influence in Europe and for control of colonial markets, England needed money: and *some* of those with the required financial expertise were Jews. But the loan-contracting and stock-jobbing involved in raising large cash sums aroused the distrust of Englishmen unaccustomed to sophisticated forms of financial speculation. The Country ideology which was used to argue against the Jew Bill of 1753 was founded on an ethic of civic virtue which maintained that society and civil government could only be preserved by the patriotic actions and public spirit of men of property, by which they meant property in land. This property, in short, had to have a real, stable, heritable value: not a fictitious and mobile one. Trade in money and shares did not confer the rights of citizenship upon financiers, because their wealth was based upon fantasy and speculation. Thus Jews, who were (like Catholics in Ireland and many Dissenters) debarred from the ownership of land and from full citizenship, and were frequently figured as rootless wanderers – landless on three counts – were suspected as potential destroyers of the political and social gains secured by the Glorious Revolution. Later I will briefly show what Edgeworth does to counter these associations; but before I do so I want to glance back again at Burke's *Reflections* and at the insidious anti-Jewishness of his attacks on men of speculation and their role in revolution.

Burke constantly brackets speculation and theory together with the betrayal of national trust, contrasting the men of great civil and military talents, the 'ornament of their age', with those who resemble 'Jew brokers contending with each other who could best remedy with fraudulent circulation and depreciated paper the wretchedness and ruin brought on their country by their degenerate councils'. Such interventions 'only change and pervert the natural order of things'. The men of letters who sympathize with the revolution partake of this characteristically Jewish unnaturalness: they may think that they're 'combating prejudice', warns Burke, but in fact they're 'at war with nature'.[55] For when property is destroyed and hereditary rights over-thrown by revellers, 'rational liberty has no existence' – is, in short, a fantasy – leaving 'a paper circulation, and a stock-jobbing constitution'.[56] The financial system of the new French republic is condemned by Burke for its 'continual transmutation of paper into land, and land into paper', by which means

> the spirit of money-jobbing and speculation goes into the mass of land itself [is literally naturalized] and incorporates with it. By this kind of operation, that species of property becomes (as it were) volatilized; it assumes an unnatural and monstrous activity…[57]

For Burke, speculation gives rise to a species of miscegenation, by which it becomes 'as extensive as life', mixed with all its concerns, diverting 'the whole of the hopes and fears of the people from their usual channels, into the impulses, passions, and superstitions of those who live on chances'.[58]

To this suspect economy of paper circulation, Burke opposes inheritance, pitting heredity and loyal affections against 'that vague speculative right' urged on the people from the 'Babylonian pulpits' of Price and his ilk.[59] I would suggest that Edgeworth is recalling and deliberately challenging Burke's meshing of monied interest, intellectual enquiry and instability when she creates the Jewish protagonist in Harrington, Mr Montenero. Montenero, through whom Harrington conquers what remains of his neurotic childhood fear of Jews, is depicted as opposite in every way to Harrington's blustering, intemperate, and intolerant father. Cos-mopolitan, restrained, cultured, and with an acute head for business, Montenero quickly gains Harrington's respect and love: far more effectively than Harrington senior, he encourages Harrington to use his rational self-control to counter both his natural tendency to enthusiasm and his old superstitions. But Harrington's conversion from anti-Semitism is first effected, significantly enough, through a textual encounter with one of the most renowned Jewish thinkers of the eighteenth century: an example, perhaps, of the paper circulation Burke finds so threatening to established order.

Reading a biography of Moses Mendelssohn given to him by a Jewish pedlar whom he has chivalrously defended against the aristocratic anti-hero of the novel, Harrington discovers that Mendelssohn also suffered from a nervous disease in childhood. In this detail, he sees a reflection of his own sensibility; and the pedlar's remark that he is 'so kind to the Jews'[60] regains its sense of *kinship* as well as sympathy. Mendelssohn was most famous, as Edgeworth would have known, for his definitive statement on the relationship between religion and government, *Jerusalem* (1783), which emphasizes the social function of religion: its role in making good citizens. Theological tenets, he argues, should not be government's concern. Mendelssohn's pluralism is based on a belief also expressed by Toland in his *Nazarenus* (1718): that the endeavour to obliterate religious distinctiveness thwarts the purposes of Providence, which had always intended that Judaism should continue to thrive alongside Christianity. Toland holds that

> the Jews, tho associating with the converted Gentiles, and acknowledging them for brethren, were still to observe their own Law thro-out all generations; and ... the Gentiles, who became so farr Jews as to acknowledge ONE GOD, were not however to observe the Jewish Law: but ... both of them were to be for ever after united into one body or fellowship ...

This desired state, argues Toland, is a 'Union without Uniformity'.[61] Such principles of religious equality, Mendelssohn felt, had at first been promised in the newly independent America, which, in the words of Richard Price, had provided 'a place of refuge for opprest man in every region of the world'.[62] Price's vision of religious liberties went beyond the limited freedom guaranteed by toleration in a state with an established Church. By liberty of conscience, he envisaged a state in which no one religious community would claim any kind of superiority over any group, and where all would be equally entitled to protection so long as they conducted themselves honestly and peaceably.

Like Mendelssohn and Price, Montenero and his daughter Berenice, with whom Harrington falls in love, look to post-Revolutionary America as just such an example of religious and social freedom, against which the illiberality of English high society is thrown into stark contrast.[63] In the events which follow, Harrington becomes increasingly conscious of the rampant anti-Semitism of his cultural inheritance, as his empathy, developed through his love for Berenice, opens his ears and his heart to the enlightening rational converse of her father.

> [W]hen her father spoke, it seemed to be almost the same as if she spoke herself, her sympathy with him appeared so strongly. I was convinced that all which he said, she thought and felt, and this gave an additional interest to his conversations.[64]

It is important to keep the close identification of Berenice with her father in mind to counterbalance the disappointment we cannot avoid feeling when it finally emerges that she is not, in fact, Jewish. Montenero's wife, it emerges, had been an English Protestant, and faithful to his promise to his wife on her death-bed, Montenero has brought Berenice up as a Christian.

But I would urge that the somewhat uneasy resolution of the novel, which ends with Harrington's betrothal to Berenice, relies much more heavily on actions taken by Montenero than on religious beliefs passively received by his daughter. Just prior to this scene of revelation and resolution is the episode in which Mr Montenero's house comes under attack during the Gordon Riots. In a sense the Riots can be seen as reprising some of the issues raised by the Jew Bill. Although it was Catholics this time who were the target of agitation, the violent antipathies expressed have much in common with those directed against Jews in 1753. The slogan Edgeworth records as the cry of the mob — 'No Jews, no wooden shoes'[65] — indicates the common ground assumed to exist between the two, since wooden shoes were associated with Catholic monasterial domination over the people of France, an emblem of French despotism as compared with English liberties. Edgeworth uses the Gordon Riots to suggest how detached Harrington has become, by virtue of his sympathetic identification with Mr Montenero and Berenice, from the xenophobic politics of his childhood loyalties so enthusiastically instilled by his father. But Edgeworth also uses the episode to show how Montenero and others like him are essential to the well-being, indeed the survival, of the principles of freedom. Harrington, Montenero, and Berenice are making the house secure against the rioters, when 'two strange female figures'[66] appear, in flight from the mob. Despite the fact that their presence in the house will attract trouble, since the rioters suspect them (wrongly) of being 'concealed papists',[67] Montenero and Berenice gladly harbour them.

This scene has a number of resonances. By providing a secure place of refuge, Montenero – himself an exile of the Inquisition – shows what real liberality is, especially as the two ladies in question are both convinced anti-Semites. In more ways than one, this episode is a prelude to the final scene of the novel, reviving the themes of protection and belonging introduced in the discussion of naturalization early in the story. Montenero's readiness to tolerate hostile opinion is contrasted with the English refusal in 1754 to consider Jews as natural citizens. The economic plot discernible in the allusions to the Jew Bill becomes plainer as Montenero steps in to save the fortunes of Harrington's father. Harrington senior is facing the threatened loss of his fortune as a result of damage caused by rioters, which has severely damaged the financial security of the bank where most of his money is lodged. Hurrying to the bank to see what can be done, he finds Mr Montenero arranging a plan whereby the bank's credit can be restored. Montenero than sets about helping Mr Harrington, giving the 'plain country gentleman'[68] the benefit of his business acumen, and then volunteering a substantial sum to the bank director as security for Harrington's savings. As a result of Montenero's generosity, Harrington senior has to review his opinion of 'dealing with the Jews',[69] forced to recognize that all would have been lost but for Montenero's intervention.

What Edgeworth does at the end of *Harrington* could be seen as an indirect response to Burke's validation of family and establishment and attack on speculation. By showing how Montenero has become a surrogate father to Harrington, setting him an admirable example of integrity, enlightened rationality, self-restraint, and toleration towards those of different religious persuasions, Edgeworth shows how elective affinities can enrich and improve social ties. The vertical forms of transmission favoured by Burke in the *Reflections*, safely contained within the concepts of undisturbed lineage and inherited values, are challenged in Harrington's emulation of and empathy with Montenero. Edgeworth thus uses an apparently conventional marriage-plot for progressive ends. The union between Berenice and Harrington with which the novel closes preserves what Toland would call a 'Union without Uniformity'; the hybridity represented by Berenice remains in the foreground, so that Jewishness is not, as some have suggested, erased. Within a framework of unity, which has the cosmopolitan Montenero joining his fortunes with English Protestants, religious distinctiveness is still given the last word. Harrington senior's ambiguous words of praise for Montenero's integrity and generosity – 'By Jupiter Ammon, none but a good Christian could do this' – is countered by Berenice, whose pointed question is left hanging in the air: 'And why,' said Berenice, laying her hand gently on my father's arm, 'and why not a good Jew?'[70] As a text, *Harrington* itself displays this pluralism, drawing on a cosmopolitan mixture of other texts, but coming to its own very individual and richly informed conclusions about prejudice and family feeling. Profoundly moral, yet far removed from Burke's nativist moral economy, it demonstrates the necessity of moving beyond the narrow religious affiliations of the 'little platoon' if a truly tolerant and stable society is to be achieved. In so doing it ratifies the rights of a new generation to remake their concepts of what is right and natural – to innovate – and to see this innovation as an enrichment rather than as the ruin of society. In the words of Toland:

> such as liv'd before us were the Children or the Youth, and we are the true Antients of the World. And if Experience ... be the most considerable Advantage which grown persons have over the younger sort, then, questionless, the Experience of such as come last into the World must be incomparably greater than of those that were born long before them: for the last Comers enjoy not only all the Stock of their Predecessors, but to it have likewise added their own Observations.[71]

In conclusion, then, we have seen that Burke's own sense of the injustice of anti-Catholic legislation led him to construct a critique of legalized exclusion which came perilously close to echoing the Lockean heresy of government – that a set of laws which persecute a majority cannot be said to be binding. Burke's doubts about the Whig ascendancy's limited concept of religious toleration create a conflict of allegiance for him which he strives to resolve in the *Reflections* by taking up a stance of religious conformity, and attacking his former allies – Dissenters. It is this conflictedness which is exposed when we discover the consistency of vocabulary in Toland's critique of prejudice and Burke's defence of prejudice, and compare Burke's revision of the idea of nature in the *Reflections* with Edgeworth's fictional exploration of the politics of naturalization in eighteenth-century England. As with the concluding words of Edgeworth's novel, we have finally to recognize that Burke's *Reflections* raises more questions about toleration and political inclusiveness than it can ever answer – in short, that it dramatizes its author's own profound ambivalence towards the regime he appears to be defending.

Notes

1 David Bromwich, 'Remember! Remember! Edmund Burke as the Last Defender of Pre-Capitalist Morality', *Times Literary Supplement*, 16 January 1998, p. 3.

2 J. G. A. Pocock, ed., Introduction, *Reflections on the Revolution in France* (Indianapolis: Hackett, 1987), p. ix.

3 J. G. A. Pocock, 'Edmund Burke and the Redefinition of Enthusiasm: The Context as Counter-Revolution', in François Furet and Mona Ozouf, eds, *The French Revolution and the Creation of Modern Political Culture*: Vol. 3: *The Transformation of Political Culture 1789–1848* (Oxford: Pergamon Press, 1989), pp. 19–35; James E. Bradley, *Religion, Revolution and English Radicalism: Nonconformity in Eighteenth-Century Politics and Society* (Cambridge: Cambridge University Press, 1990).

4 Josiah Tucker, *A Treatise Concerning Civil Government* (Gloucester and London: T. Cadell, 1781).

5 'Edmund Burke and the Redefinition of Enthusiasm', p. 25. I have drawn extensively on this article for this outline of the politics of Dissent in the late eighteenth century.

6 Ibid. p. 26.

7 John Toland, *Letters to Serena* (1704; facsimile edn, Stuttgart–Bad Cannstatt: Friedrich Frommann Verlag, 1964), Letter I: The Origin and Force of Prejudices, p. 2.

8 *Letters to Serena*, p. 3.

9 Ibid. p. 4.

10 Ibid. p. 12.

11 Ibid. p. 13.

12 *Reflections*, p. 137.

13 Ibid.

14 Ibid. p. 138.

15 Ibid.

16 Ibid. p. 146.

17 Ibid. p. 137.

18 Ibid. pp. 137, 131.

19 Ibid. p. 140.

20 Ibid.

21 *Letters to Serena*, p. 16.

22 *Reflections*, pp. 146, 138.

23 Ibid. p. 138.

24 For the importance of English Deists to French Enlightenment thought, see J. G. A. Pocock, 'Post-Puritan England and the Problem of the Enlightenment', in Perez Zagorin, ed., *Culture and Politics from Puritanism to the Enlightenment* (Berkeley and Los Angeles: University of California Press, 1980), p. 91. See also Franco Venturi, *Utopia and Reform in the Enlightenment* (Cambridge: Cambridge University Press, 1971). Venturi stresses the association between Deism and republicanism.

25 Iain McCalman, 'Mad Lord George and Madame La Motte: Riot and Sexuality in the Genesis of Burke's *Reflections on the Revolution in France*', *Journal of British Studies*, 35 (1996) p. 366.

26 *Reflections*, p. 135.

27 'Mad Lord George and Madame La Motte', p. 367.

28 *Reflections*, p. 146.

29 'Tracts Relative to the Laws Against Popery in Ireland', in *Works and Correspondence of the Right Honourable Edmund Burke*, 8 vols (London: Francis & John Rivington, 1852), vol. VI, p. 3.

30 *A Letter from the Right Honourable Edmund Burke MP ... to Sir Hercules Langrishe on the subject of the Roman Catholics of Ireland and the Propriety of admitting them to the Elective Franchise, consistently with the Principles of the Constitution as established at the Revolution* (London: J. Debrett, 1792: 2nd edn, corrected), p. 72.

31 'Tracts', *Works and Correspondence*, vol. VI, p. 6.

32 Ibid. p. 26.

33 Ibid. p. 21.

34 Letter from Maria Edgeworth to her cousin Sophy Ruxton, 19 September 1798.

35 See Marilyn Butler's account of these events in her *Maria Edgeworth: A Literary Biography* (Oxford: Clarendon Press, 1972), pp. 136–40.

36 This is amply demonstrated in numerous depictions of Burke throughout his life. See Nicholas K. Robinson, *Edmund Burke: A Life in Caricature* (New Haven and London: Yale University Press, 1996).

37 Frederick Bull MP, speech in the House of Commons in early 1780; cited in Gerald Newman, *The Rise of English Nationalism: A Cultural History 1740–1830* (London: Weidenfeld and Nicolson, 1987), p. 209.

38 Moses Mendelssohn (1729–86), philosopher, pioneer of German Aufklärung and central figure in modern Jewish history.

39 Seamus Deane, *Strange Country: Modernity and Nationhood in Irish writing since 1790* (Oxford: Clarendon Press, 1997), p. 30.

40 *Harrington, A Tale*, and *Ormond, a Tale*, 3 vols (London: R. Hunter, 1817), vol. I, p. 20. Harrington occupies the first volume. New edition published 1999, ed. Susan Manly, in *The Novels and Selected Works of Maria Edgeworth*, 12 vols, General eds: Marilyn Butler, Mitzi Myers and W. J. McCormack (London: Pickering and Chatto).

41 This letter, together with Edgeworth's reply, is reprinted in *The Education of the Heart: The Correspondence of Rachel Mordecai Lazarus and Maria Edgeworth*, ed. Edgar E. MacDonald (Chapel Hill: University of North Carolina Press, 1977), pp. 3–9.

42 Letter from Edgeworth to Rachel Mordecai Lazarus, 4 August 1816, in *Education of the Heart*, p. 8.

43 *Reflections*, p. 60.

44 *Harrington*, vol. I, p. 3.

45 Ibid. p. 15.

46 Ibid. p. 18.

47 *Letters to Serena*, p. 2.

48 Harrington, vol. I, pp. 34–41.

49 Ibid. pp. 37, 40; *Reflections*, p. 97.

50 Harrington, vol. I, p. 41.

51 [John Toland], *Reasons for Naturalizing the Jews in Great Britain and Ireland, on the same Foot with all other Nations* (1714), pp. 18–19.

52 See Thomas W. Perry, *Public Opinion, Propaganda and Politics in Eighteenth-Century England: A Study of the Jew Bill of 1753* (Cambridge, MA: Harvard University Press, 1962), and Todd Endelmann, *The Jews of Georgian England 1714–1830* (Philadelphia: J. P.S. A, 1979) for accounts of the Jew Bill fracas.

53 *Letter to Sir Hercules Langrishe*, p. 45.

54 *Reflections*, p. 61.

55 Ibid. p. 101.

56 Ibid. p. 103.

57 Ibid. p. 238.

58 Ibid. p. 240.

59 Ibid. pp. 83, 79.

60 *Harrington*, vol. I, p. 78.

61 John Toland, *Nazarenus: or, Jewish, Gentile, and Mahometan Christianity* (London, 1718), Preface, pp. iv–v.

62 Price, *Observations on the Importance of the American Revolution* (London: T. Cadell, 1784), p. 2.

63 See *Harrington*, vol. I, pp. 169–70, where Montenero describes his daughter's American childhood, and its freedom from manifestations of religious bigotry, far removed from the more vicious world of 'European prepossessions'. Edgeworth is drawing here on Rachel Mordecai's account of her upbringing as related in her first letter to Edgeworth (*Education of the Heart*, p. 6).

64 *Harrington*, vol. I, p. 202.

65 Ibid. p. 377.

66 Ibid. p. 381.

67 Ibid. p. 383.

68 Ibid. p. 438.

69 Ibid. p. 32.

70 Ibid. p. 521.

71 *Christianity Not Mysterious* (1696; Stuttgart-Bad Cannstatt: Friedrich Frommann Verlag, 1964), pp. 116–17.

8

Reflections on the Act of Union

CLAIRE CONNOLLY

This essay reads the *Reflections on the Revolution in France* as an anticipatory comment on the Act of Union between Britain and Ireland. The Act was passed in January 1800, some years after both the publication of the *Reflections* and the death of its author, and little is known of Edmund Burke's opinion of such a measure. Nonetheless, I wish to argue that the *Reflections* reflect not only on France in 1789 but also, anachronistically, on the Ireland of the future.

I am not the first critic to make a case for the proleptic wisdom of the *Reflections on the Revolution in France*, or to suggest that it has a relevance wider than its original context. Conor Cruise O'Brien exemplifies both these views when he writes that

> Burke's explicit argument is of less importance than the experience which is behind it, the acquired range of feeling both for the great forces of politics and for its detail. The feeling for the great forces reaches the level of the prophetic.[1]

The 'prophetic' ability of the *Reflections* has been understood either as evidence of Burke's political sagacity, even his 'clairvoyance' as Cruise O'Brien puts it, or as a testament to some uncanny quality of the text.[2] Distrusting such hyperbole, E. P. Thompson argues that while 'it is futile to attempt to deny Burke's foresight in anticipating the Terror and Buonopartism', an attempt ought be made to historicize this prescience. Indeed in Thompson's view, it is worth 'arguing that Burke *caused* those things' he seems merely to divine.[3] Despite tending to the mystical view, Conor Cruise O'Brien too insists, as Thompson reminds us, that 'these prophecies were in great measure self-fulfilling'.[4] Further study of the apocalyptic or revelatory tone of much Romantic political commentary, in Britain and in Ireland, or comparison with a fellow anticipator like Malthus could add to these attempts to locate Burke's prophetic abilities in their historical moment. Thomas Paine simply categorizes Burke's prognosticating tendency as another instance of his showy style. 'I can consider Mr. Burke's book in scarcely any other light than a dramatic performance', remarks Paine, reading what later critics understand as an openness to the future as merely an effect of rhetoric: 'It leaves everything to be guessed at, and mistaken.'[5] In the context of my argument here, however, I wish to draw attention to another instance of actual or promised prescience in Burke's own political writings, what W. J. Mc Cormack has described as '[t]he gathering darkness of Burke's utterances on Ireland in his last years'. Intriguingly, Mc Cormack insists that these increasingly apocalyptic pronouncements regarding Ireland's future 'should not be held apart from the stylistic experiments of the *Reflections on the Revolution in France*'.[6] This echoes Tom Paulin's claim that '[i]n Burke's style you see the next two centuries of Irish history waiting to be born'.[7]

In this essay I propose to forge a link between E. P. Thompson's question – how best to read the dimension of the future in the *Reflections*? – and W. J. Mc Cormack's more cryptic observations, which I understand as expressing a need to introduce an awareness of the tenor and texture of Burke's views on Ireland to a stylistically informed reading of the *Reflections*. Mc Cormack himself offers something of both, and is particularly aware of the politics embedded in the narrative method of the *Reflections*. Operating according to contrasting chronologies, he argues, its narrative reveals much of the 'political direction' of the argument. Thus, in the account of British history, 'we are taken back from the present occasion' on a journey which culminates in the Magna Carta. The narrative of French history, on the other hand, travels in the opposite direction and terminates in the present moment, as if in imitation of the French speculators who do not know how to 'look backward to their ancestors'.[8] This alertness to the ideology of narrative time informs Mc Cormack's call for 'a more dynamic' mode of literary history which would allow for a reading of the *Reflections* as having been influenced by later texts: 'the *Reflections*, thus read, is as much influenced by *Castle Rackrent*, the Act of Union, and Yeats's *Collected Poems* as they are influenced by it'.[9]

Locating the *Reflections on the Revolution in France* amidst these particular texts suggests that it too can be read as actively involved in promoting and shaping notions of Irish political identity. Seamus Deane has recently called for Burke's *Reflections on the Revolution in France* to be counted among the formative texts of Irish culture. His *Strange Country: Modernity and Nationhood in Irish Writing since 1790* describes *Reflections on the Revolution in France* as a foundational text, that is

> one that allows or has allowed for a reading of a national literature in such a manner that even chronologically prior texts can be annexed by it into a narrative that will ascribe to them a preparatory role in the ultimate completion of that narrative's plot.[10]

Strange Country proposes a strategic relocation of the *Reflections*'s place in cultural history, an argument made possible by a dynamic reading of the text's own temporality. In arguing that 'even chronologically prior texts can be annexed by it', and, later, that 'the *Reflections* is a text which opens a number of possibilities for the interpretation of earlier and the production of later texts', Deane assigns to *Reflections on the Revolution in France* an anachronistic place in the national narrative, in a move which correlates to Mc Cormack's 'dynamic' cultural history.[11]

Both Deane and Mc Cormack, despite holding divergent views of Burke's legacy, discern an important connection between the temporality of *Reflections on the Revolution in France* and the problematic nationality of its author. It is this nexus of concerns which my essay will explore, offering an analysis of the *Reflections*'s own historical method as the basis of an argument for its relevance to a reading of the Act of Union.

Past history

Seeking to assign blame for the 1798 revolution in Ireland, Sir Richard Musgrave locates as one among its many causes the 'decided attachment to popery' of Edmund Burke.[12] Burke died the year before the insurrection took place, but his political reputation was very much alive in 1801 when Musgrave produced his history of 1798, *Memoirs of the Different Rebellions in Ireland, from the Arrival of the English*. Musgrave analyses the events of 1798 by excavating layers of disloyalty, finding all previous instances of lawlessness to be seamlessly linked, inspired by sectarian hatred and directed towards 'subverting the constitution, and separating Ireland from England, with the assistance of France'.[13] Looking back to the 1760s, for example, Musgrave presents Whiteboy activities[14] in those years as evidence of an 'alarming spirit of insurgency' driven by a desire to overthrow crown rule. The agrarian grievances which actually motivated much Whiteboy activity were only a 'pretext', he claims, disguising seditious and specifically sectarian intent. Thus, the *Memoirs of the Different Rebellions in Ireland* discover a sequence of revolutions marring the pages of Irish history; making it impossible to ever trust in Irish Catholic loyalty and providing irrefutable evidence for the need for the Union with Britain enacted in the year the *Memoirs* were published.

Edmund Burke too was concerned to analyse and define the nature of Whiteboy activity in the 1760s (the last period he would have spent any length of time in Ireland), particularly in the early 1790s when plans to extend limited concessions to Irish Catholics were being discussed. In Kevin Whelan's estimation, 'Burke's critique of the Irish Protestant gentry stemmed in large part from his bruising encounter in the 1760s with Munster Protestants determined to implicate the Catholic gentry, subgentry, and leading merchants in Whiteboy activity.'[15] Burke wrote to Sir Hercules Langrishe in 1792, attempting to persuade him of the benefits of including Irish Catholics in the benefits of the British Constitution, and citing the Whiteboy trials of the 1760s as evidence. These trials involved agrarian outlaws being hanged for treason in a series of highly visible punishments, the public face of what Whelan calls '"red-hot" Munster Protestantism'.[16] Luke Gibbons has argued that for Burke the trials represented 'an imbalance in the calibration of State terror'.[17] Professing his reluctance to enter these controversies anew, Burke nonetheless insists that the prosecution of the Whiteboys resulted from state misreading of crime as conspiracy:

I do not desire to revive all the particulars in my memory – I wish them to sleep for ever; but it is impossible I should wholly forget what happened in some parts of Ireland, with very few and short intermissions, from the year 1761 to the year 1766, both inclusive. In a country of miserable police, passing from the extremes of laxity to the extremes of rigour, – among a neglected, and therefore disorderly populace, – if any disturbance or sedition from any grievance, real or imaginary, happened to arise, it was presently perverted from its true nature, often criminal enough in itself to draw upon it a severe appropriate punishment; it was metamorphosed into a conspiracy against the State, and prosecuted as such.[18]

Burke and Musgrave present radically different visions of the future of the Irish political nation, each drawing on the same event to present opposite conclusions as to the possibility of Catholic loyalty. Burke wishes to put aside previous instances of lawlessness in order to progress towards an enlightened future. Yet one condition of future peace is forgetfulness, and Burke admits to finding this impossible: the past is called up by present circumstances and will not sleep. Musgrave, while only too happy to dwell on the past and its instructive instances of Catholic rebelliousness, is also brought face to face with some more disturbing aspects of Gaelic Ireland. Musgrave's account of Whiteboy trials in Tipperary lingers on the notorious hanging of Father Sheehy in Clonmel,[19] and Kevin Whelan has argued that Sheehy 'haunts his narrative, reappearing like Banquo's ghost at regular intervals'.[20] The description of Sheehy's trial is also the occasion for a heated attack on the parentage and politics of Edmund Burke, whose few appearances in Musgrave's history also have something of the spectral about them. Musgrave presents a luridly detailed and highly conspiratorial account of Burke's secret conversion to Catholicism and asserts that

When the enormities committed by the white boys were about to draw on them the vengeance of the law … Mr. Edmund Burke sent his brother Richard … and Mr. Nagle, a relation, on a mission to Munster, to levy money on the popish body, for the use of the white boys, who were exclusively papists.[21]

In order to elucidate these charges, Musgrave feels it is necessary to touch on some circumstances of Burke's life, but like Burke himself professes a reluctance to delve into the past, undertaking it only as a sad but necessary evil. Musgrave has no wish 'to disparage him' or to impugn 'his exalted moral and intellectual excellence'.[22] After all,

> His book on French affairs contains more political wisdom, and more profound knowledge of practical government, than any that ever appeared; and in future ages will tend to endear the British constitution to its subjects.
>
> The bright effulgence of his genius, like the sun, raised up some buzzing insects, who cavilled at the doctrines which he advanced; but the state of France proves the futility of their assertions, and that he spoke prophetic truth.[23]

Here, it is the enduring value of the *Reflections on the Revolution in France*, Burke's 'book on French affairs', which 'in future ages will tend to endear the British constitution to its subjects'. This is in turn connected to a kind of future knowledge of events in France, the 'prophetic truth' of Burke's political vision.

Accusing the revered prophet of British constitutionalism of being a Catholic spy gets Musgrave into rhetorical difficulty, a dilemma he tries to solve by separating out (as many critics have done since) the two Burkes: one reflecting on France and turned towards the future of the British empire, the other dwelling in Ireland and the domain of the past. To this end, Musgrave seeks to prove that Burke was embroiled in Irish history. Discussing the 1641 rebellion, the uprising of Ulster Catholics remembered with particular horror by Irish and English Protestants alike, he states with certainty that 'Mr. Edmund Burke seriously intended to have written a history of that rebellion, for no other purpose but to vindicate the Roman catholicks from the odium which they brought on themselves by it'.[24] The force of this accusation is best understood in the terms offered by Joep Leerssen, who points out that in the eighteenth century '"1641" served largely as a paradigmatic example of the untrustworthiness and bloodthirst of Catholics, and, hence, as a cornerstone in the political thought of which the penal laws were the juridical expression'.[25]

Attempts to produce a more balanced or palliative account of 1641 were current from the early eighteenth century onwards, but Musgrave is openly hostile towards these revisions, and produces this last piece of 'evidence' against Burke as decisive.

Unlike the accusations of conversion to Catholicism, however, there is clear proof of Burke's interest in 1641. Describing in a letter how he has studied Irish history 'with more Care than is common', Burke delivers his opinion of 1641 with less than his customary reticence regarding Ireland:

> That the Irish rebellion of 1641 was not only (as our silly things called Historys call it), not utterly *unprovoked* but that no History, that I have ever read furnishes an Instance of any that was so *provoked*'. And that 'in almost all parts of it, it has been extremely and most absurdly misrepresented.[26]

Such was the controversy that continued to surround 1641 that Burke is certain of being himself misrepresented. Entering into discussion of the rebellion involves him in 'an ugly Dilemma': he will either be construed as 'a friend to Rebellion' or a supine follower of 'the doctrines of passive Obedience', misunderstood in either case.[27] The danger of such 'misrepresentations' greatly increased after the 1798 insurrection, which inevitably revived memories of 1641 and made it even less likely that the past would rest comfortably in 'our silly things called Historys'. The *Reflections on the Revolution in France* abhors what it calls the 'ransacking' of history to meet the angry demands of the present moment, but, I will argue, itself effects just such a fluid interpenetration of time frames.[28]

Future history

Dorinda Outram argues that, because of the way in which the French Revolution has attracted 'totalizing interpretations', 'the history of the Revolution and the history of the future have traditionally been wrapped up in each other'.[29] According to Seamus Deane, it is the revision of the past in the *Reflections* which brings the future into view. As with romantic nationalism and Anglican romanticism, Deane argues, '[n]ostalgia was the dynamic that impelled the search for the future.'[30] In what follows, I show how the *Reflections* annexes the future for the forces of counter-revolution, transforming what Deane describes as nostalgia for ancestry into the demands of posterity, understood as what future generations expect of the present.

The paradox of positing nostalgia as the motor force of the future is intensified when one considers the revolutionary charge of the idea of the future. Marquis de Condorcet's *Outline of a Historical Table of the Progress of the Human Mind* asks

> If man can predict with almost complete certainty the phenomena whose laws he understands, and even if when these laws are unknown to him he can predict future events with great probability on the basis of the past, why should it be regarded as a chimerical undertaking to delineate, with some degree of truth, the future of mankind from the results of its past?[31]

Condorcet here is describing the beginning of the progress towards human perfection (his 'tenth era') and offers the idea that the past carries the traces of the future as a revolutionary proposition.[32] The future is also the tense of Irish nationalist thought, according to David Lloyd, who reads W. B. Yeats's 'Easter 1916' as posing the question of 'the relation between the singular moment in which a nation is founded or constituted and the future history of the citizens it brings into being'.[33] Luke Gibbons observes that the United Irishmen who led the 1798 rebellion self-consciously adopted the revolutionary turn to the future, effecting 'a radical break with the past and with romantic nostalgia'.[34] In associating 'we have thought little about our ancestors and much of our posterity', declared one Dublin United Irish society.[35]

Reflections on the Revolution in France works against the grain of such assumptions, however, repeatedly invoking the future as the rationale for counter-revolution. It is the future, the *Reflections* contends, which France in its revolutionary fervour, appears to have forgotten. Discussing the social contract, for example, the text concedes that while '[s]ociety is indeed a contract', it is not one that can be dissolved at will precisely because of the obligation to the future. The social contract which constitutes the tie between state, monarch, and people 'is to be looked on with other reverence; because it is not a partnership in things subservient only to the gross animal existence of a temporary and perishable nature'.[36] Rather than a merely commercial arrangement which would end within generations, 'it becomes a partnership not only between those who are living, but between those who are living, those who are dead, and those who are to be born'.[37]

One of the central assertions of the *Reflections on the Revolution in France* is that history is best understood as a repository of moral lessons, which the current generation must learn to read, and read properly: 'In history a great volume is unrolled for our instruction, drawing the materials of future wisdom from the past errors and infirmities of mankind'.[38] To this extent, the *Reflections* partake of an eighteenth-century sense of history as an instructive chronicle, providing models of virtuous human society. It both reproduces the conventional wisdom that 'All history is only the precepts of Moral Philosophy reduc'd into Examples' and privileges history as the repository of community.[39] In Roy Porter's summary of the conservative Georgian sense of history (the line in which he places Burke) 'the past seemed to hold the key to the present, through having laid down positive (albeit fiercely contested) and binding title-deeds of legitimacy: political, legal and ecclesiastical'.[40]

Alerting readers to the potential 'perversion' of history, however, the *Reflections* also acknowledges the pliability of the past, which may,

> in the perversion, serve for a magazine, furnishing offensive and defensive weapons for parties in church and state, and supplying the means of keeping alive, or reviving dissensions and animosities, and adding fuel to civil fury.[41]

Considering some differences between eighteenth- and nineteenth-century modes of historiography, Karen O'Brien turns to Burke as a figure who sits on the cusp of a new understanding of historicity. His early *Essay Towards an Abridgment of the English History* seeks to counter a belief in the immemorial, yet it is ironic, as O'Brien notes, that it is in this essay that Burke 'discerns a tendency in British cultural life which he would later help to accelerate; the discovery of inherent value in history itself'.[42] This latter tendency is strongly present in the *Reflections,* which having warned against potential 'perversion' of the past then assigns positive value to the rhetorical figure 'history', seemingly above such corruption. The text thus invokes and indeed anticipates another understanding of the past as it looks forward to 'history, in the nineteenth century, better understood, and better employed'.[43]

Discussing the history of the next century – whether as a particular kind of narrative or a certain body of facts – draws the *Reflections* into a contemplation of the future and of posterity. This future history, the history of the future, will not invoke the past merely to excuse present atrocities, as the citizens of Paris were roused against the Archbishop of Paris when they watched an actor in the role of the sixteenth-century Cardinal of Lorraine 'ordering general slaughter' during a stage performance of the St Bartholomew's Day Massacre.[44] Instead, Burke trusts, history in the nineteenth century will 'teach a civilized posterity to abhor the misdeeds of both these barbarous ages':[45]

> It will teach future priests and magistrates not to retaliate upon the speculative and inactive atheists of future times, the enormities committed by the present practical zealots and furious fanatics of that wretched error, which, in its quiescent state, is more than punished, whenever it is embraced.

This history will teach a future establishment not to misread the past in its dealings with future revolutionaries. Furthermore,

> It will teach posterity not to make war upon either religion or philosophy, for the abuse which the hypocrites of both have made of the two most valuable blessings conferred upon us by the bounty of the universal Patron, who in all things eminently favours and protects the race of man.[46]

In dealing with the past then, which is the present of the narrative, history in the nineteenth century will work to inculcate timeless values and universal blessings.

This faith in the 'inherent value in history itself' is somewhat shaken, however, not in what the *Reflections* says, but in what it says. Marilyn Butler has commented on how 'unlike eighteenth-century history, nineteenth-century history is still with us as a current method'.[47] One of the central tenets of this method is a certain temporal continuity, whereby the account of an event follows the occurence of that event. But in writing of the Terror before it occurred, the *Reflections* reverses the usual chronology of event and narration in which an event occurs and is then followed by an account of that event. In the course of Conor Cruise O'Brien's observations on Burke's prophetic abilities, quoted above, he describes the uncanny effect generated by this reversal:

> Reading Burke with classes, I have found that undergraduates readily assume that the *Reflections* occur at a much later stage in the Revolution than is actually the case: that the September Massacres, the execution of the King and Queen, the Terror, have already happened, whereas of course they all lie in the future.[48]

For Conor Cruise O'Brien's students, the *Reflections* belong to the past and are read as unproblematically reflecting back on that past. Yet in leaping forward as it does, the rhetoric of *Reflections* disrupts that stable sequence, anachronistically anticipating the future. To further grasp the anticipatory reach of the *Reflections*, it is worth noting that the faith in linear narratives which the text upsets is in many ways a product of that nineteenth-century history so confidently predicted by Burke.

Anachronism is of course central to the process of history-writing itself. In her study of the historiography of the French Revolution, Ann Rigney argues that 'the crowd which set out in search of arms on the morning of 14 July 1789' were not to know they were participating in 'Bastille Day' or the meaning which later events would lend their actions, as '[e]ach new, unforeseen development can cast new light on the original events (the historical signifiers) and retroactively change their significance'.[49] Later events consist of the Terror, Napoleon, and 1848; but also the histories of Lamartine, Michelet, and Blanc, so that

> historical discourse must be seen as 'anachronistically' situated with respect to its object: it represents past events at the same time as it considers them retrospectively from a particular distance and reveals their significance for a later public.[50]

The position described by Rigney is clearly one of some power, and the *Reflections* offers narrative confirmation of this cultural authority, evincing a keen and productive awareness of the anachronisms of historical discourse in its account of the duties owed to the King and Queen of France.

At once drawing on historical expectations and invoking future interpretations, Burke heaps scorn on the feeble request made by a 'miserable' assembly that their equally miserable king might 'forget the stormy period' that had passed:[51]

Yielding to reasons, at least as forcible as those which were so delicately urged in the compliment on the new year, the king of France will probably endeavour to forget these events, and that compliment. But history, who keeps a durable record of all our acts, and exercises her awful censure over the proceedings of all sorts of sovereigns, will not forget, either those events, or the aera of this liberal refinement in the intercourse of mankind. History will record, that on the morning of the 6th of October 1789, the king and queen of France, after a day of confusion, alarm, dismay, and slaughter, lay down, under the pledged security of public faith, to indulge nature in a few hours of respite, and troubled melancholy repose.[52]

The certainty found here and in the subsequent famous description of the violation of the queen's chamber as to what history will record gives the passage much of its force. But this confidence as to the subsequent meaning of events is anachronistic in the sense described by Rigney, in representing past events while on the point of retrospectively revealing their significance for a later public.

Furthermore, as becomes increasingly clear in this section of the text, the process of lending retrospective significance involves the text in elaborately fictional methods and effects. Following on the image of king and queen wishing only 'to indulge nature in a few hours of respite, and troubled melancholy repose', we have the characters of the loyal sentinel and the 'persecuted woman' fleeing naked through the corridors, the palace 'swimming in blood'.[53] In depicting these events, now in the past, the text is not just alert to their future meaning, but more specifically to the way in which the meanings of history are open to narrative negotiation. The events are unfinished, awaiting the intervention of the future:

The actual murder of the king and queen, and their child, was wanting to the other auspicious circumstances of this '*beautiful day.*' The actual murder of the bishops, though called for by so many holy ejaculations, was also wanting. A group of regicide and sacrilgious slaughter, was indeed boldly sketched, but it was only sketched. It unhappily was left unfinished, in this great history-piece of the massacre of innocents.[54]

In ironically voicing the views of millenarian thinkers and

revolutionaries, the narrative entwines its reflective judgements with revolutionary rhetoric and opens up a radical view of history.

The *Reflections* pursues the metaphor of a 'history-piece', an image which underlines the ambivalent meanings of 'history'. Writing of human participation in history as a dual process of acting and narrating, Michel-Rolph Trouillot observes that 'history means ... both "what happened" and "that which is said to have happened"'.[55] In asking what will have happened, the *Reflections* is drawn into a heightened awareness of this ambivalence: 'What hardy pencil of a great master, from the school of the rights of men, will finish it, is to be seen hereafter.'[56] Here, the questions of what will happen and who will write it are seen to be inextricable from each other. The past contains the outlines of a present which the future will fill in. It is the 'hardy pencil of a great master' which will produce the truth of the event, which will determine what will have happened. For Slavoj Žižek, it is this future anterior tense (what will have happened) which best conveys the inscription of the past in language, its meaning changing 'with the transformations of the signifier's network':[57]

> The past exists as it is included, as it enters (into) the synchronous net of the signifier – that is, as it is symbolized in the texture of the historical memory – and that is why we are all the time 're-writing history', retroactively giving the elements their symbolic weight by including them in new textures – it is this elaboration which decides retroactively what they 'will have been'.[58]

As with 'history, in the nineteenth century, better understood, and better employed'[59] the future contains the key to the meaning of the past. In the terms offered by Žižek: '[s]ymptoms are meaningless traces, their meaning is not discovered, excavated from the hidden depth of the past, but constructed retroactively'.[60] History is not merely a storehouse of facts to be drawn on. The *Reflections* do not simply find helpful evidence in the facts of the Glorious Revolution, rather they enact that past. As with the revolutionaries who staged a performance of the St Bartholomew's Day massacre in order to excite the 'cannibal appetites' of the Parisian public, the past so revered in the *Reflections* is filled with what Žižek calls 'the dimension of the future'.[61]

Paper ties

Following on this reading of the *Reflections* as a text turned towards the future, I wish to offer a reading of the Act of Union as revolutionary, in the sense of that word articulated by Burke during the course of his reflections on France.

What would have been Burke's view of the Act of Union? Seamus Deane offers one answer to my question. He reimagines the history of late eighteenth- and early nineteenth-century Ireland through Burke's eyes and concludes that the French Revolution, the Act of Union and Catholic Emancipation (eventually granted in 1829) can be gathered into a gradualist narrative of Anglo-Irish relations as 'the history of a consolidated effort, frustrated by prejudice but implacable in its direction, to recruit Irish Catholics into the Union with the help of the Irish Catholic Church while appeasing the endless fears and bigotries of Irish Protestants'.[62] W. J. Mc Cormack points out that 'speculation as to whether he would have been unionist or anti-unionist is largely pointless' but also maintains that Burke desired ever closer ties between Britain and Ireland: 'England and Ireland were bound together in the imperial system: this was as firmly held by Burke as his eloquent denunciation of the Irish undertakers of English policy in Ireland.'[63]

What emerges from these free indirect voicings of Burke's beliefs is an understanding of Anglo-Irish history as progressing, albeit slowly and with some difficulty, in the general direction of greater tolerance and mutual understanding between the countries. Deane designates this liberal view, of which he is stringently suspicious, 'the Burkean programme'. Rather than further analyse or excoriate the nature of that metanarrative, however, I wish to offer an interpretation of the Act of Union which reads the *Reflections* against 'the Burkean programme'.

For Sir Richard Musgrave, the Act is a 'radical remedy' designed to secure Irish loyalty in what Kevin Whelan describes as an offensive move in 'the zero sum game of sectarian Irish arithmetic, where the oppressive weight of Catholic numbers threatened to obliterate the political control of the frail Anglican minority'.[64] Whelan quotes Musgrave on the figures: 'In a menacing tone, the papists have told us for some years "we are 3 to 1". With the Union, we may retort, "we are 11 to 3".'[65] According to the *Reflections on the Revolution in France*, 'the constitution of a kingdom' is emphatically not

> a problem of arithmetic. This sort of discourse does well enough with the lamp-post for its second: to men who *may* reason calmly, it is ridiculous. The will of the many, and their interest, must very often differ; and great will be the difference when they make an evil choice.[66]

Read alongside Musgrave's belligerent use of the number argument, the opposition of the forces of 'the lamp-post' to the men of reason may be seen as revealing the aggression of the Protestant state.

Clearly, Burke produces the argument against arithmetic as a brake on democracy, but it is possible to extend this into an analysis of the proper conduct of power, which so concerns Burke in all his political writings. In his last letter on Irish affairs, written in the 1790s, Burke insisted that the most fruitful way to improve Anglo-Irish relations was not to reform the law or to pass acts of parliament, but to work on the 'disposition of the ruling power'. Mutual trust and understanding, made possible by appeals to the 'men who *may* reason calmly', contain the best hope for the future:

> Men do not live upon blotted paper. The favourable or the hostile mind of the ruling power is of far more importance to mankind, for good or evil, than the black letter of any statute.[67]

W. J. Mc Cormack offers this description of the difference the Union makes to 'the history of Ireland's relations with England':

> In the eighteenth century this can be identified principally as the Monarchy or, more abstractly, the Protestant Succession: the king of England was also the king of Ireland. In the nineteenth century, we speak of the United Kingdom, and the significant alteration is not simply the Union but the emphasis on the kingdom, or, more abstractly, the state.[68]

In the terms offered by Mc Cormack, the Union makes the inclination of the monarchy, the 'disposition of the ruling power', visible as the force of the state.

Burke's preference for bonds of emotion over paper ties is

familiar from the *Reflections on the Revolution in France*. When Samuel Span, one of Burke's Bristol constituents, proposed the idea of a legislative union in the 1770s (believing that the issue of free trade with Ireland could be resolved in this way) Burke responds thus:

> I wish to have as close an union of interest and affection with Ireland as I can have; and that, I am sure, is a far better thing than any nominal union of government.[69]

This distinction can be recast as the difference between 'blotted paper' and the kindly sentiments of the monarchy, and it is in the light of this distrust of a 'nominal union' that I would read W. J. Mc Cormack's important observation that 'the union was (and is) universally referred to as the Act of Union' and it is here too that I would suggest Union begins to disrupt the Burkean programme.[70] In asserting rather than assuming the relationship between Ireland and Britain, the Act of Union decisively shifted Anglo-Irish relations into the statute books and thus into the realm of print, debate, and discussion.

On further examination, the nature of Burke's distrust of Union as a legislative measure relates directly to this problem of discussion, especially speculation. The letter to Samuel Span cited above reminds Span of the impropriety of even debating Union:

> You tell me, Sir, that you prefer an union with Ireland to the little regulations which are proposed in parliament. This union is a great question of state, to which, when it comes properly before me in my parliamentary capacity, I shall give an honest and unprejudiced consideration. However, it is a settled rule with me, to make the most of my *actual situation* ...[71]

Here, Union belongs to the future and thus to the realm of speculation and Burke refuses to take this conjectural discussion any further '[u]ntil it can be matured into a feasible and desirable scheme'. Burke's reluctance may be simply on practical grounds: the editors of the correspondence comment that there is no evidence that Union was being discussed in the 1770s, so it seems that Span had the Union with Scotland in mind as a model here. But in a letter written in 1794 – some sixteen years later – union is still a dangerously speculative proposition.

Writing to Earl Fitzwilliam on his being appointed viceroy in Dublin, Burke himself raises the subject of Union, but in a manner which suggests great unease:

> As to the Union, I do not exactly know in what manner it has come before you. If your Lordships Colleagues in the Cabinet have adopted the Scheme, it is probable that they have formed some plan for carrying it into execution. A great deal of the merit of the measure itself will depend on that plan. But if it be merely an Idea floating in their minds, I am of the opinion it ought not to be hastily entertaind, or even very publickly discussed.

The Union belongs to the realm of theory and is, according to Burke 'perfectly impracticable'. As in the *Reflections*, theory is dangerous territory:

> I always looked upon an Union, even under Circumstances infinitely more favourable than any that now exist, as a bold experimental remedy, justified, perhaps called for, in some nearly desperate Crisis of the whole Empire. If it were to be proposed now, it would be argued merely as a speculative question; but not with the coldness which might be expected in a dry speculation.[72]

Read in the light of the *Reflections*, what the Act of Union offers Ireland can be understood as a speculative proposition. Just as the French revolutionaries sought to replace ancient and un-written rules with 'paltry, blurred shreds of paper about the rights of man', so Ireland is being offered a new paper tie, a written arrangement, which threatens the old fealties, secured only by the 'real hearts of flesh and blood beating in our bosoms'.[73]

One contemporary commentator described the need for Union to be coupled with Catholic Emancipation as 'the plainest of all political truths' and yet the proposals gave rise to something of a paper war.[74] W. J. Mc Cormack has comprehensively documented the pamphlet debate around union and concludes that the issue gave rise to 'more than 250 separate publications'.[75] 'It has been the misfortune ... of this age, that every thing is to be discussed, as if the constitution of our country were to be always a subject rather of altercation than enjoyment', comments the *Reflections*.[76] Despite its status as a classic statement of English-ness, the *Reflections* maintains that English liberty is defined by its unwritten status, the quiet confidence most famously manifested in the image of the 'thousands of great cattle, reposed beneath the shadow of the British oak'.[77] As with Jonathan Swift, read by Seamus Deane as 'promissorily Burkean', what is striking here is 'the extraordinary rhetorical innovativeness' put to the service of an avowedly unassuming position.[78] Burke was of course well aware that Irish Catholics did not fully enjoy the benefits of the British constitution, but the possibility of 'altercation' was to be treated with great caution.

To return to Musgrave, he does finally link those aspects of Burke's career he tends to keep separate, specifically accounting for the concessions made to Catholics in 1792 by blaming Burke's 'book on French affairs'. The Dublin Catholic Committee had employed Burke's son Richard as their representative and their ensuing (limited) successes 'may be accounted for in the following manner':

> Knowing that Mr. Edmund Burke, a warm favourer of popery, had in a high degree conciliated the esteem of our gracious sovereign, and the government of England, by his ingenious and energetic writings against the extravagant theories and frantick proceedings of the French republicans; they resolved to employ his son, an over-weening, petulant young man, to be their agent, in forwarding their pretensions; hoping thereby to ensure the weight and consideration of his father for that purpose.[79]

Here, the reputation of the *Reflections* allows Richard Burke to accumulate political capital for the Irish Catholic interest. Whether Musgrave's heated accusations have any historical validity or not, it has been my argument that the *Reflections* does open up a different understanding of Anglo-Irish relations in the late eighteenth century. A focus on the Act – rather than the fact – of Union allows us to read the Union not so much as another stage in the inexorable march towards closer ties with Britain, but rather as a disruptive and even revolutionary moment; a piece of legislation which offered a problematic answer to a connection which many contemporary observers would have preferred not to call into question.

The subsequent history of the Act bears this reading out. A great number of Irish Protestants did indeed fear the revolutionary potential of Catholic Emancipation, legislation for which was originally linked with Union. The future history of

Catholic nationalism was to derive paradoxical benefit from the
'nominal union' between the kingdoms. Organizing itself around
the twin campaigns for Catholic Emancipation and for repeal of
the Union, mass Catholic nationalism emerged out of a sophisticated understanding of the basis of Anglo-Irish relations. Oliver
MacDonagh reminds us that '[l]iterally interpreted, repeal was
politically nonsensical' in the early nineteenth century, and that
the campaign constituted not so much an expression of a positive
desire to overturn the Act of Union, as 'an invitation to treat, an
attempt to *elicit* a proposition from the British government'.[80]
Read as part of the future history of *Reflections on the Revolution
in France*, the Act of Union emerges as a precarious political
gesture. Possibly the best evidence of the complexity and confusion of contemporary responses to the Union is found in a
series of drawings by Burke's friend and fellow countryman,
James Barry. As Luke Gibbons has shown, Barry was among
those who 'initially welcomed' the projected Union in the belief
that it would be linked with emancipation legislation and produced these drawings in preparation for an allegorical depiction
of the Act of Union.[81] The painting was never executed, however, and the allegory was to remain incomplete.[82]

Phantom Union

I do not wish to overemphasize what I have been describing as
the revolutionary aspect of the Union. It offered little in the way
of attention to 'the rights of man' and undoubtedly did transform
the Catholic majority of Ireland into an insignificant minority
within the empire. Yet this sense of its minority status became
politicized around the campaigns for Catholic emancipation and
Repeal of the Union, both orchestrated by Daniel O'Connell
whose 'monster meetings' of disenfranchised Irish Catholics are
sometimes credited with being the first appearance of the mob on
the Irish historical stage. For O'Connell a novel by Thomas
Moore, *Captain Rock* (1824) represented the *Uncle Tom's Cabin* of
the movement for Catholic Emancipation.[83] Its protagonist, Captain
Rock, relates the history of Ireland as a story of ancestral insur-
gence against English rule. Each generation has a new instance of
English perfidy to deal with and for him, it is the Act of Union.

Captain Rock vividly describes 'the foul bribes, out of which that unnatural measure arose' and makes use of a contemporary literary reference for effect: the Union is, 'like Frankenstein's ghastly patch-work, made up of contributions from the whole charnel-house of political corruption'.[84] He sees the Union emerging from the violent conflict of 1798 and the venality of the Irish parliament:

> the Union, a measure rising out of corruption and blood, and clothed in promises put on only to betray, was the phantom by which the dawn of the Nineteenth century was welcomed.[85]

Here Union is represented as a phantom, a bloody ghost set to haunt the future.

Disguise is given a discernibly theatrical turn in Moore's description, as the Union looms over the future like the vampires that dominated the stages of nineteenth-century theatres. The 'phantom' status assigned to the Union by Moore's protagonist transforms the actual event into a dangerous political fantasy, blurring the lines between theatrical stage and parliamentary platform. *Captain Rock* leaves the reader with a powerful image of the Union as undead, a spirit set to assume different shapes. For Edmund Burke, like Captain Rock, measures that promise reform have a spectral dimension, making it difficult to name the dangers that are passing before your eyes. 'You are terrifying yourself with ghosts and apparitions', he tells his young correspondent in Paris, 'whilst your house is the haunt of robbers'. Like the spectral spirit of wickedness, the fantasy of Anglo-Irish relations contained in the Act of Union has proved to be 'a little more inventive'.[86]

Notes

1 Conor Cruise O'Brien, Introduction to Edmund Burke, *Reflections on the Revolution in France* (Harmondsworth: Penguin, 1986), p. 71.

2 Ibid. p. 72.

3 E. P. Thompson, 'In the Gentlemen's Cause', Review of Conor Cruise O'Brien, *The Great Melody: A Thematic Biography of Edmund Burke*, *Times Literary Supplement*, 4 December 1992, 3–4, p. 3.

4 Cruise O'Brien, Introduction, p. 72.

5 Thomas Paine, *The Rights of Man, Part 1*, in Bruce Kuklik, ed., *Thomas*

Paine: Political Writings (Cambridge: Cambridge University Press, 1989), pp. 71, 73. I am grateful for Helmut Pietsch for drawing attention to the significance of Paine in this context.

6 W. J. Mc Cormack, *From Burke to Beckett: Ascendancy, Tradition and Betrayal in Literary History* (Cork: Cork University Press, 1994), p. 54.

7 Quoted in Luke Gibbons, 'Edmund Burke on Our Present Discontents', *History Ireland*, 5:4 (Winter 1997), pp. 21–5. See also William O'Brien's assertion that 'England spent six humiliating generations in learning from O'Connell and from Parnell and from the Irish revolution of 1916 what the genius of Burke would have revealed to her in a prophetic flash'. William O'Brien, *Edmund Burke as an Irishman* (Dublin: M. H. Gill and Son, 1924), p. 272.

8 Mc Cormack, *From Burke to Beckett*, p. 31; *Reflections*, p. 83.

9 Mc Cormack, *From Burke to Beckett*, p. 44.

10 Seamus Deane, *Strange Country: Modernity and Nationhood in Irish Writing since 1790* (Oxford: Clarendon Press, 1997), p. 1.

11 Ibid. p. 3.

12 Richard Musgrave, *Memoirs of the Different Rebellions in Ireland, from the Arrival of the English* (2nd edn, Dublin, 1801), p. 35.

13 Ibid. p. 33.

14 Prominent in Munster in the 1760s, the Whiteboys were one of a number of eighteenth-century Irish 'agrarian redresser movements', to use Kevin Whelan's term. Consisting of secret societies which arose in response to local injustices, often in taxation and rent, disguised men dressed in white (and sometimes as women) visited violent revenge on offending landlords. The wearing of Stuart white and the allegorical invocation of powerful female figures links the Whiteboys to the Jacobite cause, but recent historiography has attributed more complex allegiances and motivations to Whiteboy activity, connecting them to wider European trends in popular protest. See Kevin Whelan, 'An Underground Gentry? Catholic Middlemen in Eighteenth-Century Ireland', in James Donnelly Jr and Kerby A. Miller, eds, *Irish Popular Culture, 1650–1850* (Dublin: Irish Academic Press, 1998), pp. 118–72: p. 150; and Luke Gibbons, *Transformations in Irish Culture* (Cork: Cork University Press, 1996), pp. 141–3. For Burke's knowledge of Whiteboy activities see O'Brien, *Edmund Burke as Irishman*, pp. 71–85, and Louis Cullen, 'Burke, Ireland and Revolution', *Eighteenth-Century Life*, 16 (February 1992), pp. 21–42: pp. 26–33.

15 Whelan, 'An Underground Gentry?', p. 162.

16 Ibid.

17 Luke Gibbons, 'Customs in Common', paper delivered at 'Edmund Burke and our Present Discontents' conference held at Goldsmiths' College, University of London, July 1997.

18 Edmund Burke, 'A Letter to Sir Hercules Langrishe, M.P., on the Subject of the Roman Catholics of Ireland, and the Propriety of admitting them to

the Elective Franchise, Consistently with the Principles of the Constitution, as estabiushed at the Revolution, 1792' in Matthew Arnold, ed.,
Irish Affairs: Edmund Burke (London: Cresset Library, 1988), pp. 206–78:
p. 219.

19 Luke Gibbons's essay 'Customs in Common' contains a full discussion of
the relevance of the Fr Sheehy case for Burke's politics.

20 Kevin Whelan, *The Tree of Liberty: Radicalism, Catholicism and the
Construction of Irish Identity: 1760–1830* (Cork: Cork University Press,
1996), p. 135.

21 Musgrave, *Memoirs of the Different Rebellions*, p. 38.

22 Ibid. p. 35.

23 Ibid.

24 Ibid. p. 28.

25 Joep Leerssen, *Mere Irish and Fíor-Ghael: Studies in the Idea of Irish
Nationality, its Development and Literary Expression prior to the Nineteenth
Century* (2nd edn, Cork: Cork University Press, 1996), p. 332.

26 Edmund Burke to Dr William Markham [post 9 November 1771], *Correspondence*, vol. II, p. 285. Although Burke never wrote a history of the
1640s, he took it upon himself to 'urge a very learned and Ingenious friend',
Thomas Leland, to undertake the project. Leland's *History of Ireland from
the Invasion of Henry II* appeared in 1773 but Burke disapproved of
Leland's vacillating between competing accounts and his willingness to
repeat tales of Catholic atrocities.

27 Burke to Dr William Markham, *Correspondence*, vol. II, p. 285.

28 *Reflections*, p. 189.

29 Dorinda Outram, '"Rousseau's Stutter": The French Revolution, Philosophy
and the History of the Future', in Ciaran Brady, ed., *Ideology and the
Historians*, Historical Studies XVII (Dublin: Lilliput Press, 1991), pp. 66–
76: p. 66.

30 Deane, *Strange Country*, p. 2.

31 Condorcet, *Outline of a Historical Table of the Progress of the Human Mind*;
quoted in Morroe Berger, 'An Introduction to the Life and Thought of
Madame de Staël', *Madame de Staël on Politics, Literature, and National
Character* (Garden City, New York: Doubleday, 1964), pp. 1–89: p. 43.

32 Berger, pp. 42–4. Berger also discusses the Futuribles organization,
founded in the early 1960s by the French philosopher Bertrand de Jouvenel
'to promote the scientific study of the future' (p. 45).

33 David Lloyd, *Anomalous States: Irish Writing and the Post-Colonial Moment*
(Dublin: Lilliput Press, 1993), p. 71. See also David Lloyd, *Nationalism and
Minor Literature: James Clarence Mangan and the Emergence of Irish
Cultural Nationalism* (Berkeley, Los Angeles and London: University of
California Press, 1987).

34 Luke Gibbons, '"A Shadowy Narrator": History, Art and Romantic

Nationalism in Ireland, 1750–1850', in Brady, ed., *Ideology and the Historians*, pp. 99–127: p. 99.

35 R. B. McDowell, *Ireland in the Age of Imperialism and Revolution, 1760–1801* (Oxford: Clarendon Press, 1979), p. 371; quoted in Gibbons, 'A Shadowy Narrator', p. 99.

36 *Reflections*, p. 147.

37 Ibid.

38 Ibid. p. 189.

39 John Dryden; quoted in Joseph M. Levine, *The Battle of the Books: History and Literature in the Augustan Age* (Ithaca and London: Cornell University Press, 1991), p. 275.

40 Roy Porter, *Gibbon: Making History* (London: Phoenix, 1988), p. 26.

41 *Reflections*, p. 247.

42 Karen O'Brien, *Narratives of Enlightenment: Cosmopolitan History from Voltaire to Gibbon* (Cambridge: Cambridge University, 1997), pp. 18–19. See *An Essay towards an Abridgment of the English History*, in Paul Langford, ed., *The Writings and Speeches of Edmund Burke*, 3 vols, ed. T.O. McLoughlin and James T. Boulton, *The Early Writings*, vol. I (Oxford: Clarendon Press, 1997).

43 *Reflections*, p. 192.

44 Ibid. p. 191.

45 Ibid. p. 192.

46 Ibid.

47 Marilyn Butler, 'Against Tradition: The Case for a Particularized Historical Method', in Jerome McGann, ed., *Historical Studies and Literary Criticism* (Madison, Wisconsin and London: University of Wisconsin Press, 1985), pp. 25–47: p. 28.

48 Cruise O'Brien, Introduction, p. 71.

49 Ann Rigney, *The Rhetoric of Historical Representation: Three Narrative Histories of the French Revolution* (Cambridge: Cambridge University Press, 1990), p. 14.

50 Ibid.

51 *Reflections*, p. 120.

52 Ibid. p. 121.

53 Ibid. p. 122.

54 Ibid. p. 123.

55 Michel-Rolph Trouillot, *Silencing the Past: Power and the Production of History* (Boston: Beacon Press, 1995), p. 2.

56 *Reflections*, p. 123.

57 Slavoj Žižek, *The Sublime Object of Ideology* (London and New York: Verso, 1989), p. 56.

58 Ibid. p. 56. Žižek is adhering to a Lacanian psychoanalytical framework, so the 'journey into the past' refers to the process of analysis as well as the narration of history. His discussion deconstructs the opposition between personal and political history, and uses the notion of transference to examine the relationship between past, present, and future (p. 56).

59 *Reflections*, p. 192; Žižek, *The Sublime Object of Ideology*, p. 138.

60 Žižek, *The Sublime Object of Ideology*, pp. 55–6.

61 *Reflections*, p. 250.

62 Deane, *Strange Country*, p. 20.

63 Mc Cormack, *From Burke to Beckett*, pp. 35, 54.

64 Whelan, *The Tree of Liberty*, p. 139.

65 Richard Musgrave to T. Percy, 15 January 1799; quoted in Whelan, *The Tree of Liberty*, p. 139.

66 *Reflections*, p. 103.

67 Burke, 'A Letter on the Affairs of Ireland, written in the year 1797', in Matthew Arnold, ed., *Irish Affairs: Edmund Burke*, pp. 373–89: p. 381.

68 Mc Cormack, *From Burke to Beckett*, pp. 49–50.

69 Edmund Burke to Samuel Span, 23 April 1778, *Correspondence*, vol. III, p. 434.

70 Mc Cormack, *From Burke to Beckett*, p. 36.

71 Edmund Burke to Samuel Span, 23 April 1778, *Correspondence*, vol. III, p. 434.

72 Edmund Burke to Earl Fitzwilliam [*circa* 26 September 1794], *Correspondence*, vol. VIII, pp. 20–1.

73 *Reflections*, p. 182.

74 Henry Dundas to William Pitt, [May 1798]; quoted in McDowell, *Ireland in the Age of Imperialism and Revolution*, p. 684.

75 Mc Cormack, *From Burke to Beckett*, p. 442. See W. J. Mc Cormack, *The Pamphlet Debate on the Union between Great Britain and Ireland, 1797–1800* (Dublin: Irish Academic Press, 1996).

76 *Reflections*, p. 142.

77 Ibid. p. 136.

78 Deane, *Strange Country*, pp. 2–3.

79 Musgrave, *Memoirs of the Different Rebellions*, p. 91.

80 Oliver MacDonagh, *States of Mind: A Study of Anglo-Irish Conflict 1780–1980* (London: George Allen and Unwin, 1983), p. 57.

81 Gibbons, 'A Shadowy Narrator', p. 122. See William Pressly, *James Barry: The Artist as Hero* (London: the Tate Gallery, 1983), pp. 144–6.

82 See Anne Crookshank and the Knight of Glin, *The Watercolours of Ireland: Works on Paper in Pencil, Pastel and Paint c.1600–1914* (London: Barrie and Jenkins, 1994), p. 99.

83 Oliver McDonagh, *The Emancipist: Daniel O'Connell 1775–1829*, p. 17;

quoted in Marjorie Howes, 'Tears and Blood: Lady Wilde and the Emergence of Irish Cultural Nationalism', in Tadhg Foley and Seán Ryder, eds, *Ideology and Ireland in the Nineteenth Century* (Dublin: Four Courts Press, 1998), pp. 151–72: p. 161. See also Luke Gibbons, 'Between Captain Rock and a Hard Place: Art and Agrarian Insurgency', in Foley and Ryder, *Ideology and Ireland*, pp. 23–44.

84   [Thomas Moore], *Memoirs of Captain Rock, the Celebrated Irish Chieftain, with Some Account of his Ancestors, written by himself* (London, 1824), pp. 321–2.

85   [Thomas Moore], *Memoirs of Captain Rock*, p. 363.

86   *Reflections*, p. 190.

9

Reflections and correspondences: the unfamiliarity of Burke's familiar letter

ANGELA KEANE

A symptom of the status of Burke's *Reflections on the Revolution in France* as one of many pamphlets in the English 'revolution debate' in the 1790s is the critical neglect of its immediate pre-history. Critics who have paid attention to the so-called struggle for representation between Burke, Wollstonecraft, Paine, and the other respondents to *Reflections* have tended to take for granted the conventional nature of the subtitle: 'a letter intended to have been sent to a gentleman in Paris'. This essay begins with a brief exploration of the evolution of *Reflections* as a letter to a particular addressee. This is not an attempt to define the text's private moment of origin nor to mark out its place in the formal development of the eighteenth-century epistle. Rather, to look at *Reflections* as the end-point of a cross-Channel letter exchange with a young, French, political idealist, as well as the starting-point of the English 'pamphlet war', is to refresh and revise some critical commonplaces about Burke's counter-revolutionary poetic and his reactionary aestheticization of political authority. Such commonplaces have crystallized into the myth of 'the Burkean legacy': a powerful and affective Romantic symbolism, a poetics monopolized by the political right and in need of rescue by the Left.[1] While the legacy might be in place, its genesis could bear some revision.

As this essay shall suggest, to read *Reflections* through its epistolary frame is to recover a neglected political context; but there is also much to be gained from exploring the text as 'correspondence' in a less literal way. Recent theoretical and critical approaches to the form of the letter have exploited, but not exhausted, the metaphorical range of the term correspondence, and have teased out the social, political, and representational significance of a long-ignored literary category.[2] Correspondence is now understood to articulate the contingent relation of private and public, fact and fiction, subject and object; writers are 'self-authors', 'self-authenticators', 'self-fashioners'; letters are 'ex-changes'; readers are 'imagined communities'; mail effaces or exposes 'epistemological gaps'. *Reflections*, as this essay implies, is fertile ground for 'post-age' criticism. However, the eighteenth century itself, or at least Johnson's *Dictionary*, provides a gloss on 'correspondence' which helps to focus the connection between the poetics and politics of Burke's letter in a historically parti-cular way. For Johnson, the primary sense of correspondence is 'relation; reciprocal adaptation of one thing to another'. This essay will argue that the literary and political 'method' of *Reflections* is characterized by Burke's belief in correspondences: that is, in reciprocal adaptations of representation to event, of words to things, and of power to property. It is a faith which amounts less to a unifying symbolism than to a fragile empiri-cism. Burke's *Reflections* are haunted by things which do not correspond.

Letters between men: the redirection of political friendships

On 4 November 1789, Richard Price moved an address to the English Revolution Society, whose members were gathered at the Dissenters' meeting-house at the Old Jewry, to 'offer the National Assembly of France their Congratulations on the Revolution in that country'. On the same day in Paris, Charles Jean-François Depont, a twenty-two-year-old member of the Parlement of Paris, wrote a letter to Edmund Burke.[3] Since his election to the *comité patriotique* of Metz in September 1789, Depont had been keen to solicit the opinion of the man he regarded as his political mentor on the turn of events in France. Depont's letter sparked off a brief exchange between the two who had become acquainted when

Burke entertained the young Frenchman, to whom he referred elsewhere as 'Dumpling' and 'Picky Poky', on a visit to England in 1785. Burke's first reply was indulgent but reserved. Noting that Depont regarded him as 'the faint and glimmering taper' to his 'splendid flame of Liberty', Burke acknowledged the young man's right to call upon him for his 'undisguised Sentiments on whatever related to that Subject'.[4] His good wishes for the current pursuit of Liberty in France, however, were couched in an extensive series of conditional clauses: conditional on Depont's assurance of the 'liberty, property, and safety of the individual subject'.[5]

As Burke was anxious about the security of the French post, he withheld his initial letter, sending in its place a short explanation for his epistolary and political caution. Depont was undeterred by his former mentor's reservations, and wrote again in late December 1789. He cited the Revolution Society's congratulatory address to the National Assembly as his new inspiration and source of hope in England's support for France's battle for Liberty.

Burke presumably received Depont's reply in January 1790, on his return to London for parliamentary business. This would have been around the same time as he read for the first time Price's sermon, the proceedings of the Revolution Society cited by Depont, and the correspondence between the Revolution Society and the National Assembly, all of which had been published in the English press in December 1789. Despite the concern about such political developments which Burke registered in private, he seems to have been reluctant to address the subject of the Revolution in public, and condemned the imprudence of a speaker who spoke out against the Revolution at the opening of Parliament in January 1790.[6] A number of factors seem to have precipitated a sea-change in Burke's attitude to the Revolution as a subject for public debate, however, and moved him closer to the composition of *Reflections*. Firstly, the Whig statesman may well have been piqued at the discovery that his standing as Depont's political inspiration had been eroded by Richard Price. Further, while he had been worried about the diplomatic sensitivity of his avuncular letters, Depont and a large proportion of the reading public of London had been enthralled by the open correspondence of the French National Assembly and the English Revolution Society. Most significantly, perhaps, the speech that he eventually made on the Revolution late in February 1790 precipitated the parliamentary split on the matter between Burke and his erstwhile Whig colleagues, including his former ally, Charles James Fox. Burke was obviously losing credibility as a champion of Liberty. Perhaps because he recognized little point in maintaining the gap between private political sentiment and public declamation on matters relating to the Revolution, he was less circumspect with his final reply to Depont. *Reflections on the Revolution in France ... In a Letter intended to have been sent to a gentleman in Paris* appeared on 1 November 1790, sold thirteen thousand copies in the first five weeks of publication, and ran through eleven editions by September 1791.[7]

In the interval between the production of the private letter of 1789 and the publication of the pamphlet in 1790, Burke had reinvented his young acquaintance, in a manner which is not difficult to read as a veiled attack on 'misguided' Whig colleagues: from a libertarian whose flame had been lit by Burke's taper, to a victim of the hysterical enthusiasm which had been whipped up by 'literary caballers' and 'intriguing philosophers'.[8] More significantly, Burke revised his mode of address to produce the famous political letter which is simultaneously public and private in its address, rational and sentimental in its register, and classical and 'organic' in its form.

Attention to the context of the polyphonic epistolary poetic of *Reflections* unearths a broad pattern of shifting political relations. Burke's attitude to the Revolution is after all informed by his sense of the changing role of the politician in Britain. The new, and to Burke, apparently unwieldy political alliances which were forming around and beyond him, not least between his revolutionary antagonists, his erstwhile protégé Depont and his former ally Fox, were indications that the character of political patronage, of the determining force of private relationships between men in matters of state, was being thrown into question. This was partly a generational issue for Burke, as can be gleaned from some of the most frequently cited passages of *Reflections*, where he seems only too aware of his passing moment, and hams it up for a new breed of political readers with his lament for the age of chivalry. It would be to misunderstand Burke's social and political status, however, to read *Reflections* as the last gasp of the urbane letter of patronage in an age demanding more open and immediate forms of political correspondence. Burke was a man whose polite urbanity was always under pressure, as he brought middle-class 'ability' to a world of aristocratic privilege and Irish Catholic sympathies to an Anglican establishment. This tension is registered in the form and the content, the poetics and the politics of his counter-revolutionary letter.

Familiar letters and strange readers

To some extent, *Reflections* continues a tradition of political letter-writing to which Burke had subscribed throughout his career. He had long made use of the 'letter to an eminent person', a form of public epistolary address which was a popular form of journalistic and political discourse between the late seventeenth and the early nineteenth centuries. Such letters provided writers outside the 'inner circle' of parliamentary decision-making with a means, albeit conventional, of seeking patronage or of calling the attention of an influential figure to a matter of political concern. They were often, of course, vehicles of satire, in which the 'eminent' addressee was subjected to vehement criticism. As Frans de Bruyn has suggested in his recent study of Burke's literary genres, the 'letter to an eminent person' was a response to a social context in which 'individuals of ability, but modest means and connections' were seeking a place, or at least a voice, in a still hierarchical political world.[9]

Burke's most famous exploitation of this form was his *Letter to a Noble Lord*, which was published in 1796.[10] Provoked by derogative comments about the pension he had been receiving from the Pitt administration since 1794 (comments which were made in both the House of Lords and the House of Commons in November 1795), Burke began to compose a private letter to William Windham, to thank him for publicly defending the merit of his financial reward. Although this private letter was never finished, Burke completed it in a public polemic in which he launched a vociferous attack on his detractors: the Duke of Bedford, the Earl of Lauderdale and John Curwen. The deliberate clash of form and content on which the satire of *Letter to a Noble Lord* depends, its play on the history of the dedicatory address from the meritable, but déclassé politician to the potential patron, exposes in more ways than Burke may have intended the tensions in his own political position towards the end of his life. The apparent disdain for political professionalism, and the penchant for gentlemanly amateurism which he expressed in *Reflections* and elsewhere could just about be reconciled with the calls he made for reform of the civil list and his apparent belief in political independence. However, the impecunious circumstances in which he found himself during his last few years, and his acceptance of a royally sanctioned pension, exposed the problem of eschewing patronage without the comfort of independent wealth.

Reflections, like *Letter to a Noble Lord* is written in several voices and embodies a complex social register. Both texts began as private correspondence and, in their later public form, gestured to a classical tradition of political letters and the perform- ance of an intimate exchange between men. In *Reflections*, of course, Burke writes *as* rather than to an 'eminent person' and eschews classical epistolary motifs, favouring the more loosely structured 'familiar letter', with its display of the writer's individuality over decorum. At least, this is the rationale he provides for his friend Philip Francis. When Francis complained that the composition of an early draft of the 'Paris Letter' was 'loose', Burke replied disarmingly:

> I am quite sure it is. I never intended it should be otherwise; for purporting to be, what in Truth it originally was, a Letter to a friend, I had no Idea of digesting it in a Systematick order. The Style is open to correction, and wants it. My natural Style of writing is somewhat careless; and I should be happy in receiving your advice towards making it as little viscious as such a Style is capable of being made. The general character and colour of a Style which grows out of the Writers peculiar Turn of mind and habit of expressing his thoughts must be attended to in all corrections. It is not the insertion of a piece of Stuff though of a better kind which is at all times an improvement.[11]

He asks advice, then, not on firming up the structure, but on making it as 'little viscious as such style which grows out of the

Writers peculiar Turn of mind', simultaneously sketching a portrait of the 'looseness' and singularity of his reflections, and the artlessness of his composition. Superficially, the epistolary poetic that Burke embraces in 1790 seems to be consistent with the pattern of formal and social changes in eighteenth-century letters, as noted in a number of recent cultural histories of the form. Broadly, these studies chart the shift from the classical model which dominated fictional and non-fictional correspondence in England in the early part of the century, and which signified 'agreement' and 'harmony' in poetic composition and social order, to the more egalitarian register of familiar letters which emerged in the middle of the century. Decorous exchange and social hierarchy, it seems, are eclipsed by sentimental correspondence and 'sympathetic' relations: the 'adaptation of one thing to another'.

Burke was, of course, writing to a French man, and commenting, in part, on the incendiary political role of *French* men of letters, so it seems appropriate to address that context too. According to Janet Gurkin Altman, the formal and political fortunes of the classical French letter seems to have been similar to that of the English epistle. The author of the classical epistle was the court subject, who construed himself as a loyal servant to the monarch; his epistles were, in Altman's terms, 'public speech acts that constitute a predictable and universally imitable model of courtesy'. Running counter to, but co-existent with this model was epistolary art 'interpreted as inimitable but inspiring emulation because it is understood to emanate from differing, private literary spaces that articulate the particularities of historical contingency'. Altman attributes to this inimitable 'romantic' letter the generation of an array of 'discourses of cultural difference' which, in their new ascendancy towards the end of the eighteenth century in France, 'position writers in a reconfigured, politically powerful Republic of Letters'.[12]

The cultural democracy which Altman is ready to attribute to the French 'Republic of Letters' has been contested in recent approaches to the gender politics of the emergent political constituencies of France in the 1790s.[13] Such critiques argue that while the Revolution promoted greater class inclusiveness in political decision-making, women had greater authority in courtly culture and through the literary exchanges of the aristocratic salon. However 'closed' the emergent literary political world of France was to many writers, the fact that Burke was ready to attribute the French Revolution, at least in part, to 'men of letters' demonstrates at least *his* sense of a new, large, politicized, and socially inclusive constituency of readers: a public. It is partly in resistance to the idea of the emergence of a broadly politicized public in England as well as in France that Burke maintains the fiction of a single addressee in *Reflections*. This was a significant discursive gesture at a moment when the reality of politics as the limited exchange of ideas between men of a certain class was under pressure from new, less urbane methods of political communication and the emergence of new, and newly powerful, political friendships. Still principally, but not exclusively, conducted between men, the letter-writing activities of the London Revolution Society, the Society for Constitutional Information, the rise of the London Corresponding Society and the many other radical societies established in the provinces from 1790 onwards, threatened to establish an active citizenship which constituted far more than the estimated 400,000 political men that Burke was ready to acknowledge in 1796.[14]

Burke attempted to turn the tension between his mode of address and his possible addressees to political advantage. *Reflections* performs the social register and rhetorical intimacy of the classical epistle for an unknown public, who may have been more attuned to the informal composition of the familiar letter. Burke adapted his idiom accordingly, forcing a correspondence between performance and readership: by force of the 'reciprocal adaptation of one thing to another another', an inchoate public may develop the manners of private men.

Sentimental correspondences

Bearing in mind Burke's epistolary ruse, it is possible to return to one of the prevalent literary fictions about Burke's *Reflections*: that its political power lies in its rhetorical mastery of the Romantic symbol. *Reflections*, according to this view, is an extended piece of literary and political synthesis, epitomized in Burke's naturalization of the representative power of monarchy, church, and aristocracy and axiomatic to his anatomy of nationhood in which the part and the whole are as one. Such readings, like all readings, are genealogical effects, interpreting *Reflections* through the framework of its subsequent critical and political legacy. One such framework, not specific to Burke's *Reflections* but frequently applied to it, is provided in Coleridge's famous definition of Romantic symbol in *The Statesman's Manual*, which bears repetition here:

> a Symbol … is characterised by a translucence of the Special in the Individual, or of the General in the Especial, or of the Universal in the General. Above all by the translucence of the Eternal through and in the temporal. It always partakes of the Reality which it renders intelligible; and while it enunciates the whole, abides itself as a living part of that Unity, of which it is the representative.[15]

Disputing claims of the connection between Coleridge's Unifying method and Burke's poetic, John Whale has argued that the symbolism in *Reflections* is 'dominantly pragmatic', deployed at 'moments of crisis' which call for the 'unifying power of "spirit"'.[16] Similarly, David Fairer distances Coleridge's aesthetic from Burke's, reminding us that for the latter, symbol is 'associative and dependent on accrued meaning … a medium through which things are seen, and as such it does not contain a truth but transmits it'.[17] Both Whale and Fairer, then, point to the residual empiricism which informs Burke's symbolism, establishing an 'eighteenth-century' rather than a 'Romantic' context for his poetic. I would go further, however, to suggest that Burke's 'symbolism' is no more than a haunted empiricism. His faith in correspondence, in the adaptation of one thing to another over time is disrupted by the unprecedented things which come into view. From this perspective, the quasi-symbolic moments in *Reflections* can be read as junctures which speak of rather than resolve crisis. In passages where syntax slips, and tenses oscillate, Burke grammatically articulates things yet to come. These thing are unimaginable social relations which emerge as spectres and revenants: 'ideal' things which exceed the empirical basis of Burke's corresponding vision. For instance, in a passage to which I shall return later in this essay, Burke argues that the new social relations initiated by the French Revolution are simply old kinds of 'mischief'. He tries (and, I shall argue, he fails) to represent this new historical epoch as a repetition of the past, and argues that those who think otherwise are beguiled by form, by the 'shell and the husk of history':

> Seldom have two ages the same fashion in their pretexts and the same modes of mischief. Wickedness is a little more inventive. Whilst you are discussing the fashion, the fashion is gone by. The very same vice assumes a new body. The spirit transmigrates; and, far from losing its principle of life by the change of its appearance, it is renovated in its new organs with the fresh vigour of a juvenile activity. It walks abroad; it continues its ravages; whilst you are gibbeting the carcass, or demolishing the tomb. You are terrifying yourself with ghosts and apparitions, whilst your house is the haunt of robbers. It is thus with all those, who attending only to the shell and husk of history, think they are waging war with intolerance, pride, and cruelty, whilst, under colour of abhorring the ill principles of antiquated parties, they are authorising and feeding the same odious vices in different factions, and perhaps in worse.[18]

Before attending to the slippages in this passage, which I shall argue are symptomatic of the logic of disavowal in Burke's *Reflections* (a logic which conjures up what it seeks to dispel) I want to explore more fully the 'material' poetic which informs Burke's *Reflections*, and with which he tries to contain the spectre of the new.

In some ways, of course, there is nothing new about my claims for Burke's poetic of correspondence, in the Johnsonian sense of that term. *Reflections* has long been understood in a tradition of British empiricism, particularly, and problematically, as the political 'application' of the aesthetic theory he concocted over three decades earlier in his *Philosophical Enquiry into the Origins of the Sublime and Beautiful*.[19] From its earliest reception, Burke's *Reflections* was read as a libertine's letter in a sentimental envelope, as though, like Sterne's Yorick, Burke was using sympathy and the immutable reflexes of the body to seduce his reader into submission to his will. Mary Wollstonecraft was alert to a duplicity in Burke's correspondence when she berated him for his bathetic depiction of Marie Antoinette, and tried to expose him as a middle-class aesthete with aristocratic pretensions. This portrait has informed a number of contemporary analyses of Burke's 'sensibility', which have traced the 'ideology' of his aesthetic treatise, and which in turn have used this as an explanatory framework for Burke's later political writing.[20]

As such analyses suggest, Burke's sketch of the operations of the social passions in the *Enquiry* forces a correspondence between poetics and politics. Like other eighteenth-century treatises on the sublime, the *Enquiry* breaks with neo-classical poetics by emphasizing the authenticity of individual experience. According to recent 'politicized' readings of the *Enquiry*, this poetic shift not only has political parallels but political repercussions. Broadly, Burke is understood to set up a 'correspondence' between the pleasures and pains of the individual body and the body politic. By this sleight of hand, Burke naturalizes a historically particular version of social relations. Thus, the *Enquiry* is understood to play a significant part of the mid-century construction of bourgeois ideology, as Burke invests in, if not invents, the heroism of labour, champions commerce and masculine ambition, and downgrades the aristocracy, luxury, women, and femininity.

Such readings have cogently drawn out the politics of the aesthetic treatise, and 'exposed' the aesthetics of Burke's most famous political text, *Reflections*: its infamous sublime obfuscations. Little attention has been paid, however, to the significance of the more obvious aspects of Burke's attitude towards representation in the *Enquiry*: a less transcendent, and more fragile poetics of power. A dominant feature of Burke's poetic in the treatise, for instance, is its mimetic argument that the greatest pleasure is yielded from the representation which most closely approaches reality. This is most memorably illustrated in his portrait of the effects of tragedy:

> I imagine we shall be much mistaken if we attribute any considerable part of our satisfaction in tragedy to a consideration that tragedy is a deceit, and its representation no realities. The nearer it approaches the reality, and the further it removes us from all idea of fiction, the more perfect is its power. But be its power of what kind it will, it never approaches to what it represents. Chuse a day on which to represent the most sublime and affecting tragedy we have; appoint the most favourite actors; spare no cost upon the scenes and decorations; unite the greatest efforts of poetry, painting

and music; and when you have collected your audience, just at the moment when their minds are erect with expectation, let it be reported that a state criminal of high rank is on the point of being executed in the adjoining square; in a moment the emptiness of the theatre would demonstrate the comparative weakness of the imitative arts, and proclaim the triumph of the real sympathy.[21]

Burke translates this mimetic understanding of representation, or at least, his understanding of our natural pleasure in imitation – the 'triumph of real sympathy' – into his model of social relations. As he describes them in the *Enquiry*, social passions are authentic performances, feelings which bypass the 'reasoning faculty' and 'which merely arise from the mechanical structure of our bodies, or from the natural frame and constitution of our minds'.[22] Complicated and various, the passions are 'agreeable to that variety of ends they are to serve in the great chain of society'.[23] They correspond naturally to the social good.

Burke characterizes three principal links in this great chain: sympathy, imitation, and ambition. The latter, ambition, exposes the historical, class-based particularity of his universal claims. Sympathy and imitation are axiomatic in the sentimental worldview: 'as sympathy makes us take a concern in whatever men feel, so this affection [imitation] prompts us to copy whatever they do'.[24] Ambition, however, requires more explanation:

Although imitation is one of the great instruments used by providence in bringing our nature towards its perfection, yet if men gave themselves up to imitation entirely, and each followed the other, and so on in an eternal circle, it is easy to see that there never could be any improvement amongst them ... To prevent this, God has planted in man a sense of ambition, and a satisfaction arising from the contemplation of his excelling his fellows in something deemed valuable amongst them.[25]

It is through upwardly mobile, strenuous correspondences, the sublime 'swelling' of ambition that the self improves by claiming 'some part of the things which it contemplates'.[26] The operation of ambition ensures society's progressive adaptation; it performs a providential service to a society which risks entropy through empathy.

On this evidence, it is not difficult to see how the *Enquiry* has been read as a charter for economic individualism and as a

timely, wartime, rejection of luxury. However, the most sugges-
tive of recent readings of the *Enquiry* do not reduce it to a mono-
lithic or coherent programme of social transformation which
continues unbroken to the *Reflections*. Tom Furniss for instance,
drawing on Macherey and Jameson, argues that to read the
Enquiry as an ideological text is to unfix it, to unearth the historical
unconscious which 'fissures' and 'haunts' it. For Furniss, one such
haunting is the anxiety that the luxury which Burke 'locates elsewhere than in economic individualism' might indeed threaten
with dissolution the commercial interest on whose behalf he
writes.[27] If there is a continuity between the *Enquiry* and the
Reflections, it is to be found in the return of the repressed: the
repressed association between the 'commercial interest' and an
indolent 'luxury', which haunted the aesthetic treatise, returns
in the political letter in the form of an unpropertied 'monied
interest'.

Groundless speculation

In Burke's relatively conventional aesthetic treatise lies a fragile
vision of social relations which anticipates his later political
anxieties about commercial society in relation to the monied
interest: the class of financial speculators who, he claims, have
come to dominate France by 1790. 'By the vast debt of France', he
explains in *Reflections*, 'a great monied interest had insensibly
grown up, and with it a great power.'[28] There is some continuity
here with the poetic and social vision of the aesthetic treatise.
These men have rejected a mimetic, improving form of ambition
in favour of speculation. In this new economic context, as he
complains to Depont, expenditure is no guarantee of return:

> With you a man can neither earn nor buy his dinner, without a
> speculation. What he receives in the morning will not have the
> same value at night. What he is compelled to take as pay for an old
> debt, will not be received as the same when he comes to pay a debt
> contracted by himself; nor will it be the same when by prompt
> payment he would avoid contracting any debt at all.[29]

When labour does not correspond with remuneration, 'industry
must whither away'.[30] With the emergence of this unpredictable

model of social relations, the repercussions of which were unimaginable to Burke, he saw fit to recuperate some old enemies. So, in 1790, idleness became sociability and luxury a stimulus to industry and culture:

> In every prosperous community something more is produced than goes to the immediate support of the producer. This surplus forms the income of the landed capitalist. It will be spent by a proprietor who does not labour. But this idleness is itself the spring of labour; this repose the spur to industry. The only concern of the state is, that the capital taken in rent from the land, should be returned again to the industry from whence it came; and that its expenditure should be with the least possible detriment to the morals of those who expend it, and to those of the people to whom it is returned.[31]

Although it is not quite clear from this context why idleness is 'the spring of labour', or 'repose the spur to industry', it is apparent that the morality of Burke's economy depends on the visibility of its rewards and expenditures. In the speculative economy of the reviled 'monied interest', the value of labour and of profit are not immediately apparent. In an invisible economy, imitation gives way to improvisation. In the absence of the middle link of the chain of society, ambition has no connection with sympathy.

Burke does not retreat from his empirical model of correspondences in order to accommodate the vagaries of speculation. On the contrary, he places an even greater moral imperative on known relations, on reciprocal adaptation. Thus, the primary social relation is the 'little platoon ... the first link in the series by which we proceed towards a love to our country and to mankind'.[32] Similarly, authority must be visible. Hence, Burke's portrait of the natural relation between monarch and subject, so often read as a naturalization of state mystery, is an injunction 'to approach to look into' the defects or corruptions of state 'with due caution'. It is to the 'faults' of state, not the state itself, that we should approach with 'awe and trembling sollicitude', as to the 'wounds of a father'. His is 'the wise prejudice' by which:

> we are taught to look with horror on those children of their country who are prompt rashly to hack that aged parent in pieces, and put him into the kettle of magicians, in hopes that by their

poisonous weeds, and wild incantations, they may regenerate the paternal constitution, and renovate their father's life.[33]

The revolutionaries' attempt to 'regenerate' and 'renovate' that which they have torn apart violates the Burkean poetic. The 'thing' they are bound to create will not correspond with things that went before: it will be a monster.

Thus, in 1790, the enemies to social progress are not the indolent aristocrats who haunted the mid-century treatise, but the revolutionaries and their bastard creations. The revolutionaries include the new financiers, who generate the fancies of speculation, and the political men of letters, who peddle the 'monstrous fiction' of equality to mask their assault on society.[34] According to Burke, in the passage I cited earlier, this monstrous fiction has left Depont and his fellow revolutionary sympathizers terrified by a speculative fancy: by the 'ghosts and apparitions' of the *ancien régime*. In a telling prioritization of matter over mind, Burke warns Depont not to be distracted by such phantoms and to look to his house which has become the 'haunt of robbers'.[35] The robbers it seems are those arch traders of empty promises, the philosophes and speculators who threaten to divest France of all its valuable things.

Burke addresses Depont as though he were the naive protagonist of a romance by Ann Radcliffe; an Emily St Aubert of *The Mysteries of Udolpho* who is so preoccupied with the phantoms at the family estate that she fails to notice the banditti who loot her property and use the house as a storehouse for their stolen goods.[36] As in Radcliffe's text, the disembodied voices and shadows in the family home turn out to be those of banditti not of ghosts. In this modern romance, the robbers are dispelled, and the property passes into the hands of the next generation: the daughter of the house who heralds the start of a new feminized order, an enlightened and moral bourgeoisie. The transition is not quite complete in the course of Radcliffe's narrative. Although the ghosts turn out to be robbers, the estate remains haunted: by the ghosts of an *ancien régime* which have not been fully exorcized and by the spectre of an as yet unrealized order which threatens to overwhelm property itself.

This unrealized order haunts Burke's *Reflections* as much as Radcliffe's romance. It circulates in the form of a revolutionary energy. When Burke rails against the 'ability', 'talent', and 'innovation' of the men of letters, he articulates his fear of the uncontainable energy of a new political order. Ironically, these are the qualities Burke was seen to bring to British political life. Perhaps his first-hand knowledge of political upstarts gave him a special insight into the pragmatic means of containing them. Whilst *Reflections* is famed in this respect for Burke's attempt to match natural authority to political symbols, his most strategic manoeuvre is to recommend a correspondence between figurative and material hegemony. Rather than mystify power, he makes it literal. Thus, he argues that the way to combat ability is to match authority with property:

> Nothing is due and adequate representation of a state, that does not represent its ability, as well as its property. But as ability is a vigorous and active principle, and as property is sluggish, inert and timid, it never can be safe from the invasions of ability unless it be out of all proportion, predominant in the representation. It must be represented too in great masses of accumulation or it is not rightly protected.[37]

Implicitly, if authority corresponds with property, the representation of power is made visible. Ability has no material signs; to match power with this 'vigorous', active, and immaterial, principle is to double the mystery of representation. Contrary, then, to the quasi-mysticism which is attributed to Burke's outline of the social contract, his attack on the revolutionaries' claims for 'rights' and first principles, his corresponding vision depends on the adaptation of 'things'. The 'partnership in all science ... in all art ... in every virtue', the ends of which 'cannot be obtained in many generations' depends on the repetition and sublimation of the past: on the reciprocal adaptation of one thing to another. The 'partnership between those who are living, those who are dead, and those who are to be born' is held in place by the *stuff* not the spirit of culture. Although society is 'not a partnership in things subservient only to the gross animal existence of a temporary and perishable nature', the contract is underwritten by property.[38]

'The things in some shape must remain'

In his social vision, and in his method of historical explanation, Burke clings to his mimetic model of correspondence and a model of historical progress through adaptation. In an attempt to account for things which do not seem to correspond, Burke notes the difference between permanent historical content and temporary historical forms, generational adaptations of things which have always been and always will be. The vigilant historian, Burke suggests, will notice the difference:

> You might change the names. The things in some shape must remain. A certain quantum of power must always exist in the community, in some hands, and under some appellation. Wise men will apply their remedies to vices, not to names; to the causes of evil which are permanent, not to the occasional organs by which they act, and the transitory modes in which they appear. Otherwise you will be wise historically, a fool in practice.[39]

It is Burke's confidence in his ability to discriminate between permanent and temporary adaptations that gives him the power of prophecy, to predict turns of events according to immutable historical laws. Thus, 'History will record', he says, before inventing his most famous historical spectacle: the persecution and flight of the French royal family on 6 October 1789.[40] The dramatic scene turns to prophecy in a disorientating passage where Burke moves freely between a condemnation of the ethics of the event and its representation. Claiming, with melodramatic resignation, that the scene of the flight was played out and commemorated in the 'Theban and Thracian Orgies' of French revolutionaries, he points ominously to the applause it received in the Old Jewry, and to the darkness at the heart of the over-zealous thanksgiving:

> There was ... in the midst of all this joy something to exercise the patience of these worthy gentlemen, and to try the long-suffering of their faith. The actual murder of the king and queen, and their child, was wanting to the other auspicious circumstances of this 'beautiful day.'[41]

Like the audiences of a tragedy who quit the theatre for the promise of an execution, the English revolutionaries have a taste for 'real spectacle': a monstrous taste which elsewhere he might have described as a natural proclivity. Again, conflating event with its representation, he predicts that it will be left to the 'hardy pencil of a great master, from the school of the rights of men' to finish the sketch of 'regicide and sacrilegious slaughter … this great history-piece of the massacre of the innocent'.[42] In his own representation of this spectacle, Burke attempts to master history by living out his fears. The difference between Burke's tragic sketch and the revolutionaries' sacrilegious spectacle is a difference of aesthetic and moral perception. French sensibility, he suggests, has become so corrupt that monarchy is seen as a simulacrum of power, displaced as truth by the new authority, the representatives of republicanism. As Burke was to claim in his *Letter to a Member of the National Assembly*, the author of this perverse poetic is Rousseau:

> Under this philosophic instructor in the ethics of vanity, they have attempted in France a regeneration of the moral constitution of man. Statesmen, like your present rulers, exist by every thing which is spurious, fictitious and false; by every thing which takes the man from his house, and sets him on a stage, which makes him an artificial creature, with painted theatric sentiments, fit to be seen by the glare of candlelight, and formed to be contemplated at a due distance.[43]

The distinction between the natural theatricality of monarchy and the 'painted theatric sentiments' of French republicans depends for Burke not on the transhistorical authority of one and the temporary contractual nature of the other, but on their relative ability to bear close inspection. Ultimately, Burke justifies his own faith in one over the other on pragmatic, formal grounds: on the adaptability of monarchy over the formal rigidity of republicanism. In a telling and admittedly rare move in *Reflections*, he professes to agree with Bolingbroke's sentiment that 'he prefers monarchy to other governments; because you can better ingraft any description of republic on a monarchy than any thing of monarchy upon the republican forms'.[44]

Unfinished correspondence

For all the empirical bluster of Burke's political railings against the speculative fancies of the French monied interest, the monstrous fictions of the *philosophes*, and the painted theatrical sentiments of the republicans, *Reflections* is haunted by things which do not correspond and which bear no relation to historical or material precedent. Burke's mastery of historical event struggles to contain his own sense that the spirit of history is free of his narrative control. Burkean prophecy belies his fear of history deciding for itself. Symptomatically, the grammatical confidence of the phrase 'History will record' also concedes that history is a consciousness outside of text, which *becomes* under its own volition.

Burke's historical account is often stymied by its own explanatory structure: history as adaptation, continuity with difference. He succumbs to the paradoxical pressure of his imperative to place the Revolution in a historical continuum. Unable to countenance the arrival of the new, Burke must invent another category of historical repetition: a malign spirit, old evils disguised as new events, which return infinitely and in ever-regressing forms. This has unforeseen consequences, best illustrated by citing again the passage to which I referred above, where Burke is expounding on the folly of trying to root out social ills by abolishing the organs of authority (monarchs, ministers of state, the gospel). Here, Burke becomes subject to his own analysis and to the revolutionary potential of his explanatory account:

> Seldom have two ages the same fashion in their pretexts and the same modes of mischief. Wickedness is a little more inventive. Whilst you are discussing the fashion, the fashion is gone by. The very same vice assumes a new body. The spirit transmigrates; and, far from losing its principle of life by the change of its appearance, it is renovated in its new organs with the fresh vigour of a juvenile activity. It walks abroad; it continues its ravages; whilst you are gibbeting the carcass, or demolishing the tomb. You are terrifying yourself with ghosts and apparitions, whilst your house is the haunt of robbers. It is thus with all those, who attending only to the shell and husk of history, think they are waging war with intolerance, pride, and cruelty, whilst, under colour of abhorring

the ill principles of antiquated parties, they are authorising and
feeding the same odious vices in different factions, and perhaps in
worse.[45]

'Power' is first represented here as a constant, a neutral deep
content in a continuous historical narrative, which changes form
in each generation. The contingent forms of revolutionary change
soon overwhelm Burke-the-historian's facility for order; from
malign repetitions (comprehensible, already existing in nature)
they become unforeseen things. No longer subject to the laws of
historical continuity, 'wickedness' has a being outside of narrative: it does not correspond. The autonomous 'thing' is a shape-
shifter, elusive to the detection of the most vigilant historian.
Whilst Burke attempts to intervene as the omniscient and
rational voice, in order to dispel the apparitions of the *ancien
régime* which have been conjured up by the men of letters, he
subjects himself to an even scarier spectre. In this proto-
Malthusian vision, Burke evokes a scene of social devastation
wrought by a spectre in an ever-regenerating body; its power
accumulates because it is free of the drag of history and the
permanence of property. It is perpetually young, and circulates
endlessly with incremental vigour. This re-embodied spirit is a
bad repetition, a historical counterfeit; its horror lies in its shape-
shifting autonomy. It does not and will not correspond with
what has gone before.

As a logical effect of Burke's own historical imagination, this
revenant walks off the page: it is a revenant, perhaps, of Burke's
repressed revolutionary energy, or of speculation and of other
kinds still unknown. Tellingly, it reappears in the first of Burke's
Letters on a Regicide Peace, as a spirit untethered by social
relations or the agreed customs and correspondences of deep
historical structure. In this extract, the spirit has no material
form:

> out of the tomb of the murdered monarchy in France has arisen a
> vast, tremendous, unformed spectre, in a far more terrifick guise
> than any which ever yet have overpowered the imagination, and
> subdued the fortitude of man. Going straight forward to its end,
> unappalled by peril, unchecked by remorse, despising all common
> maxims and all common means, that hideous phantom over-
> powered those who could not believe it was possible she could

exist at all, except on the principles, which habit rather than nature had persuaded them were necessary to their own particular welfare, and to their own ordinary modes of action.[46]

The spectre, which is by definition a visual presence, has taken on a guise yet it is 'unformed'. It has no body, or at least no body which has existed in nature. Propertyless, it is thus insensible and historically untrue. It does, however, have a gender. 'She' moves forward relentlessly to an undisclosed telos by the force of visual deceit. She subdues those who see her into believing she exists. She is, however, a phantom; a ghost without history, a thing of the fancy. But what is 'she'? This spectre resembles Burke's abhorred 'public opinion' and the politics of reform. Burke fears that he glimpses, as J. G. A. Pocock suggests, 'a revolution in communications and the growth of a society where "there was no longer any means of arresting a principle in its course"'.[47]

As the spectre of reform and of new forms of political representation, she has remained a phantom, at least from some historical points of view. One such perspective is rehearsed by Pocock in his analysis of Burke's anticipation of both sides of the 1832 Reform debate. He imagines a dialogue of the dead in which Karl Marx explains to Burke that he 'had simply failed to recognise that one system of property relations was replacing another, and that "the dreadful energy" was that of the revolutionary and triumphant bourgeoisie'; that 'all human energy was by its nature involved in productive activity and the generation of new property relationships'. Burke, as Pocock notes, would not find consolation in such a reading, since he had seen 'a vision of human energy turned wholly and systematically destructive' aimed at a 'liberal commercial society'.[48] Burke had been haunted first by luxury, then by speculation: he had intimations of reform and finally of Marx's own spectre, the spectre haunting Europe in the nineteenth century, the spectre of communism. In 1790, this spectre is a revenant returned from the future, a ghost without history, a spirit without a body. She is beyond the compass of Burke's corresponding vision, and is impossible to imagine, impossible to dispel. She embodies the dreadful potential of open political exchange and society without property.

Spectres of Burke

In his reflections on the contemporary fortunes of Marxism, published in 1994 as *Spectres of Marx*, Jacques Derrida provides an account of the paradoxical disavowal of Marxist history which has followed the fall of communism.[49] This is a formulation of the relationship between political denial and historical belief which has, in a number of ways, informed my rereading of Burke's Romantic symbolism as haunted empiricism, and has various implications for the Left's current engagement with the counter-revolutionary power of *Reflections*.

Derrida reads Marxism as a messianic, eschatological narrative, a spectral presence which, like democracy 'is always still to come and is distinguished, like democracy itself, from every living present understood as plenitude of a presence-to-itself'. Capitalism is a hegemony which represses the ghost of communism: a ghost which is bound to return:

> Capitalist societies can always heave a sigh of relief and say to themselves communism is finished since the collapse of the totalitarianisms of the twentieth century and not only is it finished, but it did not take place, it was only a ghost. They do no more than disavow the undeniable itself: a ghost never dies, it remains always to come and to come-back. [50]

Derrida reminds us that ghosts are conjured by the structure of repression; that repression is itself a 'confirmation of a haunting. Haunting belongs to the structure of every hegemony'.[51] According to both of these models, capitalism as hegemonic repression, and Marxism as spectral history, the unformed spectre which haunted Burke's empirical vision cannot yet be dead, as the formless generations, untethered by property relations, are always about to be.

Although Marxist historical narrative is temporally spectral, it is motivated by a desire to still dispel spectres: the spectre of capital and the alienated automata who are subjected to its rule. Marx sought to dispel spectres and, as Derrida sees it, believed in 'what is supposed to distinguish them from actual reality, living effectivity'.[52] According to the inexorable grammatical logic of deconstruction, however, Marx succeeds only in disavowing not dispelling ghosts; their disappearance is also a conjuring trick, a structural conceit:

He believes he can oppose them like life to death, like vain appearances of the simulacrum to real presence. He believes enough in the dividing line of this opposition to want to denounce, to chase away, or exorcise the specters but by means of critical analysis and not by some counter-magic. But how to distinguish between the analysis and the counter-magic that it still risks being?[53]

Burke, too, risked counter-magic by basing his counter-revolutionary arguments on a belief in the dividing line between vain appearances and authentic performances. A moral society depends on the visibility of its political representation, a visibility which he imagined depended upon matching power to property. Property gives a body and a presence to the virtual relation that is 'society'; it is the stuff of culture, to be worked upon, though not completed by future generations. Through a kind of transubstantiation, property plays host to the spirit of history. Burke's familiar letter between men is haunted by unfamiliar things, however. It conjures unimaginable social relations which are free from the precedent of history and which do not correspond with things as they have been.

In the light of the dialectical logic which produces such a reading of *Reflections*, there seems to be a continuum between the spectres produced by the revolutionary energy of Burke's counter-revolutionary rhetoric, the uncanny capital which haunts nineteenth-century communism and the unmourned communism which haunts late twentieth-century capitalism: the opposition of magic with counter-magic, virtual reality with nostalgic, impossible self-presence. It is, of course, a purely formal continuum, which belies the matter of historical difference, and the disarmingly simple difference between form and content; differences which the current political Left in Britain needs to bear in mind.

I began by suggesting that in recent literary analyses of *Reflections*, its mythical Romantic poetic is portrayed as its most powerful legacy. The Left in particular is beguiled and fascinated by the notion of a unifying, affective symbolism which fills property with spirit, which absorbs the particular in the general, and which can oscillate omnipotently between the two as the political need arises. This is, as I have argued, a poetic which does not belong to Burke, but to Coleridge and a later generation of critics who have mobilized the myth of Burke's symbolic politics to inform their own readings of history.[54] By rereading *Reflections* as a residually mimetic 'will-to-correspondence', it is possible to retrieve not only the historical specificity but the conceptual fragility of *Reflections*, and of Burke's fraught fixation with property as the basis of moral being. The Left can end its compulsive correspondence with Burke's counter-revolutionary vision when it begins to understand the content and the form, the letter as well as the spirit of his *Reflections*.

Notes

1 See: Terry Eagleton, *The Ideology of the Aesthetic* (Oxford: Blackwell, 1990); Deidre Lynch, 'Nationalizing Women and Domesticating Fiction: Edmund Burke and the Genres of Englishness', *The Wordsworth Circle*, 25: 1 (1994), pp. 45–9; W. J. Mc Cormack, *Ascendancy and Tradition in Anglo-Irish Literary History from 1789–1939* (Oxford: Clarendon Press, 1985); David Simpson, *Romanticism, Nationalism, and the Revolt Against Theory* (Chicago: University of Chicago Press, 1993).

2 See: Janet Gurkin Altman, *Epistolarity: Approaches to a Form* (Columbus, OH: Ohio State University Press, 1982) and 'The Letter Book as a Literary Institution 1539–1789: Toward a Cultural History of Published Correspondences in France', in *Yale French Studies*, Special Issue, 'Men/Women of Letters', ed. Charles A. Porter, 71 (1986) pp. 17–62; Jacques Derrida, *The Post Card: From Socrates to Freud and Beyond*, trans. Alan Bass (Chicago: University of Chicago Press, 1980); Mary A. Favret, *Romantic Correspondence: Women, Politics and the Fiction of Letters* (Cambridge: Cambridge University Press, 1993); *Prose Studies*, ed. Amanda Gilroy and W. M. Verhoeven, 19:2 (1996); Dena Goodman, *The Republic of Letters: A Cultural History of the French Enlightenment* (Ithaca: Cornell University Press, 1994); Linda S. Kauffman, *Discourses of Desire: Gender, Genre, and Epistolary Fictions* (Ithaca and London: Cornell University Press, 1986).

3 The three letters which make up this brief correspondence are in *Correspondence*, vol. VI, pp. 31–2, 39–50, 59–61.

4 Ibid. p. 40.

5 Ibid. p. 46.

6 Ibid. p. 81.

7 *Reflections*, p. 15.

8 Ibid. p. 61.

9 Frans De Bruyn, *The Literary Genres of Edmund Burke: The Political Uses of Literary Form* (Oxford: Clarendon Press, 1996), p. 19.

10 Edmund Burke, *Letter to a Noble Lord*, *The Writings and Speeches of*

    Edmund Burke, vol. 9, ed. R. B. McDowell (Oxford: Clarendon Press, 1991).

11 *Correspondence*, vol. VI, p. 89.

12 Altman, 'The Letter Book as a Literary Institution', p. 62.

13 Goodman, *The Republic of Letters*; Joan Landes, *Women in the Public Sphere in the Age of the French Revolution* (Ithaca: Cornell University Press, 1988).

14 De Bruyn, *The Literary Genres of Edmund Burke*, p. 14.

15 S. T. Coleridge, 'Lay Sermons', *The Collected Works of Samuel Taylor Coleridge*, vol. 6, ed. R. J. White (London: Routledge and Kegan Paul), p. 30.

16 John Whale, 'Literal and Symbolic Representations: Burke, Paine and the French Revolution', *History of European Ideas*, 16:1–3 (1993), pp. 343–9: p. 348.

17 Fairer, David, 'Organizing Verse: Burke's *Reflections* and Eighteenth-Century Poetry', *Romanticism*, 3:1 (1997), pp. 1–19: p. 12.

18 Ibid. p. 190.

19 Edmund Burke, *A Philosophical Enquiry into the Origin of our Ideas of the Sublime and Beautiful*, ed. Adam Phillips (Oxford: Oxford University Press, 1990).

20 See: Eagleton, *The Ideology of the Aesthetic*; Tom Furniss, *Edmund Burke and Aesthetic Ideology: Language, Gender and Political Economy* (Cambridge: Cambridge University Press, 1993).

21 *Enquiry*, p. 43.

22 Ibid. p. 41.

23 Ibid. p. 40.

24 Ibid. p. 45.

25 Ibid. p. 46.

26 Ibid.

27 Furniss, *Burke's Aesthetic Ideology*, p. 48.

28 *Reflections*, p. 158.

29 Ibid. p. 241.

30 Ibid. p. 310.

31 Ibid. p. 209.

32 Ibid. pp. 97–8.

33 Ibid. p. 146.

34 Ibid. p. 24.

35 Ibid. p. 190.

36 For this reading of Radcliffe's romance, I am indebted to Natalka Freeland, 'Theft, Terror and Family Values: The Mysteries and Domesticities of Udolpho', in Peter Buse and Andrew Stott, eds, *Ghosts: Deconstruction, Psychoanalysis, History* (London: Macmillan, 1999).

37 *Reflections*, p. 102.

38 Ibid. p. 147.

39 Ibid. p. 190.

40 Ibid. p. 122.

41 Ibid. p. 123.

42 Ibid.

43 *Letter to a Member of the National Assembly, Writings and Speeches*, vol. 8, p. 315.

44 *Reflections*, p. 175.

45 Ibid. p. 190.

46 *First Letter on a Regicide Peace, The Writings and Speeches of Edmund Burke*, vol. 9, ed. R. B. McDowell (Oxford: Clarendon Press, 1991), pp. 190–1.

47 J. G. A. Pocock, *Virtue, Commerce and History* (Cambridge: Cambridge University Press, 1985), p. 208.

48 Ibid.

49 Jacques Derrida, *Specters of Marx: The State of the Debt, the Work of Mourning, and the New International*, trans. Peggy Kamuf (New York and London: Routledge, 1994).

50 Ibid. p. 99.

51 Ibid. p. 37.

52 Ibid. pp. 46–7.

53 Ibid. p. 47.

54 Again, I am referring in particular to Eagleton, Mc Cormack, and Simpson, whose critiques of Burke's politics are founded on their understanding of his symbolic poetic.

Notes on contributors

GREGORY CLAEYS is Professor of the History of Political Thought at Royal Holloway, University of London. His many publications include: *Thomas Paine: Social and Political Thought* (Unwin Hyman 1989), *Citizens and Saints: Politics and Anti-Politics in Early British Socialism* (Cambridge University Press 1989), (ed.) *Political Writings of the 1790s*, 8 vols (Pickering and Chatto 1995), and *The Chartist Movement in Britain* (Pickering and Chatto 1998).

CLAIRE CONNOLLY is a Lecturer in English Literature and Cultural Criticism at Cardiff University. She has published essays on gender and nationality in late eighteenth- and early nineteenth-century Irish writing, and has edited Maria Edgeworth's *Letters for Literary Ladies* (Everyman 1995), and *Ormond*, *Manoeuvring* and *Vivian* (as two volumes in the Pickering and Chatto *Novels and Selected Works of Maria Edgeworth*, 1999).

TOM FURNISS is a Senior Lecturer in the Department of English Studies at the University of Strathclyde. He is the author of *Edmund Burke's Aesthetic Ideology* (Cambridge University Press 1993) and of a number of articles on the Revolution Controversy. He is currently working on a book about the discourse of nationalism.

KEVIN GILMARTIN is an Associate Professor of Literature at the California Institute of Technology. He is the author of *Print Politics: The Press and Radical Opposition in Early Nineteenth-Century England* (Cambridge University Press 1996), and is currently working on a book on counter-revolutionary culture in the Romantic period.

ANGELA KEANE is a Lecturer at Sheffield University. She has published a number of articles on British women's writing of the Romantic period, and is the author of *Romantic Belongings*: *Women Writers and the English Nation in the 1790s* (forthcoming from Cambridge University Press). She is also the co-editor with Avril Horner of *Body Matters: Feminism, Textuality and Corporeality* (Manchester University Press 2000). She is currently researching the role of women in anti-consumerist movements in the Romantic period.

F. P. LOCK is Professor of English at Queen's University, Kingston, Ontario. He is the author of *Susanna Centlivre* (1979), *The Politics of 'Gulliver's Travels'* (1980), 'The Text of "*Gulliver's Travels*"', *Modern Language Review* (July 1981), *Swift's Tory Politics* (1983), and *Burke's 'Reflections on the Revolution in France'* (1985). With Claude Rawson, he edited *The Collected Poems of Thomas Parnell* (1989). While researching a biography of Burke, he discovered thirty new Burke letters, which he has edited as 'Unpublished Burke Letters', *English Historical Review* (February 1997 and June 1999). The first volume of his biography, *Edmund Burke: Vol. 1, 1730–84*, has recently been published

(Clarendon Press 1998). He is currently working on the second volume, which will cover 1784–97.

SUSAN MANLY is a Lecturer in the School of English, University of St. Andrews. She is the editor of Maria Edgeworth's *Harrington* and the co-editor of *Helen* and *Leonora*, all published as part of the *Novels and Selected Works of Maria Edgeworth* (Pickering and Chatto 1999).

W. J. MCCORMACK is Professor of Literary History at Goldsmiths College, University of London. He is the author of *From Burke to Beckett: Ascendancy, Tradition and Betrayal in Literary History* (Cork University Press 1994) and editor for Penguin and World's classics of novels by Edgeworth, Le Fanu, and Trollope. At present he is completing a biography of J. M. Synge, and turning his thoughts to editing Sir John Temple's *History of the Execrable Rebellion*, a volume roundly condemned by Burke.

JOHN WHALE is a Senior Lecturer in the School of English at the University of Leeds. His publications include *Thomas De Quincey's Reluctant Autobiography* (1984) and, as co-editor with Stephen Copley, *Beyond Romanticism: New Approaches to Texts and Contexts, 1780-1832* (1992). He has just completed *Imagination Under Pressure 1789-1832: Aesthetics, Politics and Utility* (forthcoming from Cambridge University Press), and is currently engaged in editing a volume of *The Works of Thomas De Quincey* for Pickering and Chatto.

Select bibliography

Editions

The Writings and Speeches of Edmund Burke, ed. Paul Langford *et al.*, 12 vols (Oxford: Clarendon Press, 1981–).

The Correspondence of Edmund Burke, ed. Thomas W. Copeland *et al.*, 10 vols (Cambridge: Cambridge University Press; Chicago: Chicago University Press, 1958–78).

Edmund Burke: Reflections on the Revolution in France, ed. Conor Cruise O'Brien, (Harmondsworth: Penguin, 1968).

Edmund Burke: Reflections on the Revolution in France, ed. J. G. A. Pocock (Indianapolis, Indiana: Hackett, 1987).

Biographies

Kramnick, Isaac, *The Rage of Edmund Burke: Portrait of an Ambivalent Conservative* (New York: Basic Books, 1977).

Lock, F. P., *Edmund Burke*, 2 vols (Oxford: Clarendon Press, 1998–).

O'Brien, Conor Cruise, *The Great Melody: A Thematic Biography of Edmund Burke* (Chicago: University of Chicago Press, 1992).

Critical studies

Blakemore, Steven, *Burke and the Fall of Language: The French Revolution as Linguistic Event* (Hanover and London: University Press of New England, 1988).

—, ed., *Burke and the French Revolution: Bicentennial Essays* (Athens and London: University of Georgia Press, 1992).

Boulton, J. T., *The Language of Politics in the Age of Wilkes and Burke* (London: Routledge and Kegan Paul, 1963).

Canavan, Francis P., *The Political Reason of Edmund Burke* (Durham, NC: Duke University Press, 1960).

Chandler, James K., *Wordsworth's Second Nature: A Study of the Poetry and the Politics* (Chicago and London: University Press, 1984).

Crossley, Ceri and Small, Ian, eds, *The French Revolution and British Culture* (Oxford: Oxford University Press, 1989).

Crow, Ian, *Edmund Burke: His Life and Legacy* (Dublin: Four Courts Press, 1997).

Deane, Seamus, *Strange Country: Modernity and Nationhood in Irish Writing since 1790* (Oxford: Clarendon Press, 1997).

—, *The French Revolution and Enlightenment in England 1789–1832* (Cambridge, MA, and London: 1988).

De Bruyn, Frans, *The Literary Genres of Edmund Burke: The Political Uses of Literary Form* (Oxford: Clarendon Press, 1996).

Dryer, Frederick, 'The Genesis of Burke's *Reflections*', *Journal of Modern History*, 50:3 (1977), pp. 462–79.

Eagleton, Terry, *The Ideology of the Aesthetic* (Oxford and Cambridge, MA: Basil Blackwell, 1990), pp. 31–69.

Fairer, David, 'Organizing Verse: Burke's *Reflections* and Eighteenth-Century Poetry', *Romanticism*, 3:1 (1997), pp. 1–19.

Furniss, Tom, *Edmund Burke's Aesthetic Ideology: Language, Gender and Political Economy in Revolution* (Cambridge: Cambridge University Press, 1993).

Gibbons, Luke, 'Edmund Burke on Our Present Discontents', *History Ireland*, 5:4 (Winter 1997), pp. 21–5.

Gray, Tim and Hindson, Paul 'Rhetoric and Representation in Burke's *Reflections*: Edmund Burke and the French Revolution as Drama', *History of European Ideas*, 14:2 (1992), pp. 203–11.

—, eds, *Burke's Dramatic Theory of Politics* (Aldershot: Avebury, 1988).

Hampsher-Monk, Iain, 'Rhetoric and Opinion in the Politics of Edmund Burke', *History of Political Thought*, 9:3 (Winter 1988), pp. 455–84.

Hughes, Peter, 'Originality and Allusion in the Writings of Edmund Burke', *Centrum*, 4:1 (1976), pp. 32–43.

Kaufman, Pamela, 'Burke, Freud, and the Gothic', *Studies in Burke and his Time*, 23 (1972), pp. 2179–92.

Lock, F. P., *Burke's Reflections on the Revolution in France* (London: George Allen and Unwin, 1985).

Macpherson, C. B., *Burke*, Past Masters series (Oxford: Oxford University Press, 1980).

Mc Cormack, W. J., *From Burke to Beckett: Ascendancy, Tradition and Betrayal in Literary History* (Cork: Cork University Press, 1994).

Mahoney, Thomas H. D., *Edmund Burke and Ireland* (Cambridge, MA: Harvard University Press, 1960).

Mitchell, W. J. T., *Iconology: Image, Text, Ideology* (Chicago: University of Chicago Press, 1986).

O'Gorman, Frank, *Edmund Burke: His Political Philosophy* (London: Allen and Unwin, 1973).

Pocock, J. G. A., *Virtue, Commerce and Society: Essays on Political Thought and History, Chiefly in the Eighteenth Century* (Cambridge: Cambridge University Press, 1985).

—, 'Edmund Burke and the Redefinition of Enthusiasm: The Context as Counter-Revolution', in Furet, François and Ozouf, Mona, eds, *The French Revolution and the Creation of Modern Political Culture*, Vol. 3, *The Transformation of Political Culture 1789–1848* (Oxford: Pergamon Press, 1989), pp. 19–35.

—, 'Burke and the Ancient Constitution: A Problem in the History of Ideas', *The Historical Journal*, 3:2 (1971), pp. 125–43.

Paulson, Ronald, *Representations of Revolution (1789–1820)* (New Haven: Yale University Press, 1983).

Reid, Christopher, *Edmund Burke and the Practice of Political Writing* (Dublin and New York: Gill and Macmillan, 1985).

Robinson, Nicholas K., *Edmund Burke: A Life in Caricature* (New Haven and London: Yale University Press, 1966).

Simpson, David, *Romanticism, Nationalism and the Revolt Against Theory* (Chicago and London: University of Chicago Press, 1993).

Smith, Olivia, *The Politics of Language 1791–1819* (Oxford: Clarendon Press, 1984).

Stanlis, Peter, *Edmund Burke and the Natural Law* (Ann Arbor: University of Michigan Press, 1958).

Whale, John, 'Hazlitt on Burke: The Ambivalent Position of a Radical Essayist', *Studies in Romanticism*, 25:4, pp. 465–81.

White, Stephen K., *Edmund Burke: Modernity, Politics, and Aesthetics, Modernity and Political Thought*, vol. 5 (Thousand Oaks, London, and New Delhi: Sage, 1994).

Wilkins, Burleigh Taylor, *The Problem of Burke's Political Philosophy* (Oxford: Clarendon Press, 1967).

Wood, Neal, 'The Aesthetic Dimension of Burke's Political Thought', *Journal of British Studies*, 4:1 (1964), pp. 41–64.

Index

Note: 'n' after a page reference refers to a note on that page.